AQA Music

AS

A2

Exclusively endorsed by AQA

Rosemary
Broadbent

Andrew S. Coxon

Nelson Thornes

Published in 2009 by:
Nelson Thornes Ltd
Delta Place
27 Bath Road
CHELTENHAM
GL53 7TH
United Kingdom

09 10 11 12 13 / 10 9 8 7 6 5 4 3 2

A catalogue record for this book is available from the British Library

ISBN 978 1 4085 1389 7

Cover photograph: Tim Pannell/Corbis

Page make-up by Hart McLeod Ltd, Cambridge

Printed and bound in Spain by Graphycem

Contents

AQA introduction   v

Studying AQA A Level Music   vii

AS LEVEL

Unit 1	Influences on music	2
Chapter 1	Listening	2
Chapter 2	Set work – Mozart's *Symphony No. 41*, first and third movements	14
Chapter 3	Historical study for AS	38

Unit 2	Creating musical ideas	82
Chapter 4	Introduction to composing and arranging	82
Chapter 5	Developing your composing skills for AS	84
Chapter 6	Choosing a composing option for AS	97
Chapter 7	Managing your time	107

Unit 3	Interpreting musical ideas	110
Chapter 8	Introduction to performing	110
Chapter 9	Acoustic performances	113
Chapter 10	Technology-based performances	124

Changes to AQA specification

For the June 2012 examination and until further notice the AS set work will be:
Beethoven – Symphony No. 1, first and second movements

For the June 2013 examination and until further notice the set works for A2 will be:
Elgar – Symphony No. 1
Shostakovich – Symphony No. 5

Chapters 2 and 12 of this book have been revised to reflect the new set works, and can be found at: **www.nelsonthornes.com/go/13897**

A2 LEVEL

Unit 4	Music in context	138
Chapter 11	Listening	138
Chapter 12	Set works – Mahler's *4th* or Vaughan Williams' *5th Symphony*	144
Chapter 13	Historical study for A2	166

Unit 5	Developing musical ideas	200
Chapter 14	Developing your composing skills for A2	200
Chapter 15	Choosing a composing option for A2	207
Chapter 16	Writing the review	218

Unit 6	A musical performance	220
Chapter 17	Introduction to performing at A2	220
Chapter 18	Developing your performing skills	222
Chapter 19	Choosing a performing option	228
Chapter 20	Preparing acoustic performances	231
Chapter 21	Preparing technology-based performances	236

Glossary		244
Reference works		248
Index		249
Acknowledgements		254

AQA introduction

Nelson Thornes and AQA

Nelson Thornes has worked in partnership with AQA to ensure this book and the accompanying online resources offer you the best support for your GCSE course.

All resources have been approved by senior AQA examiners so you can feel assured that they closely match the specification for this subject and provide you with everything you need to prepare successfully for your exams.

These print and online resources together **unlock blended learning**; this means that the links between the activities in the book and the activities online blend together to maximise your understanding of a topic and help you achieve your potential.

These online resources are available on **kerboodle!** which can be accessed via the internet at **www.kerboodle.com/live**, anytime, anywhere. If your school or college subscribes to this service you will be provided with your own personal login details. Once logged in, access your course and locate the required activity.

For more information and help visit **www.kerboodle.com**

Icons in this book indicate where there is material online related to that topic. The following icons are used:

How to use the handbook

This book supports the specification for your course and is arranged in a sequence approved by AQA. There is no one way of working through the handbook, as all students will come to the course with differing levels of experience and ability, so you may need to study some areas in greater detail than others.

To complete the course successfully, we recommend that you should previously have acquired the skills and knowledge associated with a GCSE Music course, or its equivalent. These should include a fairly wide experience of listening to a range of music from different periods, styles and genres, performing music as an individual or as part of a small group, working with music technology, and composing music for a variety of media and purposes.

The features in this book include:

Learning objectives

At the beginning of each section you will find a list of learning objectives that contain targets linked to the requirements of the specification.

Key terms

Terms that you will need to be able to define and understand.

Hint

Hints on useful study techniques.

Did you know?

Interesting background to the ideas covered in the main text.

Music to seek out and listen to.

Activities to help you understand the ideas in the handbook or better prepare for your exams.

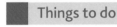 **Examiner's tip**

Hints from AQA examiners to help you with your study and to prepare for your exam.

AQA Examination-style questions

Questions in the style that you can expect in your exam. AQA examination questions are reproduced by permission of the Assessment and Qualifications Alliance.

Weblinks in the book

Because Nelson Thornes is not responsible for the third-party content online, there may be some changes to this material that are beyond our control. In order for us to ensure that the links referred to in the book are as up-to-date and stable as possible, the websites provided are usually homepages with supporting instructions on how to reach the relevant pages if necessary.

Please let us know at **webadmin@nelsonthornes.com** if you find a link that does not work and we will do our best to correct this at reprint, or to list an alternative site.

About the AQA Music specification

How the specification is structured

The A Level specification (2270) consists of three AS units and three A2 units, with the AS and A2 Levels each being worth 50 per cent of the final A Level. One AS unit – Unit 3 (Performing: Interpreting Musical Ideas) is internally assessed coursework. For this unit your work will be assessed initially by the subject teacher and then sent to an AQA-appointed moderator. Unit 2 (Creating Musical Ideas) and Unit 5 (Developing Musical Ideas) are externally assessed. For these units the examination will be completed in a number of supervised sessions. Units 1 and 4 are assessed by terminal examination.

Assessment objectives

The three assessment objectives are common to both the AS and A2 A Level Music units:

■ **AO1** Interpret musical ideas with technical and expressive control and awareness of occasion and/or ensemble *(performing/realising)*.

■ **AO2** Create and develop musical ideas with technical control and expressive understanding, making creative use of musical devices, conventions and resources *(composing/arranging)*.

■ **AO3** Demonstrate understanding of, and comment perceptively on, the structural, expressive and contextual aspects of music *(appraising)*.

These tables show how the assessment objectives relate to each unit of the specification:

Weighting of assessment objectives for AS

Assessment objectives	Unit weightings (%)			Overall weighting of area of study (%)
	Unit 1	Unit 2	Unit 3	
AO1			40	40
AO2		30		30
AO3	30			30
Overall weighting of units (%)	30	30	40	100

Weighting of assessment objectives for A2

Assessment objectives	Unit weightings (%)						Overall weighting of area of study (%)
	Unit 1	Unit 2	Unit 3	Unit 4	Unit 5	Unit 6	
AO1			20			15	35
AO2		15			15		30
AO3	15			20			35
Overall weighting of units (%)	15	15	20	20	15	15	100

Studying AQA A Level Music

The AS examinations

Unit 1: Influences on music

This unit is worth 30 per cent of the AS marks and 15 per cent of the total A Level marks. It is assessed through a written examination lasting 1 hour 45 minutes and marked out of 80. The examination takes place in May of the examination year. There are three sections:

Section A: Listening

You will study a range of musical language and context by listening to music from across a wide range of genres and through exploration of two areas of study. The examination will be in the form of questions, with or without a musical excerpt, questions based on a score excerpt and/or comparison of two sections from a piece of music, or two performances of the same piece.

Section B: The Western Classical tradition

This Area of Study (AoS) is compulsory and consists of close consideration of the first and third movements of Mozart's *Symphony No. 41 in C major*, K.551 against the key musical elements: form, harmony, instrumentation and timbre, melody, rhythm and metre, texture, tonality and context.

Section C: Areas of Study 2

You will choose **one** from a choice of **three** areas of study:

- Choral music in the Baroque period
- Music theatre: a study of the musical from 1940 to 1980
- British popular music from 1960 to the present day.

Unit 2: Creating musical ideas

This unit is worth 30 per cent of the AS marks and 15 per cent of the total A Level marks. The unit is coursework based, assessed externally and marked out of 60. You will have up to 20 hours of controlled time in which to complete your chosen brief(s). Sessions of controlled time will be arranged by your centre but the work must be submitted in May of the examination year. You will be able to choose from **three** different options or briefs and, for all of them, recordings can be made using acoustic instruments or voices and/or ICT technology.

Brief A: Compositional techniques

Two questions will be set:

- **Harmonisation of a 16-bar diatonic melody:** You will be given a traditional 16-bar diatonic melody in a major or minor key, for which you will have to create a four-part harmonization. You can compose for any group of four melodic instruments or voices.
- **Controlling texture:** You are given up to 24 bars of keyboard accompaniment. You are to show your ability to control texture by creating a piece of music using the given chords in two parts. You can compose in your own choice of style and can use any two melodic instruments or voices.

Submissions must be as a score in staff notation and there must be a recording on CD or minidisk.

Brief B: Free composition or pastiche in response to a given genre

Within this brief, there is a choice between **four** different musical genres:

- **Vocal music:** accompanied or unaccompanied. If accompanied, you can write for one voice or more; if unaccompanied, there must be at least two voices. There is no upper limit to the number of voices used.
- **Small ensemble:** any small group of instruments, traditional or otherwise. There must be at least two instruments.
- **Electronic music:** this can be for any electronic sound source, including loops and samples. However, you must always make sure that there is a significant amount of original material.
- **Keyboard music:** this can be for a single keyboard or up to four keyboards of the same or different types. For the purposes of this brief, tuned percussion and electronically produced keyboard sounds are also permissible.

Your composition should last 3–6 minutes and can be in any appropriate diatonic style. It must be accompanied by a recording on CD or minidisk and there must be a score and/or chart and/or annotation.

Brief C: Arranging

You will be given a traditional folk song melody and the lyrics to one or more verses. You are to arrange this for any group of voices and/or instruments. Your arrangement should last 3–6 minutes and can be in any appropriate style. It must be accompanied by a recording on CD or minidisk and there must be a score and/or chart and/or annotation.

Unit 3: Interpreting musical ideas

This unit is worth 40 per cent of the AS marks and 20 per cent of the total A Level marks. The unit is internally assessed and then externally moderated and is marked out of 80. Performances will last 10–16 minutes and must be completed for a deadline in May of the examination year, although the performances can be recorded at any time during the course.

You will offer **two** performances from six options:

- a solo performance on an instrument
- a solo performance on voice
- a solo performance on a second instrument
- an ensemble performance
- a technology-based performance: 1 – sequencing
- a technology-based performance: 2 – multi-track/ close microphone recording.

Your performance within each option will last 5–8 minutes and can consist of a single piece or a number of shorter pieces. You can perform your own composition if it will make the necessary demands in terms of technique and expression. When you submit your recorded performances (on CD or minidisk), you must provide a score, lead sheet/detailed annotation, or the recording of the original work.

The A2 examinations

Unit 4: Music in context

This unit is worth 20 per cent of the total A Level marks. It is assessed through a written examination lasting 2 hours 15 minutes and marked out of 100. The examination takes place in June of the examination year. There are three sections:

Section A: Listening

As at AS, you will study a range of musical language and context by listening to music from across a wide range of genres and through exploration of two areas of study. Examination will be in the form of questions, with or without a musical excerpt, questions based on a score excerpt, and/or comparison of two sections from a piece of music or two performances of the same piece.

Section B: The Western Classical tradition

This Area of Study is compulsory and consists of close consideration of one of the following set works:

- Gustav Mahler: *Symphony No. 4 in G major*.
- Ralph Vaughan Williams: *Symphony No. 5 in D major*.

As at AS, these works will be considered against the key musical elements: form, harmony, instrumentation and timbre, melody, rhythm and metre, texture, tonality and context.

Section C: Historical study

You will choose **one** from a choice of three areas of study:

- English choral music in the 20th century
- chamber music from Mendelssohn to Debussy
- four decades of jazz and blues from 1910 to 1950.

Unit 5: Developing musical ideas

This unit is worth 15 per cent of the total A Level marks. The unit is coursework, assessed externally, and is marked out of 60. You will have up to 20 hours of controlled time in which to complete your chosen brief(s). Sessions of controlled time will be arranged by your centre but the work must be submitted in May of the examination year. You will be able to choose from **three** different options or briefs:

Brief A: Compositional techniques

Two questions will be set on:

- harmonisation of a chorale melody in the style of Bach
- completion of an extract from a Classical string quartet. Submissions must be as a score in staff notation and there must be a recording on CD or minidisk.

Brief B: Free composition or pastiche

You will compose a substantial single piece of music (5–8 minutes) in any style or genre and for any combination of voice(s) and/or instrument(s), using acoustic and/or electronic sound sources. As an alternative, you could write up to **three** separate, related sections, thus forming a type of suite.

It must be accompanied by a recording on CD or minidisk and there must be a score and/or chart and/or annotation.

Brief C: Arranging

You will be given a piece of 'popular' classical music. You are to arrange this for any group of voices and/or instruments. Your arrangement should last 5–8 minutes and can be in any recognised pop, rock or jazz style. It must be accompanied by a recording on CD or minidisk and there must be a score and/or chart and/or annotation.

Additionally, for A2, there must be a **review** of the process of composition for Unit 5 which evaluates its success in relation to the brief and refers to the contextual considerations of the composition.

Unit 6: A musical performance

This unit is worth 15 per cent of the total A Level marks and is externally assessed. It is marked out of 60. Performances will last 10–15 minutes and must be completed for a deadline in May of the examination year, although the performances may be recorded at any time during the course. You will offer **one** performance of 10–15 minutes from **three** options using acoustic instruments or music technology:

- solo acoustic performances
- technology-based performances
- one solo performance and one technology-based option: each of these performances is to last at least 5 minutes.

Your performance within each option must include two (or more) contrasting pieces, showing a variety of style, technique, period and/or approach. You can perform your own composition if it will make the necessary demands in terms of technique and expression. When you submit your recorded performances (on CD or minidisk), you must provide a score, lead sheet/detailed annotation or the recording of the original work.

The candidate record form

For each of Units 2, 3, 5 and 6 you will also have to submit a candidate record form (CRF). Advice and guidance on how best to complete this will be given with each individual unit.

1 Listening

Learning objectives:

- to understand the range of skills required by Section A of the specification

- to look, in detail, at the range of aural skills listed within Section A

- to look at ways of acquiring those skills

- to become aware of the specialist musical vocabulary used within this section

- to study examples of many of the aural skills to be assessed

- to learn where to access music that will help you develop the aural skills required.

Introducing listening

For Section A, the first part of the Unit 1 examination, you will need to develop your aural (i.e. listening) skills to meet the range of requirements listed in the specification. These will be covered in detail in this chapter. The focus is firmly on *listening skills* rather than *historical knowledge*. The excerpts will be recorded on a CD by AQA and you will fill in the answers in an examination answer booklet, which will also contain the questions set for the other parts of the unit.

What musical extracts can you use?

Any music may be used as you prepare for this first section, as the musical excerpts used for the listening tests can be taken from any period within musical history. There will be no questions requiring you to identify either a composer or a period.

The excerpts you use can be from recordings or from live performance. For example, if the theme of your lesson is writing cadences and learning how to use them, it will be logical to incorporate suitable exercises for aural recognition; similarly with work done on modulation, chord inversions, sequence, riff, notes of anticipation, timbre and texture. You will already have gained many of the skills you will need during KS3 and GCSE, by participation in music making at various levels and through general listening. There will be different levels of ability within any group, so programmes of aural training will have to be either wide-ranging or almost individually tailored, though software such as *Auralia*, from *Sibelius*, might be useful.

Work together to practise your listening skills

You can work with another member of your class to practise listening skills. You should make sure that you get a full list of the skills needed from your teacher, especially as they relate to you: in other words, there needs to be some preliminary work done, either at the end of your GCSE year, or at the start of the AS year, to judge the level of your aural skills.

What do you need to cover?

This listening section will test your ability to cover some of the following points, so work will need to be done in all areas, especially those in which a lack of skill or a measure of difficulty is perceived:

- cadences
- chord identification
- compositional techniques
- technical terms
- completion of a diatonic melody
- tonality and modulation
- instrumentation
- texture
- ornamentation
- time signatures
- intervals
- melodic/rhythmic devices

The rest of this chapter covers each of these areas in detail.

Cadences

There are four main cadences:

- perfect ⎱ 'final' or
- plagal ⎰ 'full close'
- imperfect (or 'half close')
- interrupted.

Each cadence, at its simplest, consists of a two-chord progression.

Perfect and plagal end on the tonic chord, achieving a 'full close', a sense of finality, if the tonic is in root position. The *perfect cadence* moves from dominant to tonic (V– I).

Play these examples of perfect cadences:

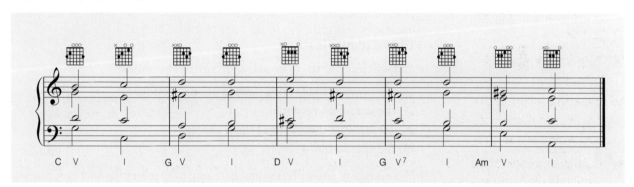

The *plagal cadence* moves from subdominant to tonic (IV–I) and is traditionally linked with the singing of *Amen* at the end of hymns, a practice less common in churches nowadays.

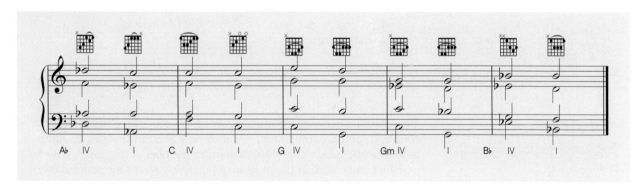

You should now work out some examples of your own, in other keys.

The *imperfect cadence* offers, as it were, an incomplete moment of pause at the end of a phrase. It leaves the ear unsatisfied and awaiting the chord's resolution as the music resumes its progress.

The *interrupted cadence*, while appearing to be approaching a full close or perfect cadence, veers away, interposing one or more chords. The cadence moves from dominant to submediant (major-to-minor chords in a major key and major-to-major chords in a minor key).

Try these examples – two imperfect cadences and two interrupted cadences – before working some of your own:

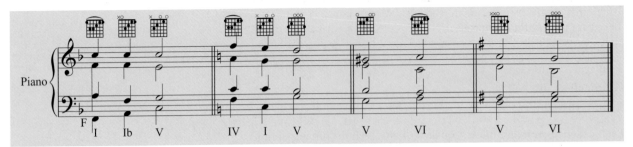

Additional exemplar materials can be found in the course of your study of the set work and your chosen second area of study; whether it be *Choral Music in the Baroque Period*, or *Music Theatre: A Study of the Musical from 1940 to 1980*, or *British Popular Music from 1960 to the present day*.

Chord identification

You will be expected to be able to recognise, in context:

■ the primary triads (tonic, subdominant, dominant)

■ the dominant seventh

■ 1st and 2nd inversions of these chords

■ the cadential 6–4.

You should practise playing and listening to these, either as a group or with a partner.

The following example shows each of these chords and their inversions in C major, with a short phrase in the margin to demonstrate the use of the cadential 6–4, i.e. the tonic chord in second inversion resolving to the dominant in root position.

There will be many opportunities, within your studies elsewhere in the course, to practise recognition of chords and their inversions. In addition to your work in this unit, you, or another member of the group, may be a pianist and could, in the process of practising pieces for performance, play individual chords and/or extracts that would be suitable for chord identification purposes.

Example of a cadential 6–4

Compositional techniques

For AS Listening, you need to be able to recognise, and differentiate between, the following techniques.

Canon

A canon is a composition where the melody is repeated at regular intervals by other voices *exactly* in one or more other parts, which enter *before* the first part has finished. Subsequent statements can be at pitches other than the original (see round).

Round

This is a particular type of canon where the melody is restated by the other entries only at the unison or octave. You might like to look at, and perform, *Sumer is icumen in*, the earliest example of the round to have survived. Some English composers wrote examples of the round, including Henry Purcell (1659–95).

Imitation

This describes a passage in which a figure or phrase is repeated by another voice, if not exactly. There are many imitative passages within the Mozart *Symphony No. 41 in C*, K. 551, such as bars 56–65 and 244–253 in the first movement, and bars 44–50 in the third. (See Chapter 2.)

Ostinato

An *ostinato* is a repeated melodic or rhythmic pattern. There is also a *basso ostinato*, as in a 'ground bass'. Examples of the former can be found in, for example, African drum patterns, and popular or minimalist music; while Baroque music is a rich source of the latter (for example, the music of Purcell, such as the duet for soprano and bass *Hark! Each tree* in his *Ode on St Cecilia's Day (1692)*.) Perhaps the simplest rhythmic *ostinato* is that used by Queen in *We will rock you*, consisting of this pattern, at a slow tempo (shown in the margin).

Pedal

A note sustained or repeated below changing harmonies (also known as a 'pedal point' or 'bass pedal'). If the sustained note is not in the bass then it forms an 'inverted pedal' – an 'inner pedal' if in the middle of the texture and an 'upper pedal' if above it. Many examples of pedal points can be found within the movements set from Mozart's *Symphony No. 41 in C*, K. 551. Examples include:

- Bass pedal/pedal point: first movement, bars 39–46, 49–55 and 81–86, though in the first two examples there are additional pedal notes in other parts of the texture.
- Inner pedal: first movement, bars 56–60³, bars 94–96; third movement, bars 1–8 G, 9–13 D and 52–55 G.
- Upper pedal: first movement, bars 125–129.

Riff

A repeated pattern, as with *ostinato*, but more usually applied to popular music contexts. Many well-known popular songs begin with an instrumental riff, including *Ticket to ride* by The Beatles.

Sequence

The repetition of a musical phrase at a higher or lower pitch. If the intervals remain exactly the same, it is a *real sequence*; if they are slightly altered to avoid moving out of key, it is a *tonal sequence*, though this level of differentiation will not be required.

Examples can be found in:

- Mozart: *Symphony No. 41 in C*, K. 551: first movement: bars 132–154, bars 299–300; third movement: bars 1–8 and bars 28–40.
- The musicals: *Sunrise, sunset* and *Matchmaker* from *Fiddler on the Roof* by Jerry Bock and Sheldon Harnick, and *I feel pretty* and *Somewhere* from *West Side Story* by Leonard Bernstein and Stephen Sondheim.

Technical terms

You will need to know the following technical terms:

Appoggiatura and acciaccatura

Written   Played

The *appoggiatura* is an unessential note falling (or, less frequently, rising) to a harmonised note (or one where the harmony is implied). In the 18th century, these notes were in common usage and denoted by a smaller type, as in the example alongside, which is followed by notation showing how it is played.

Nowadays, it is written as in the 'played' version above and is heard as a temporary dissonance resolving by step to a harmony note. One of the most obvious (and famous) examples is in the song *Maria* from *West Side Story* where the second syllable is set to an F♯, an appoggiatura (in fact, a chromatic appoggiatura) to the ensuing G.

The *acciaccatura* is often referred to as a 'crush note' (from its Italian derivation) to denote the fact that the note in question is 'crushed' – in other words, played in as short a time as possible. When this note is written, there is a cross through the stem to denote the fact that it has no real value. In a listening test, the difference is basically that of the duration of the first pitch: if very short before resolving to the harmony note, it is an acciaccatura; if longer, perhaps the same value as the harmony note that follows, it is an *appoggiatura*.

Passing note

This is a note that moves by step between two harmony notes. Play through these examples, listening closely to the off-beat, unaccented quavers, helping to smooth out the melody line:

Note of anticipation

As the name suggests, this is a note that 'anticipates' the note (and harmony) that follows, and it is not to be confused with a note suspended from the previous chord.

The principle of the 'note of anticipation' can be applied to more than one note, as in this following example, again balanced by the same notes used as a triple suspension or *appoggiatura*:

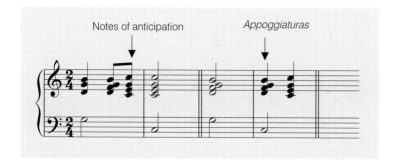

Completion of a diatonic melody

In the examination situation, this type of test will normally consist of listening to an excerpt, then filling in notes missing from a skeleton score (an outline of the musical excerpt being used). On some occasions, you will be given the rhythm to use, as in this excerpt from *Symphony No. 40 in G minor*, K. 550 by Mozart (bars 1–9):

To help with this type of question, you will need to be able to recognise intervals as well as step-wise movement, and you can use the openings of tunes you may know to help remember a range of intervals: some of the most common include:

- Minor third: the opening of *Greensleeves*.
- Major third: the opening of *While shepherds watched their flocks by night* or *Once in royal David's city*.
- Perfect fourth: *Amazing grace*, *Matchmaker (Fiddler on the Roof)*, *America* or *Tonight (West Side Story)*, *Master of the house (Les Misérables)*.
- Perfect fifth: *Twinkle, twinkle, little star*.
- Minor sixth: *When Israel was in Egypt's land*, or *To life (Fiddler on the Roof)*.
- Major sixth: *My Bonny lies over the ocean*.
- Minor seventh: *Somewhere* from *West Side Story*.

Bali Ha'i from *South Pacific* can help with the octave and the major seventh, as its opening three notes leap an octave and then drop back a semitone, identifying the major seventh:

Similarly, the melody of *The lonely goatherd* from *The Sound of Music* gives the sounds of the octave, minor seventh and major sixth:

Tonality and modulation

You will need to be able to recognise modulations to the dominant, subdominant and relative minor, which are the three keys most closely related to the opening tonic. The first thing to do, when confronted with this type of question, and before listening to it (in other words, during the preparation/reading time), is to work out the names of these three keys relative to the excerpt to be heard (if there is a skeleton score). When actually listening to the music, you must first note the initial key and then work out the possible modulations.

Thus, if the starting key is, for example, C major, the possible modulations are to G major (dominant), F major (subdominant) and A minor (relative minor); if the starting key is A minor, the possible modulations are to E minor (dominant), D minor (subdominant) and C major (relative major).

Having established the starting key, you must next determine whether the key reached is major or minor. Our first example starts in a major key, so if the new key reached is also major, your choice is dominant or subdominant; if it is minor, your choice is self-evident, in that there is only one possible minor key – the relative minor (in this case, A minor). In our second example, which starts in a minor key, if the new key reached is also minor, then it is a choice between dominant and subdominant; if it ends in a major key, then that key must be the relative major – C major in our example.

In all cases, it is vital that you are able to retain the pitch of the tonic in your mind so that you can then relate the new key back to it by simply singing up or down the scale (in your head!) and counting how many steps it takes to reach the original key note.

Instrumentation

You will have learnt to recognise many instruments during earlier music lessons and should, by this stage, be familiar with their characteristic sounds. You can be practising for this type of question whenever you listen to any piece of music, by trying to identify the instruments playing and any special techniques being used. Some of the more common instruments are listed here by family:

Strings	Woodwind	Brass	Percussion (tuned)	Percussion (untuned)
Violin	Piccolo and flute	French horn	Timpani	Bass drum
Viola	Oboe and cor anglais	Trumpet	Glockenspiel	Snare drum
Cello	Clarinet	Trombone	Xylophone	Triangle
Double bass	Bassoon	Tuba	Piano	Tambourine
Harp	Double bassoon		Celesta	Wood block

The basic string techniques of playing with a bow (*con arco*) or plucking the strings (*pizzicato*) should pose no problems by this stage.

You will also need to recognise instruments found in basic jazz and pop music situations, so will need to be familiar with the sounds of saxophones, keyboards, synthesisers, guitars and drum kits.

Instrumentation also covers voice recognition, so you should be aware of the main voice types:

Female		Male	
Soprano	High vocal range	Tenor	High vocal range
Mezzo-soprano	Middle vocal range	Baritone	Middle vocal range
Alto (Contralto)	Low vocal range	Bass	Low vocal range

The most common are the high and low vocal ranges within each group but many female vocalists, especially in the world of popular music, have a range that really fits that of the mezzo-soprano, though soprano would invariably be accepted within an examination answer.

Another vocal feature to recognise is that of 'falsetto': this is where men sing in a vocal range higher than any of the above – it is, literally, a 'false' voice. It is a vocal style commonly met within popular music and is commonly associated with the Bee Gees, in songs such as *Night fever*. It is also the sound produced by the male alto or countertenor, though, in this case, the singers use this voice all the time.

The instruments and layout of an orchestra

Texture

The main types of texture to differentiate between are 'harmonic/homophonic' and 'contrapuntal/polyphonic'. 'Homophonic' and 'polyphonic' derive from the Greek and mean 'one sound' and 'many sounds' respectively. The contrast between these styles or features can be found in many areas of potential AS study.

Here is an example to illustrate the differences, from *Messiah*, chorus no. 26: *All we like sheep*. The opening phrase in this quotation – 'ev'ry one to his own way' – is in a homophonic style, with the four parts singing their own line but in the same rhythm; the rest, setting 'we have turned', is an example of polyphonic or contrapuntal music, where each part sings independently, entering at different times (although the lines are based on the same musical idea).

Many other examples can be found in *Messiah*, in Bach's *B minor mass* and in musicals.

Other textures you will need to be able to recognise include:

■ Imitative texture: where a part imitates one that has gone before, as in the contrapuntal section of the above quotation.

■ Unison: where all players/singers perform at the same pitch. This must not be confused with playing and/or singing in octaves, where the same tune/melody is played and/or sung but at different octaves.

■ Single melody line: quite literally, an unaccompanied melody, although it can be (and is) applied to music where the melody *could* stand alone but has a light accompaniment.

Ornamentation

Trill

Basically, a trill, or shake, is the rapid alternation in pitch of two adjacent notes a semitone or a tone apart. In the Baroque era, the trill tended to begin on the note above the written pitch as in this example:

while, in later periods, the trill would begin on the note itself:

However, as far as this listening test is concerned, your ability to recognise the sound of the trill aurally will be sufficient.

Turn

When the music contains a turn you will hear notes played very quickly, revolving around a central pitch, as here (although other rhythms can be employed):

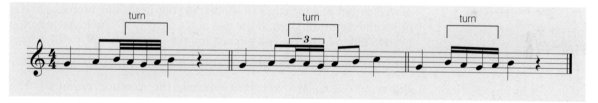

Mordent

There are two types of mordent: an upper mordent and a lower mordent. Aurally, the mordent can be recognised as a rapid single movement, by step, away from and returning to the main pitch. Thus:

an *upper* mordent: a *lower* mordent: written as:

Play these examples of ornaments, and others at different pitches, so that you become accustomed to their sound and can differentiate between them.

The three ornaments

In the listening section of this examination you will need to concentrate on the following to identify these ornaments:

- ■ The trill: an extended alternation of two adjacent pitches.
- ■ The turn: movement above and below the same note, with the upper and lower notes occurring just once.
- ■ The mordent: there will be three notes, with the first and last being the same and the additional notes being one step higher (upper mordent) or one step lower (lower mordent).

Time signatures

At AS Level, this will cover the recognition of simple, duple, triple and quadruple time, for example: $^2/_4$, $^2/_2$, $^3/_4$ and $^4/_4$. Thus, your main task in a listening test is to decide whether the basic pulse falls into groups of two, three or four. It is usually accepted that, in some pieces of music, it is difficult to differentiate whether the music has two or four beats in a bar and, in such cases, either answer would be acceptable. You will not be expected to recognise compound time signatures or music with five or seven beats in a bar until A2 Level.

Intervals

You will be expected to recognise major, minor and perfect intervals. This has been covered partially in the section on Completion of a diatonic melody (see page 7).

Perfect intervals can be the fourth, fifth and the octave. It is easy to confuse the sound of the fourth with that of the fifth. If the notes are played as part of a melody, you should, in your head, sing from one to the other and count the steps. If the two notes are played simultaneously, you need to differentiate the two pitches and then sing from one to the other.

All other intervals at this level are either major or minor.

Where notes are played as part of a melody, the 'counting' techniques should be applied, although, while practising this type of exercise, you should also aim to acquire the skill of being able to memorise the phrase.

Where two notes are played simultaneously, you should first determine whether the sound is dissonant or consonant. If it is dissonant, you are, really, restricted to a second or a seventh, whether major or minor. Seconds 'crunch' together as they are 'next-door' notes; sevenths cover a wider range with the major seventh being the more dissonant of the two as the two notes involved are just a semitone away from being an octave. It may help you to identify a minor seventh if you practise singing the notes which form a 'dominant seventh': for example, if you think the two notes are:

try playing then singing:

Where two notes are consonant, there is a wider range of possibilities and there is no real short cut to the acquisition of the aural skills you will need. They will develop and improve through regular practice.

To summarise the major and minor intervals:

You should practise playing and listening to these and then repeat the process in different keys. Working with someone else will make it easier to listen to a range of intervals and you will be able to track your progress and identify any intervals that you find harder to recognise or confuse. These can then become the focus of more intensive aural work.

The perfect intervals are:

Melodic/rhythmic devices

These are identified as ***ostinato*** pattern, **passing note**, **riff** and **sequence** and have been dealt with under Compositional techniques on pages 4–5.

■ Summary

This chapter has dealt, in some detail, with the range of listening skills you will be required to address during the first part of this Unit 1 Influences on Music examination. Many of these are covered on past papers set by AQA at GCSE and A2, and your teacher will undoubtedly be able to access those that are appropriate. Additionally, AQA provide specimen listening materials. However, as was pointed out at the beginning of this chapter, listening skills can be gained during any and all musical activities: listening, performing, composing, appraising.

You need to ascertain which aural skills you already have, those you can acquire relatively easily and those you find difficult, and then ensure that you gain the help, advice and the opportunities to hear musical examples that you need, to gain all skills identified.

Above all, listen closely and carefully to a wide range of music from different periods and in different genres.

■ Hint

You might prefer to think of the minor 2nd as a semitone and the major 2nd as a tone.

■ Key terms

Ostinato: a short phrase, persistently repeated.

Passing note: a note that moves by step between two notes of a chord.

Riff: a repeated pattern of notes. This term is usually applied within popular music.

Sequence: repeated use of a short phrase moving up a step on each repetition. Descending sequences are also used.

2 Set work – Mozart: *Symphony No. 41,* first and third movements

Learning objectives:

- to study the set work: Mozart: *Symphony No. 41 in C,* K. 551, first and third movements

- to look closely at the exposition section of the first movement

- to examine how themes and motifs grow out of each other

- to study Mozart's use of the musical elements

- to consider how Mozart varies, extends and alters his musical ideas within the development section

- to study how the themes return within the recapitulation and compare their return here with their initial appearance in the exposition

- to examine how Mozart brings this movement to a conclusion in the coda section, considering to what extent this is based on the codetta (or epilogue) from the end of the exposition

- to look closely at minuet and trio form and how it is used in the third movement.

Methods of study

You will be able to take an unmarked copy of the score into the examination room, and will be required to write *one* essay from a choice of two. Realistically, you will have about 40 minutes in which to plan and write your essay, so it is essential that you take every opportunity to learn how to plan and write an essay.

You will need to learn the techniques of musical analysis, probably through simple piano pieces, or, perhaps, utilising any music you and your fellow students are currently learning for a concert or a grade examination. From such pieces you will be able to appreciate phrase structure, development of motifs, overall form, modulation, and so on.

You will need to understand the meaning of forms such as binary, ternary, rondo, **minuet and trio**, and sonata form. You may well be aware of some of these through KS3 and/or GCSE studies.

Specifically, for this symphony, you will need to learn about and understand binary, ternary and sonata forms. These are all explained fully below. Phrase structure, tonality, modulation, use of instruments, awareness of texture and form can also be integrated with compositional work.

Key musical features

Use of instruments

The core of the 'Classical orchestra' was the string section, with the wind sections often having a more subsidiary role. However, although the brass instruments were limited to notes of the 'harmonic series' (see explanation within the analysis on page 22), Mozart was still able to use brass and woodwind instruments as an independent group acting as a contrast to the predominant string sound. Despite using fairly limited resources, Mozart was able to write for a wide range of combinations of instrumental timbres, producing a great variety of textures.

Phrase structure

In the Classical period, phrasing was balanced and usually regular. Examples of 'question and answer' or 'antecedent/consequent' phrasing can be found in both movements under consideration, but there are also occasional examples of irregular-length phrases and these should be borne in mind in any question focusing on phrasing.

Tonality

This includes consideration of the use of both major and minor tonalities. (There is no modal writing in this symphony.) It also covers the possible reasons behind the choices.

Modulation

During the Classical period, most modulation was to a key closely related to the original tonic, and you should be familiar with such links, as shown:

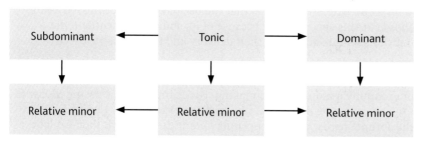

As both movements are in the same key, this can be summarised easily for both:

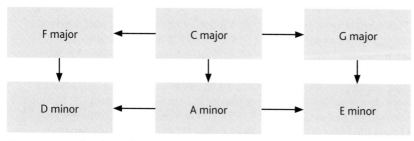

However, study of the first movement will reveal that Mozart did not confine himself to these keys, and was prepared to modulate outside this scheme to accommodate his music's direction and aspirations.

Texture

This refers to whether the writing is 'homophonic' or 'polyphonic': these key musical terms are explained in the previous section on page 9, where examples are given of each. The definitions are reproduced here:

- 'Homophonic' and 'polyphonic' derive from the Greek and mean 'one sound' and 'many sounds' respectively.

Thus, *homophonic music* (sometimes referred to as an 'harmonic texture') is where all parts have independent pitches but the same rhythms.

- *Polyphonic* or *contrapuntal music* is where each line has its own melody and rhythm, although there are often close similarities between the lines.

■ Analysing the music

After initial guidance on the process of analysis from your teacher, you should analyse short pieces of music or sections of longer pieces. Concentrating on a small number of features is likely to be beneficial at first. Thus you might, with different works, analyse the composer's use of:

- melodic shape/phrase structure
- melodic/motivic development
- use of texture
- choice of timbre
- choice of and use of tonality, including modulation
- structure.

Key terms

Minuet and trio: the minuet was a stately dance in ¾ time that originated in the 17th century. Composers would pair the minuet with a second dance that contrasted in style and texture, called the trio, before returning to a repeat of the minuet. Note that 'trio' does not refer to the number of players in this instance. Although the orchestration would usually be lighter, there would usually be more than three people playing. The term 'trio' is also used to refer to a lighter, contrasting section in the middle of a scherzo movement.

Things to do
- Identify the key signatures of all the keys involved in the example on the left, which has C major as its starting point.
- Note the differences in key signature.
- In the case of the minor keys, work out the harmonic minor scale to show the leading note.

You should never just *describe* what the composer is doing: rather, you should comment on the *effect* of the modulation, melodic shape, choice of timbre and so forth, under discussion. It is a matter of *observation* to be able to point out that the word-setting is syllabic; it is the role of *analysis* to state, for example, that the use of syllabic setting has been chosen at this specific stage because of its ability to accentuate the individual words and make their delivery and impact more direct.

With this set work, musical quotations are not required – just precise reference to the score. However, any such reference should be to illustrate or exemplify a point you are making. For example, if discussing Mozart's use of contrasting dynamics, you might refer to bars 1–4 and point out the abrupt change from the opening *forte* (*f*) to *piano* (*p*), then explain what effect this has.

Background information

This symphony was the third of a group of three written over a period of six weeks in the summer of 1788 towards the end of Mozart's life. (The other two are *Symphony No. 39 in E♭*, K. 543 and *Symphony No. 40 in G minor*, K. 550). *No. 39* was completed on 26 June, *No. 40* a month later on 25 July and *No. 41* just two weeks after that. The symphonies were composed in Vienna after his opera *Don Giovanni* and the D major *Coronation* Piano Concerto, K. 537, but before the final three operas of *Cosi fan tutte* (1790), *Die Zauberflöte* (1791) and *La Clemenza di Tito* (composed quickly during the summer of 1791 for the coronation of Leopold II as King of Bohemia), and the *Piano Concerto in B♭ major*, K. 595. He was also still to write his motet *Ave verum corpus* and the *Requiem* (which, of course, he left unfinished at his death). Also still to come were the two pieces written for his friend Anton Stadler – the famous *Clarinet Quintet in A major*, K. 581 of 1789 and the *Clarinet Concerto in A major*, K. 622, written in 1791, plus some late chamber music and piano solos.

Mozart had been living in Vienna since 1781 and had, initially, been very popular and had prospered, idolised by Viennese society as both pianist and composer. It was during these ten years, till his death in 1791, that most of the works that led to Mozart's lasting fame and popularity were written. During his time in Vienna, he continued to study the works of Haydn and discovered the music of J.S. Bach. The extent to which he was influenced by Bach can be seen in the increasing use of contrapuntal texture in later works.

In this later period of his life, Mozart wrote fewer piano concertos, reflecting, perhaps, a waning of interest in his playing among Viennese concertgoers. Perhaps also, following the success of Haydn's symphonies, Mozart wanted to be seen in a different light. The fact that he wrote three symphonies is symptomatic of the fact that publishers liked to package 'sets' of works: six small-scale works, such as quartets; three larger-scale, such as symphonies. During 1788, Mozart was constantly short of funds and it is inevitable that these works will have been written with concerts in mind. To write three substantial symphonic works without any such aim was not the way of 18th-century composers.

Wolfgang Amadeus Mozart (1756–91). Unfinished portrait by his brother-in-law Joseph Lange, 1783

These works can in no way be seen as an attempt to make his final symphonic statements, though, obviously, they sum up his developments as a symphonist thus far. Nor is there any surviving evidence of their performance in Vienna, although there were many concerts and it is likely that at least one of them was performed. Mozart also undertook concert tours and would have included performances of symphonies within the programmes. He had been interested in the possibility of a trip to England for some time and there was a concert tour in Germany in 1789.

The fact that Mozart wrote a set of three symphonies points to his knowledge of Haydn's earlier 'London' Symphonies (for a trip later aborted), *Nos. 76–8*. In fact, from this point, Haydn tended to write his symphonies in sets, with an eye to publication. The 'Paris' Symphonies (Nos. 82–7) start with symphonies in C major, G minor and E♭ major (the same keys used in reverse order by Mozart). Haydn's E♭ symphony starts with a slow introduction, as does Mozart's in that key.

The symphonies were not actually published until after his death. The finale of the *Symphony No. 41 in C major* gave rise to the title in Germany of *Symphony with fugue finale*, while the nickname 'Jupiter' was first applied by the London-based impresario Salomon, the moving force behind Haydn's late symphonies.

Mozart's choice of keys for these last symphonies continues associations with specific keys that are present in his style across his composing output: E♭ major with a lyrical warmth and a richness of overall sound; G minor with urgency and drama; C major with ceremony, martial rhythms and figuration.

Mozart's choice of woodwind instruments is interesting and helps define the character of each of these symphonies: *No. 39* has clarinets (but no oboes), and they are used *par excellence* in the trio of the minuet, where the qualities of two different registers of the instrument are superbly demonstrated; *No. 40* originally had no clarinets but Mozart revised the scoring, assigning the softer oboe passages to the clarinet. *No. 41* has just one flute and no clarinets.

The Classical orchestra

Many symphonies of this period were written for what is widely referred to as 'the Classical orchestra', which was characterised by a string section with pairs of wind, brass and percussion instruments.

To see how the Classical orchestra's composition compares with that used by Mozart in *Symphony No. 41*, see the tables overleaf.

The Classical orchestra

Italian	English
Flauti	Flutes
Oboi	Oboes
Clarinetti	Clarinets
Fagotti	Bassoons
Corni	Horns
Trombe	Trumpets
Timpani	Timpani invariably tuned to tonic and dominant
Violino I	1st violins
Violino II	2nd violins
Viola	Violas
Violoncello	Cellos
Contrabasso	Double basses

The orchestra for *Symphony No. 41* is written for a smaller woodwind ensemble, with only one flute and no clarinets. In fact, Mozart uses only one flute in each of the last three symphonies.

The Classical orchestra as used by Mozart in *Symphony No. 41*

Italian	English
Flauto	Flute
Oboi	Oboes (2)
Fagotti	Bassoons (2)
Corni in C	Horns in C (2)
Trombe in C	Trumpets in C (2)
Timpani in C G	Timpani (2), tuned to C and G
Violino I	1st violins
Violino II	2nd violins
Viola	Violas
Violoncello	Cellos
Contrabasso	Double basses

The Classical symphony

By this time, the symphony had settled into a four-movement form, usually:

1 a lively opening movement, often in 'sonata form', sometimes with a slow introduction

2 a contrasting slow movement, which could also be in sonata form, or in binary, ternary, *da capo*, variations or rondo form

3 a minuet and trio, or scherzo and trio

4 a fast finale, in rondo form, sonata form or sonata-rondo form.

Sonata form

Not to be confused with compositions called sonatas, sonata form was developed during the Classical period and was the mainstay of musical form for a very long time because of its inbuilt flexibility.

There are three main sections:

- exposition
- development
- recapitulation.

To these, composers would sometimes add:

- a slow introduction
- a codetta or short 'rounding-off' section to the exposition
- a coda or longer rounding-off section after the recapitulation.

Exposition

Here, the main themes – or, as they are more usually named, 'subjects' – are presented.

In its simplest form, the pattern is:

- first tune or subject in the tonic key; this is usually a strongly rhythmic melodic idea, or 'masculine' tune
- bridge passage, modulating and leading to
- second tune or subject in the dominant; this is traditionally a gentler, more cantabile or 'feminine' melody.

The exposition is usually repeated, allowing listeners to remember the subjects better and thus appreciate the composer's skill in the ensuing development section.

Where the tonic key is minor, the second subject is usually in the relative major.

Development

Here, the composer uses material from the exposition and develops or varies it, with the music passing through a range of keys before returning towards the tonic for the recapitulation.

Recapitulation

The main themes return, sometimes exactly as in the exposition, sometimes varied:

- first subject in the tonic
- bridge passage, modified and leading to
- second subject, also in the tonic (or tonic major if the original tonic was minor).

AQA Examiner's tip

As you will have an unmarked copy of the score with you in the examination room and the examiner will have a copy as your answer is marked, there is usually no need to write out musical quotations, though precise reference is essential.

Additional considerations

■ In the exposition, there may be more than one melodic idea as a first or second subject.

■ The development section may use only part of the musical material from the exposition. It might introduce new ideas.

■ The recapitulation will often vary the orchestration of the subjects.

■ The coda, where used, might extend ideas from the music already used in the codetta or elsewhere, or even introduce new material.

■ Analysing Mozart's *Symphony No. 41 in C*

In the ensuing analysis, bar numbers are given to identify passages, themes or quotations: for example, 56–71 refers to bars 56 to 71. Where a small number follows a bar number, this refers to the actual beat in the bar, so 100^1 means the first beat of bar 100.

Miniature scores are usually printed with a bar number every 10 bars.

The recommended edition is published by Eulenburg.

Looking at the first movement – *Allegro vivace*

The exposition

The **exposition** is one organic whole, with ideas being interconnected and leading inevitably from one to another.

Bars 1–4

These bars contain the **first subject**, which consists of two contrasting ideas: **a**, which emphasises tonic and dominant and **b**, which introduces a dotted rhythm. The juxtaposition of these two ideas also underlines, from the outset, the importance Mozart will place on contrast of dynamics – from loud to quiet, or quiet to loud, without any use of *crescendo* or *diminuendo*:

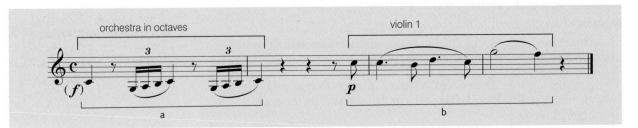

The opening phrase **a** is played *f* establishing the tonic, C, and is played in octaves by flute, oboes, bassoons and all the strings. Horns, trumpets and timpani emphasise C on the first and third beats. By contrast, the second phrase **b** is marked *p* and is played by violins, violas and cellos only, coming to a close on V⁷b, the first inversion of the **dominant seventh**. Thus, within the first subject, we have strongly contrasting phrases: the dramatic assertion of tonic and dominant **a** and the gentle, upwardly yearning phrase **b**.

Bars 5–8

a and **b** are restated, starting on the dominant and closing on the tonic with a IVc–I ending to a phrase starting Ib–Vc.

Bars 9–23

Returning to an *f* dynamic, a **tutti** motif appears, firstly a 'fanfare-like' figure **c**, with a striking dotted rhythm; extra emphasis of this dotted rhythm is provided by trumpets and timpani on beats two and three.

Initially (bars 9 – 15^2), this is over a tonic pedal with the other elements of this tutti: double or triple stopped chords from violin I on the first and third beats of each bar and a rushing demisemiquaver descent in violin II and violas (aI: inversion of the figure I). The harmony is I, IV and V (twice) over this tonic pedal.

From bars 17 to 20, the move is away from the chord of C major to alternating chords of tonic and dominant and then, finally, the dominant for two bars, ending on a G sustained by the whole orchestra.

Bars 24–55

What starts as a restatement of the opening bars with two **countermelodies** becomes, seamlessly, the **bridge passage** to the second subject.

Initially, the opening phrase **a** is played *p* by 1st and 2nd violins. To this is added a rising octave in flute and oboe 1, balanced by a **staccato** quaver descent **d**, plus a tonic arpeggio in octaves in the horns **e**.

AQA Examiner's tip

The important aspect here within an examination answer would be to highlight the *additions* – in other words, the *countermelodies* – to the original motif.

■ Key terms

Tutti: Italian word for 'all', meaning that everyone plays.

Countermelody: the addition of a second melody to the original.

Bridge passage: this provides the link from the first subject to the second and effects the modulation needed.

Staccato: to play the notes crisply, detached. Dots are placed above or below notes to be performed in this style.

The second phrase **b** is scored for flute, oboe 1, bassoon 1 and violins in octaves. As in the opening bars, there is a half-close on the dominant seventh. There follows the balancing restatement, starting on the dominant; the triad **e** is now played by bassoons in octaves, because the natural horns used in Mozart's day were incapable of playing the notes G, B and D as they were not part of the **harmonic series**. When this phrase first occurs, the notes – C, E and G – are within the harmonic series and, therefore, playable by the horns.

Mozart takes the last three notes of the rising phrase **b** and extends them into a sequential passage, the first bassoon dropping chromatically C♯–C–B–B♭–A, with a chord progression that can be summarised as:

Key terms

Harmonic series: the notes that can be played on a brass instrument just by altering the pressure of the lips on the mouthpiece.

Cm add⁶: the chord of C minor with the addition here of a major sixth.

Half-diminished seventh: this is built up: minor third – minor third – major third (a diminished seventh is built entirely of minor thirds).

Dominant pedal: a sustained or repeated bass note on the fifth note of the scale above which the harmony changes.

Second subject: second tune or 'subject' in the dominant; this is traditionally a gentler, more cantabile or 'feminine' melody.

Did you know?

71¹ means the first beat in bar 71.

Strings (without the double bass) complete this section with a sequence of suspensions ending with a VII–I cadence into G major for the balancing statement of this decorated repeat of the main subject starting in bar 37. For this, all the strings play motif **a** in octaves, the upper strings starting with double- or triple-stopping notes of the chord of G major. The dynamic is raised to *f* and the 2nd oboe adds another octave to the bassoons' G major triad, which is figure **e**. Figure **d** is again played by flute and 1st oboe while horns, trumpets and timpani play G on the first and third beats.

The balancing phrase **b** maintains the *f* dynamic played by violins I and II, bassoons and cellos; while flute, oboes, horns, trumpets, timpani and double bass support this with a tonic G pedal across five octaves. Note how the fanfare rhythm **c** is incorporated into the pedal in the brass parts. The G pedal continues as figure **b** is repeated a tone higher and then a further tone up, while the last three notes are taken and treated sequentially from the last quaver of bar 44.

Finally, from bar 47, the G pedal stops and Mozart adds two bars to lead to a return of the musical motifs from bars 9 onwards, now in G major and over a **dominant pedal**, closing on the dominant in bar 55.

Bars 56–71¹

Mozart now introduces the **second subject**. Typically, it includes chromatic movement and it is interesting to note how the opening violin I figure, figure **f**, is echoed in the viola and cello part two bars later.

The second subject, like the first, is made up of two main ideas, falling into two four-bar phrases. Its first statement (bars 56–61) ends on the dominant. Its restatement (bars 62–67) ends on V⁷d – the dominant seventh in third inversion before resolving onto Ib for a rounding-off phrase (bars 68–71¹), which ends with a perfect cadence in G major.

Bars 72–100

Now, with a further twist, above figure **b** from the first subject we hear the second motif of the second subject **g**. The interweaving of new with earlier motifs in bars 72–6 is an example of the 'organic' nature of Mozart's writing in this first movement and should be emphasised wherever possible and relevant.

For the answering phrase (bars 75–79), Mozart emphasises the three-crotchet figure, ending on a *staccato* G^7 in second inversion, V^7c in C major and then a bar of total silence. Mozart exploits the dramatic potential of silence: what will happen next?

AQA Examiner's tip

Regular phrasing such as at bars 74–5 is a feature of 'classical' music and you should make this point if relevant to your essay/answer.

Key terms

Tremolando: the rapid repetition of a note (or the rapid alternation of two different pitches) designated by several lines being drawn through the stem of the note affected.

The answer is equally dramatic: at bar 81 there erupts a full orchestral explosion of C *minor* – the tonic minor. Amid **tremolando** strings and **acciaccaturas**, the tonality changes to C major (bar 83) and then side-slips with a chromatic rise from G to G♯ (augmented 5th) onto F major, then F minor, before returning to C major and a rise through its arpeggio across two octaves. However, the tonality then moves off via a D pedal to the dominant, G major, using the sequence Ic–V–I.

With the emphasis firmly on G major and a tonic pedal very much in evidence, this section is rounded off from bar 89 with a figure that combines rhythms from the first and second subjects: dotted crotchet–quaver from the first, dotted quaver–semiquaver from the second. It is also a diminution of figure **b**:

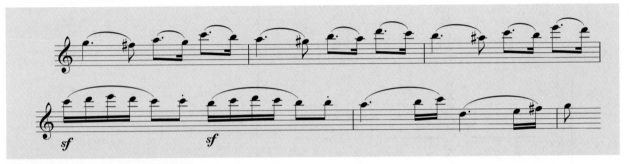

Key terms

Acciaccatura: also known as 'crush notes': a type of grace note where the note is literally 'crushed in' and played in as short a time space as possible. It is notated as a small note with a diagonal line through the stem.

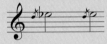

Codetta: a short 'rounding-off' section to the exposition.

This five-bar phrase is repeated from bar 94, re-orchestrated so that part of the pedal G is played to a syncopated rhythm by the 1st violins, further helping to drive the music along. The cadence is imperfect and the 1st violins, dropping to *p*, descend through the arpeggio of D[7] in bars 99–100[1]. The rest of this bar is silent – a second general rest.

Bars 101–120

Codetta: Mozart introduces a new theme for this final section of the exposition, referred to by several commentators as an epilogue.

Mozart first used this theme earlier the same year with this text:

Neal Zaslaw (1988), offers this translation: 'You are a bit innocent, my dear Pompeo; go study the way of the world'.

Remaining firmly in G major, 1st and 2nd violins sing out the melody in octaves over **pizzicato** viola and double bass and flowing quaver triadic patterns in the cello. After two bars, the oboes enter with a dominant pedal and, at the third statement of the opening phrase, the 1st bassoon adds its distinctive voice.

A seemingly innocuous figure is introduced in bar 108: this will become very important in the **development** section:

The dynamic increases to *f* from bar 111^2 as a three-bar phrase is played twice, and the codetta ends with a final reference to **al** and the chords first heard in bars 15–16. This final passage of tonic/dominant in G major leads to a perfect cadence and the end of the exposition (bar 120). As was the convention of the time, the exposition is marked to be repeated. This is not observed on all current recordings, but in Mozart's time, it enabled members of the audience – to whom this would be a new work and who would be following the musical argument aurally – to appreciate and remember the main ideas presented in this exposition. It would allow the listeners to follow the development of these ideas more easily and recognise their return in the recapitulation.

Development

The development in bars 121–188 is based on the following themes from the exposition:

◼ the first theme with its two contrasting motives (bars $1-2^1$ and 2^4-4^3)
◼ the *tutti* figure, contrasting dotted rhythms with a demisemiquaver figure (from bar 9)
◼ the countermelody to the main theme (from bar 24)
◼ the second subject (from bar 56)
◼ its secondary motif (from bar 72) and
◼ the codetta/epilogue (from bar 101).

◼ **Key terms**

Pizzicato: plucking the strings rather than playing with the bow (con arco).

Development: this is where the composer uses material from the exposition and develops or varies it. The music passes through various keys before returning to the tonic for the recapitulation.

From the exposition's final chord of G major, Mozart repeats the final G as a pivot note, deflecting the tonality from G major to an unexpected (and, considering the period in which this was written, quite unusual) E♭ major – the flat submediant of G:

Notice how Mozart features just the woodwind instruments, their unison statement covering three octaves.

As in the final section of the exposition, the codetta/epilogue theme is presented by the strings (bars 123–128), combining *pizzicato* with bowed playing and harmonised with alternate tonic and dominant chords, now in E♭ major. From the melody's third bar (bar 125), flute and 1st oboe add a dominant B♭ pedal for 17 beats. As in the exposition, two woodwind instruments repeat the last two bars, though now 1st oboe, 1st bassoon and the violins are silent, the lower strings re-entering only to underline the dominant seventh harmony under the last two beats for the second bar. The phrase, heard first in bar 108, features in bar 130 and now takes on a significant role:

Overlapping this, woodwind instruments enter at bar 133^2 playing chords in a dotted rhythm, reminiscent of bars 49–52 and cadencing into E♭ major, F minor, F major and then G minor:

There now commences (bar 139) a modulating sequence based on antiphonal entries of this final one-bar phrase, moving from G minor to F minor and back to E♭ major. As is quite typical in Mozart's music, he takes only part of this phrase – the first four quavers from bar 130 – and develops this motif:

and uses it to reverse the modulation through F minor and to G minor.

From bar 143, just the last four quavers – crotchet pattern in the lower strings is the basis of the next passage of development – begin a further modulating sequence, setting violins against flute and lower strings, before returning to use other snippets of this theme. Parts of it are gradually restored between bars 143–150.

Bars 143–145:

Bars 145–147²:

Bars 147–148²:

Modulations in these bars are from E♭ major to its relative minor, C minor, on to its dominant, G minor, before moving further afield into D minor and A minor and finally arriving at its dominant, in E major at bar 153 – a chord extremely remote from the starting point of E♭ major!

Taking up the last quaver phrase, Mozart uses it to reinforce the E major chord (bars 153–158), firstly in the upper strings, then the woodwind and then returning to the strings for a magical move from E major into the key of F major. He does this using the following sequence:

E major – E **diminished seventh** in **third inversion** – C⁷

The first subject returns in F major in its role as a transitional theme, as in bars 24 onwards. The rising motif is played by unison strings while bassoons add the countermelody. Violins continue with the next phrase in octaves, while horns sustain C (the dominant of F major) and bassoons play stepwise descending minims in parallel thirds.

Key terms

Diminished seventh: a chord formed using intervals of a minor third. In this case: E–G–B♭–D♭.

Third inversion: a seventh chord played so that the seventh is the lowest pitch, the bass note.

Did you know?

The diminished seventh consists of two interlocking diminished fifths or tritones, and this interval was often connected with the devil.

The motif and its countermelody are now taken up as the next section of the development and give rise to a modulating sequence, each repetition being one step higher after the restatement on the dominant, C. Thus, the music is heard in D major (bars 167–168) and E major (bars 169–170), though, throughout this section, the chords used are dominant sevenths. E⁷ cadences onto A minor for the next section.

From bar 171, the rhythm of the main motif is combined with the demisemiquaver rhythm first heard in bars 49–54 to produce this energetic figure over a chromatically descending bass line, shown here with the outline harmony:

Starting in A minor, Mozart moves the music rapidly through major and minor keys, B⁷ cadencing onto E major to be immediately contradicted as E minor; the B is then flattened to produce a diminished fifth chord to move chromatically to **A⁷d**, which, in turn, cadences onto D major with a further immediate change to the minor. Again, the fifth (A) is flattened leading to G⁷d. The modulations proceed with C major becoming C minor (bar 177) before a **German augmented sixth** chord is used to return the tonality to G major.

In bars 179–180, alternating tonic and dominant chords in G major (the dominant of C major) are linked by demisemiquaver phrases in bassoons and lower strings. The sheer dynamic energy that has driven this section of the development now immediately subsides to *piano*, and the gentle cadence figure derived from the end of the codetta theme, and already used extensively, returns again at this point (bars 181–183¹) in upper strings, emphasising G major. It is taken up by woodwind over a long sustained G (dominant of C major) pedal and repeated Gs from trumpets and timpani. This is the final preparation for the return to C major and the recapitulation, but, before we get there, Mozart uses this cadential figure to take the tonality from G major (where he has used a progression from **F♯ diminished seventh** to G in bars 183–185¹) to D minor and sequentially to C major (bars 185³–187), before a downward scale passage in *staccato* parallel thirds leads to the recapitulation.

Key terms

A⁷d: this is the third inversion of a chord, in this case of A⁷:

German augmented sixth: this chord is formed by taking the sixth note of the scale, flattening it, adding a third, a fifth and an augmented sixth. It resolves here to the dominant, though it often resolves to the tonic chord in third inversion:

F♯ diminished 7th: the chord built on F♯ using intervals of a minor third:

Key terms

Recapitulation: the main themes
return; sometimes exactly as in the
exposition, sometimes varied.

AQA Examiner's tip

Make a comparative list between the
exposition and the recapitulation to
be able to summarise similarities and
differences, for example:

Exposition

- Bars 1–4: **first subject** –
  two contrasting ideas – **a**,
  emphasising tonic and dominant
  and **b**, introducing a dotted
  rhythm; in C major – tonic;
  contrast of dynamics, *f* to *p*.

- Bars 5–8: **a** and **b** restated,
  starting on the dominant and
  closing on the tonic.

Recapitulation

- Bars 189–192: exact return of
  bars 1–4: **first subject** – two
  contrasting ideas – **a** and **b**,
  in C major – tonic; dynamics
  contrasted as before.

- Bars 193–196: exact
  restatement of bars 5–8.

Key terms

Harmonic series: as explained
on page 22, the series of notes
that can be played on a brass
instrument just by altering
the pressure of the lips on the
mouthpiece. As the pitch gets
higher, so the available notes are
closer together.

Things to do

Look at Mozart's use of the wind
instruments in this movement.

Recapitulation

Starting in bar 189, in C major, the **recapitulation** is exact until the
pause on the dominant in bar 211 (= bar 23 of the exposition).

Simply by altering the C major broken chord (horns) to C minor, Mozart
sets in motion a modulation to the flattened leading note, B♭. These
two nine-bar passages (28–36 and 216–224) use the same melodic and
rhythmic ideas but explore different tonalities.

Here, the harmonic progression can be summarised thus (shown along
with the imitative motif in the violins):

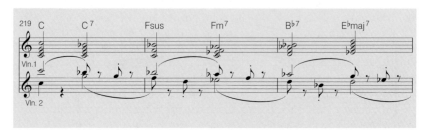

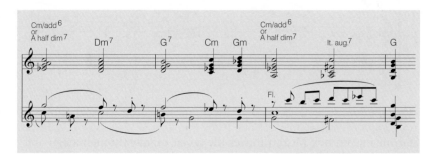

Basically, this is a sequence of seventh chords with the last three chords
providing a chromatic approach to the dominant (G major).

The recapitulation now continues exactly as did the exposition until bar
235 (the equivalent of bar 47 of the exposition). Mozart needs to alter
the course of the bridge passage so that the second subject can enter
in C major rather than G major. He does this by the simple device of
modulating into G major, rather than D major, as happened in bars 47–
49. Following this, bars 237–243[1] correspond to bars 49–55[1], though over
a G (dominant of C) pedal rather than over a D (dominant of G) pedal.

For the first five bars of the second subject (244–248) the scoring remains
faithful to that of the exposition, though the melodic outline is altered by
a simple octave shift from bar 246[2]. The ensuing changes are subtle but
significant.

At bar 249, instead of Violin I having the rising scale (partly chromatic),
this is taken over by the flute and then the bassoon. In the exposition,
the bassoon doubled the 1st violin from this point; now the doubling is
on bassoon and flute. A further alteration to the scoring takes place from
the last beat of bar 253, where it is the 1st oboe rather than the bassoon
that doubles the 1st violin. Notice the additional colour from the horns
from bar 254: this is possible because this range of notes is available to
them as part of the **harmonic series** (as they are pitched in C).

The flute is added later than the corresponding passage in the exposition,
entering only to highlight the cadence into C major at bars 258–259,
rather than for a section of the dotted rhythm.

Bars 71–79 of the exposition are now re-scored with the addition of 1st bassoon and the horns. The bassoon doubles the 1st violins an octave lower, while the horns add their warm colour to the harmony. The oboes and a flute are added for the balancing four bars and the music comes to a halt after three *staccato* crotchet chords of C^7 in 1st inversion (V^7b). In the exposition at this point, the chord was the dominant seventh of C major (G^7) and in 2nd inversion (V^7c).

After a bar's dramatic silence (bar 268), the chord resolves *ff* (*fortissimo* – 'very loud') onto F minor, the subdominant minor, to balance the exposition's resolution onto C minor, at that point the tonic minor. Again, *tremolando* strings and repeated timpani notes add to the contrast, although after just two bars the timpani stop: the only note available within this key was C, the dominant of F minor, and this would have created a different 'feel' to the music from that produced by the tonic pedal in the exposition had it continued. The timpani return from bar 273 on a G, a dominant pedal in C major, which is achieved in bar 277 following a Ic–V^7–I perfect cadence. Beginning on the F, Mozart initially uses a chromatically descending bass line to underpin the chord sequence which moves the music from F minor to C major, here summarised as:

Once the tonic key, C major, is regained in bar 277, the five-bar phrase from bar 89 returns, now, of course, anchored firmly over a tonic pedal in C major. The music is slightly re-orchestrated so that the pedal is provided by all the violins now doubled by all the woodwind instruments. Further variations to the instrumentation take place within the repetition of this phrase, the most notable, perhaps, being the addition of a simple stepwise sequential phrase in flute and bassoons:

The ensuing cadence approach – bars 285–288[1] – follows the same chord pattern, here transposed, as in the exposition (bars 97–100[1]), finishing with a downward dominant seventh arpeggio (G^7) from the 1st violins.

The codetta theme returns, now in C major. Because of the change of key here, as compared to the exposition, Mozart is able to augment the dominant oboe pedal with one in the horns (see bars 291–295[1] and compare with bars 103–107[1]) and follow the same procedure at the cadence points (compare bars 108[3]–111[1] to bars 296[3]–299[1]).

Continuing in C major, the coda follows the pattern of the codetta until bar 309[1] (bar 120[1]). From this point, Mozart adds five triumphant bars, emphasising the tonic chord and ending the movement in a blaze of full orchestral colour.

Key terms

Sus: shortened form of 'suspended' or 'suspension'. It refers to the device of holding on to, or sustaining, a note from the previous chord and delaying its resolution.

Further listening

Initially, listen to Mozart's *Symphonies Nos. 39*, K. 543 and *40*, K. 550, written in the same period as *No. 41*.

Listen to other symphonies by Mozart, such as:

- K. 183, *No. 25* – the so-called 'little' *G minor*
- K.200, *No. 28 in C Major*
- K. 201, *No. 29 in A Major*
- K. 297, *No. 31* – the 'Paris' Symphony.

Listen to symphonies by Haydn – in particular, any of:

- *Nos. 82–87*, the so-called 'Paris' symphonies
- *Nos. 93–104*, the last 12 symphonies, referred to collectively as the 'London' or 'Salomon' symphonies.

Things to do

1. Summarise the form of this first movement.

2. Make a chart of Mozart's use of the different motifs in this movement.

3. Plot a diagram to show Mozart's use of keys and key relationships.

4. Compare the recapitulation and the exposition, pointing out similarities and differences.

5. Look in detail at Mozart's use of texture and instrumental timbre.

■ Looking at the third movement: *Menuetto allegretto*

The established third movement of a symphony was a minuet and trio: an overall ternary form movement, with the minuet and trio each being in binary form, thus:

Minuet:	Section **A** repeated; Section **B** repeated
Trio:	Section **C** repeated; Section **D** repeated. At this point is added the instruction: *Menuetto D.C.* (that is, *Menuetto da capo*, meaning 'go back to the Minuet' and, conventionally, play without repeats. The additional instruction, *senza replica* ('without repeats'), is rarely used in this type of movement but is always understood.
Minuet:	Section **A**; Section **B**

- Section **A** often, but not always, modulates from the tonic to the dominant.
- Section **B** restores the tonic and often includes a repeat of Section **A**.
- The trio, though really a second minuet, will usually provide a contrast of timbre, ensemble and style from the minuet.

Summary of standard minuet and trio form:

‖: **A** :‖: **B** :‖: **C** :‖: **D** :‖ **A** ‖ **B** ‖

Minuet

The preceding slow movement was full of delicate demisemiquaver tracery in F major (the subdominant of C major), though with some strong dynamic contrasts. Here, the emphasis is on the opening chromatic descent in the 1st violins which is the basis of the movement and then the contrasting trio, full of elegance and grace.

The structure of this minuet is:

- **A**: bars 1–16
- **B**: bars 17–59.

The minuet, in the tonic key of C major, starts gracefully with just the two violins, the melody being typically Mozartian in its use of chromaticism/semitones. Lower strings, brass and timpani enter in bars 3 and 4 to point the **imperfect cadence** (I–Ic–V). The movement starts on the chord of C but without its root, and the two violins move in parallel 10ths around an inner dominant pedal (G). Whereas most of Mozart's minuet movements start loudly, this starts quietly; a firm pulse and full tonic chord is not established until the *forte* entry of horns, trumpets, timpani and lower strings in bars 3–4.

■ Key terms

Imperfect cadence: one that ends on the chord of the dominant. Often the two chords are simply I (tonic) to V (dominant). In this cadence, or half-close, chord I is used in 2nd inversion (Ic) to resolve by step to the dominant, giving Ic–V.

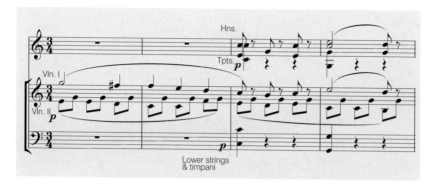

This opening phrase is balanced by a second four-bar phrase following the same pattern and ending with a double *appoggiatura* to the tonic. Again, violins I and II move in parallel 10ths around the same dominant pedal. This inner pedal is a feature throughout these opening eight bars.

At bar 9, there is a sudden dynamic increase from **p** to **f** and the full orchestra effects the modulation to the dominant (G major) with an extension of the opening idea, combining the chromatic movement with the *staccato* quavers, while the inner pedal is maintained by the violas and cellos – though the dominant note is now D:

The cadence in bars 15 and 16 is **perfect**.

This first section **A** is repeated.

The second section **B** begins **p** (*piano* – quietly) over a tonic G pedal in repeated crotchets from the horns, while trumpets, timpani, cellos and basses reinforce this on the first beat of bars 17, 19 and 21–24. The theme itself is, like the themes in the **A** section, chromatic, with the oboes playing an octave higher than the violins (whose pitches are given in this quotation):

Key terms

Perfect cadence: a 'final' cadence that uses the progression V–I (dominant to tonic), though here it is V⁷–I, simplified from the end of this phrase thus:

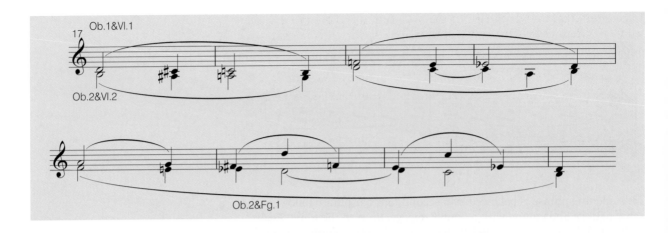

Key terms

F♯ diminished seventh: A chord built on F♯ and consisting of intervals of a minor third, thus:

![AQA Examiner's tip]

Make a note of Mozart's use of contrast of timbre and texture in this trio.

The final return to the tonic chord (23^3–24^1) uses an **F♯ diminished seventh** over the tonic pedal. Having contrasted the dynamics to start this **B** section, Mozart now contrasts them again, with a *f* (*forte* – loud) broken chord of C major (the subdominant of G) in strings and horns, repeated by woodwind and all the brass, underpinned by the timpani (bars 24^2–28^1). At this point, the opening theme from section A returns but is continued differently. There are three sequential statements by flute, oboe 1 and 1st violins, each echoed a fifth lower by bassoons, cellos and basses. The first (bar 28) starts on G, the second on A (bar 32) – but notice how Mozart varies the third bar of the flute/oboe/1st violin on this second appearance (bar 34) so that the third entry can be on D (bar 36), rather than B, and thus lead to the cadential phrase that leads back into C major (though with a passing modulation to F major).

In keeping with the usual form of the minuet and trio in this period, this second section has been longer than the first, the music is a development of that heard in the first section and the music from that first section has been restated.

Trio

The structure of the trio is:

■ **C:** bars 60–67
■ **D:** bars 68–87.

The trio afforded a contrast to the minuet, usually most notably in its scoring. Mozart follows that pattern, starting with a simple V^7–I cadence in C major for flute, bassoons and horns, followed by a skittish quaver figure in 1st oboe and 1st violins over a simple V^7b–I–V harmony:

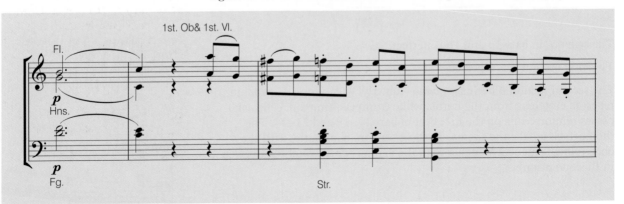

In fact, the eight bars that make up the first section of this trio are a wonderful example of what is meant by 'classical' balanced phrases:

- ■ the first phrase (bars 60–63) moves from tonic to dominant
- ■ the second (bars 64–67) cadences firmly, but simply, in the tonic
- ■ the two phrases are based on very similar rhythms and melodic shape:

This delicate, lightly scored first section is followed by a dramatic outburst over an E pedal (from bar 68), starting and ending on a chord of E major, the mediant major. The initial feeling is of A minor, the relative minor, though Mozart uses two diminished seventh chords in the course of this passage: D♯ diminished seventh in bars 70 and 74, resolving to E major on each occasion, and G♯ diminished seventh in bar 72 resolving onto A minor. The strong rhythmic drive of the pedal is another striking feature of this section, lasting seven bars (68–74):

Again, there is a sudden dynamic change: nowhere in this movement does Mozart use a *crescendo* or a *diminuendo*. Strings play two perfect cadences in sequence in bars 76–79, first in E major then in D major, before a full restatement of the first section of this trio, with some revisions to the scoring, most notably the addition of flute and 1st bassoon to reinforce the final cadence in C major.

Menuetto D.C.

The minuet is now restated without repeats.

Things to do

1. Summarise the form of this third movement.

2. Comment on Mozart's use of instruments.

3. Plot a key scheme for this movement.

4. Comment on the areas of contrast between the minuet and the trio sections.

5. Listen to other examples of this form, perhaps starting with *Symphonies Nos. 39*, K. 543 and *40*, K. 550.

6. Look closely at Mozart's use of dynamics and dynamic contrast.

AQA Examination-style questions

Questions in the examination will relate to Mozart's use of form, tonality, instrumentation and the other elements of music. One, two or three elements may be included within the scope of the question. Alternatively, the question may take the form of a quotation that would engage you in a more general discussion, perhaps relating to genre, context or a more general analysis of the use of the musical elements.

Questions will focus on a movement, a large section of a movement (such as exposition, development or recapitulation) or may ask you to make a comparison between the two prescribed movements. Therefore, there will be no questions focusing on very short passages.

You must make sure that you identify the precise meaning of the question and keep it in mind as you plan and then write your essay. Keep your comments succinct and try to find as many points as you can; referring to specific bars, phrases or passages in the symphony to support and illustrate your answer.

Exam practice question on the first movement

1 Consider to what extent the first movement follows a traditional pattern of sonata form.

Key words here are:

- *Consider:* weigh up the arguments for and against
- *to what extent:* you are being asked to come to a conclusion, having presented your evidence
- *a traditional pattern:* you will need to set out what you consider to be the 'normal' pattern for sonata form and then look at what Mozart does.

A possible approach would be to outline sonata form, referring to:

- exposition
- development
- recapitulation

and pointing out the function and position of the 'optional' sections: slow introduction, codetta and coda.

In the course of this, you will need to refer to expectations as to key relationships between the different sections.

- Outline Mozart's use of sonata form in this first movement.
- Point out where he follows the 'standard' pattern and where he deviates.
- Finally, draw conclusions as to the extent to which he follows or deviates from the 'standard' form.

Exam practice question on the third movement

2 Describe the ways in which the third movement is typical of a Classical minuet and trio.

Notice that it *does not* ask you to 'discuss to *what extent* the third movement is typical of a Classical minuet and trio'. Therefore, you are being asked, specifically, to point out features that support the view that this movement is typical of a Classical minuet and trio.

Having made this important distinction, you should now make a list of what you consider to be the salient points. These might well include:

- the minuet and trio's 'Classical' design, overall, of each part having two repeated sections with the second section being longer, similar in style and melodic material to the first and including a (re-orchestrated) restatement of the first section
- the time signature of $3/4$
- the regular beat (the minuet was a dance, after all)
- the choice of tempo – *Allegretto* – quite fast – appropriate for this type of dance and typical of other minuet and trio movements from this period
- the main theme's regular, balanced four-bar phrasing
- the use of chromatic passing notes
- the gently rocking accompaniment supporting the melody
- the question/answer, antecedent/consequent nature of the melodic material
- the modulation to the dominant at the end of the first section
- dependence on primary chords to reinforce the tonic
- the slow rate of harmonic change – often more than one bar on each chord
- the reduced orchestration of the trio
- strong tonic–dominant feel in the harmony in the trio
- strong, contrasting outburst from bar 68 over pedal E
- smooth modulation to the dominant's dominant (very typical of this period) before returning to C major (the tonic) via G^7
- further use of regular, balanced four-bar phrasing in the trio
- music developed by sequence and by use of imitation
- wide use of single line melody over (largely) homophonic accompaniment.

This would be enough to produce an excellent response, making judicious and precise references to the score. Be sure to use appropriate musical terminology within your answer.

Do:

- keep your answer focused on the question at all times
- make a list of what needs to be covered
- get on with the answer straight away
- conclude by referring to the question via a brief summary.

Do not:

- answer the question you wish the examiner had asked!
- simply write down everything you know about the topic referred to in the question and leave it to the examiner to pick out any relevant facts
- repeat the question as an introduction: the examiner has the question in front of him or her
- give generalised background information.

3 Historical study for AS

Learning objectives:

- to understand the content of each of the three areas of study

- to understand the focus of each of the areas of study

- to become familiar with the basic vocabulary of each of the areas of study

- to learn more about the main topics to be studied within each area of study

- to discover areas for further individual study.

Areas of study

You will choose one AoS from the following three options:

- choral music in the Baroque period
- music theatre: a study of the musical from 1940 to 1980
- British popular music from 1960 to the present day.

Examination will be by a choice from two essay questions about your chosen area of study. The specification gives a list of composers or groups/singers of the genre, but this should not be seen as indicating *either* that you must study all of these *or* that you cannot study other suitable composers/groups/singers within the period. However, within each area of study, various features are bullet-pointed and you must make sure that you cover these through your choice of composers/groups/singers and works.

Choral music in the Baroque period

This option covers the period c.1625–1750 and, therefore, a very wide range of composers and compositions, even within the parameters of this specification.

You would be well advised to concentrate on learning, initially, about the main forms that make up this unit and the main types of vocal setting. Then you should look closely at several examples of each type of composition:

- arias
- recitatives
- choruses.

These should cover a range of styles from different composers, such as:

- Charpentier
- Buxtehude
- Purcell
- Vivaldi
- Bach
- Handel.

Comparison can be made between secular and sacred compositions.

Having made initial choices on which works to study:

- Be selective about which movements you look at: a judicious choice of arias, recitatives and choruses is required rather than close attention to entire works.
- Be able to compare different styles of these movements, both from within a work, and between two (or three) works.
- Be able to discuss the composer's use of form and tonality.
- Be aware of the use of texture.

For any essay, you will need to understand the precise thrust of the question: key words and phrases in examination questions are 'describe', 'write informatively', 'analyse', 'comment in detail on', 'write a critical commentary on', and so on. All require that you provide a focused, logical and always relevant answer, supported by a comprehensive range of specific evidence.

Music theatre: the study of the musical from 1940 to 1980

Again, this is a very rich period and there are many very important works you could study. An excellent starting point is to realise that 'musical theatre', by its very name, consists of both a play following a narrative and the music; both songs and dances. The musicals to concentrate on are those wherein the characters are clearly defined and differentiated through their music rather than those where a single style of music permeates the entire musical.

You should therefore research:

- the context of the musical and its characters
- how these are presented through the music, whether in songs or dance.

You should select a range of:

- solo songs
- small and large ensembles
- dance movements.

Again, the breadth of your work should enable you to answer questions that require comparison of two songs, ensembles or dances from the *same* musical, as well as one that invites comparison between the work of two different composers.

Composers might include:

- Richard Rodgers
- Leonard Bernstein
- Jerry Bock
- Lionel Bart
- Andrew Lloyd Webber
- Claude-Michel Schönberg.

Musicals might include:

- *Oklahoma!*
- *West Side Story*
- *Fiddler on the Roof*
- *Oliver!*
- *Evita*
- *Cats*
- *Les Misérables.*

British popular music from 1960 to the present day

This option offers the opportunity to focus on the areas of music that interest you most, as well as increasing your understanding of the historical perspective and development of popular music. In many ways, the music of the Beatles will be integral to any study of 1960s music, though other groups and artists from that period should not be ignored. The defining styles of each decade could well form the basis of your work, looking at how specific musical styles, the changing use of instruments, the introduction of technology, the role of the lyrics (in terms of topics covered by songs and the influence of the internet) have impacted on this aspect of popular culture.

Your studies will focus on the key musical figures in popular music since 1960 and should include the roles played by arrangers, composers and record producers. There are several 'definitive sounds' in popular music, including Motown, folk rock, and punk, the 'big' sounds of some studio producers, the move away from the use solely of guitars and a drum kit as the backing, the use of technological and recording effects, and so on.

Here are some initial suggestions.

British bands of the 60s:

■ Beatles
■ Rolling Stones.

Sounds of the 70s:

■ punk rock: Sex Pistols, Stranglers, Pogues
■ folk rock: Fairport Convention, Steeleye Span
■ progressive rock: Genesis, Pink Floyd.

The technological revolution of the 80s and 90s:

■ Oasis
■ Blur.

Recent trends: this area, especially, is where you might be exercising your own strong and precise interests. However, it is vitally important that you can write about the musical features of each song you study – in the same way as in the 'musicals' topic – so it is important to be able to explain the singer's or group's use of some, or all, of the following:

■ melody
■ harmony – chord progressions and so on
■ rhythm
■ texture – the way the instruments and voices are used
■ form and structure
■ the relationship between the vocal parts and the accompaniment
■ manipulation of sound – synthesisers, keyboards, drum machines, multi-tracking and so on
■ special effects.

■ Choral music in the Baroque period

Within this area of study, you will study settings for solo voices and for choir. The types of composition to cover are:

■ the cantata
■ the oratorio
■ the mass
■ the anthem

although the Ode and settings of the *Gloria* and *Te Deum* could also be included.

The Baroque period is generally regarded as covering *c.*1625–1750 and, therefore, includes composers such as Luigi Rossi (1597–1659), Giacomo Carissimi (1605–74), Marc-Antoine Charpentier (1634–1704), Diderik (or Dietrich) Buxtehude (1637–1707), Henry Purcell (1659–95), Alessandro Scarlatti (1660–1725), François Couperin (1668–1733), Antonio Vivaldi (1685–1741), Johann Sebastian Bach (1685–1750) and George Frederic Handel (1685–1759).

The cantata

There are two main types of cantata:

- the Baroque solo cantata: featuring lyrical but quite vocally agile melodic lines. These cantatas consisted of a dramatic or pastoral narrative poem set to a mixture of aria, *arioso* and *recitative*
- an extended choral work, with or without solo voices.

The inclusion of the chorale in the Baroque solo cantata form led to the church cantata. Those of Dietrich Buxtehude (1637–1707) use *arioso* (see page 43), strophic variations, ground basses and **canto fermo** treatment of the chorale; those of Georg Böhm (1661–1733) and Johann Pachelbel (1653–1706) consist of a series of extended variations on the chorale melody.

Erdmann Neumeister (1571–1676) wrote texts along more openly operatic lines, regarding the cantata as 'a fragment of an opera', initially discarding any biblical passages or hymn/chorale texts in favour of a more poetical style to be set as *recitativo secco* (see page 44) or as *da capo* arias. Choruses were added to a later cycle and then biblical texts.

His works were set by Philipp Krieger (1649–1725). Further developments were made by Friedrich Wilhelm Zachau (1663–1712), who taught Handel, and Johann Kuhnau (1660–1722), both of whom preferred to set the first verse of the chorale as a large choral and orchestral movement, while treating the second with a simple harmonisation. This became by far the most common form of the cantata adopted by later composers.

Bach's *Christmas Oratorio* is, in fact, a set of six cantatas for solo voices, chorus and orchestra. There remain, from Bach's vast output, some 16 secular cantatas and about 200 church cantatas.

Bach's well-known cantata *Wachet auf* (Sleepers wake), BWV 140 (1731), was written for the 27th Sunday after Trinity and is based on the parable of the ten virgins as related in the gospel for the day (Matthew XXV 1–13). A grand *Maestoso* introduction leads into verse 1 of the chorale for orchestra and four-part chorus. Sopranos have the chorale melody above moving parts in alto, tenor and bass. Note the extensive use of imitation and the fugal setting of *Alleluia*. A tenor recitative leads to the first of two duets where the image of Christ appears as the heavenly bridegroom: here, a slow and passionate setting includes an obbligato for *violino piccolo* (a small violin, tuned a minor third higher than the normal instrument). The soprano seeks assurance that the saviour will come and Jesus gives the longed-for answer. The famous setting of the chorale melody is next, opening with this instrumental phrase:

The duet that follows resolves all anxiety in one of the happiest pieces Bach wrote. The cantata closes with a dignified, homophonic setting of the chorale's third verse.

Purcell's odes are often regarded as cantatas for chorus, soloists and string orchestra, with frequent reinforcing from trumpets, recorders and oboes. First and last movements maintain unity of key, while middle

Key terms

Ground bass: a repeating pattern in the bass over which the composer weaves melodic and harmonic variations. The ground bass – often 2, 4 or 8 bars long – is usually heard either alone or just with simple harmonies at the beginning of the work.

Chaconne: the term derives from an obsolete dance, probably of Spanish origin. It was usually in triple time, with an accent on the second beat, at a slow tempo, and constructed as a series of variations on a ground bass, usually 8 bars in length.

Passacaglia: an early Italian or Spanish dance, similar to the chaconne, constructed over a ground of 2, 4 or 8 bars. If anything, the passacaglia seems to be of a more solemn character than the chaconne.

Did you know?

The *Crucifixus* in Bach's *B minor Mass* is a '**chaconne**' or '**passacaglia**', which uses a ground bass. In this case, the ground bass appears in the continuo line (played in all likelihood by the organ, cellos and basses), while the strings and flutes fill in the harmonies implied by the bass line. A ground bass always has strong harmonic implications even when it stands alone; here, Bach's scoring leaves no doubt as to the chords he intended.

sections use related keys. Purcell's favourite device of the **ground bass** is well in evidence. In the *Ode on St Cecilia's day* (1692), 'Hail bright Cecilia', No. 3 *Hark, hark each tree* and No. 8 *Wondrous machine* (both for bass voice) are written over such a bass. No. 10 *In vain the am'rous flute* (a duet for alto/countertenor and tenor voices) contains a chromatic phrase, which formed the ground bass for *Dido's lament* in his opera *Dido and Aeneas* (1689).

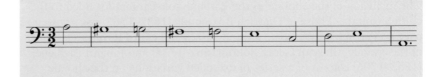

Purcell's ode begins with an overture on a grand scale, varying tempi, timbre and texture. It opens very much in the French style with dotted rhythms and antiphonal use of strings and oboes against trumpets. The ensuing *Canzona* showcases Purcell's contrapuntal skills before further antiphony leads to a perfect cadence in D major (the tonic). An *Adagio* follows, its minor tonality contrasting sharply with the brightness of D major. Trumpets are silent as Purcell varies the music's phrase lengths (five and four bars) with chromaticism increasing during the closing ten bars and a final close on the tonic major, heralding the return to D major and trumpet fanfares.

Choral concert at St Patrick's Cathedral on Fifth Avenue, Manhattan, New York

The oratorio

This is the setting of a dramatic poem or other text which is usually of a sacred character. It is sung throughout by solo voices and chorus (choir) and accompanied by orchestra. It is invariably performed without scenery or costume and was regarded by some, initially, as a way of achieving a large-scale vocal and orchestral performance without the expense of staging an opera. In fact, in a dictionary of music by Grassineau from 1740, *oratorio* was described as 'a sort of spiritual opera' and *oratorio* and *sacred drama* were virtually interchangeable.

Vocal settings fall into three main categories:

- aria
- recitative
- chorus.

Aria

An aria is an elaborate setting for solo voice, often in a ternary form when it is known as the *da capo* aria. In all types of aria, words and phrases from the text were readily repeated. The box lists the many different styles of arias from this time.

The *da capo* aria: Handel: *Messiah*, no. 48, *The trumpet shall sound*

This is, additionally, an example of an *aria obbligato* (with a solo instrument). Other excellent examples worthy of study are *Laudamus te*, *Quoniam tu solus sanctus*, *Et in spiritum sanctum Dominum* and *Benedictus* from Bach's *Mass in B minor*. Many further examples of the *da capo* aria can be found in these two works as well as in Bach's *Christmas Oratorio* (for example, in Part I: *Prepare thyself, Zion* and *Mighty Lord and King all glorious*).

Handel's aria is preceded, as is so often the case, by a short, introductory recitative, which effects a change from a simple *recitativo secco* (see page 44) to fanfare-like chords that herald the introduction of the solo trumpet.

The aria, marked *Pomposo, ma non allegro* (Pompously, but not too fast), begins with a 28-bar instrumental introduction, dominated by the solo trumpet. The bass voice enters alone with a rising arpeggio, sustaining the final note to support the return of the trumpet's opening motif:

Melismatic: where a word or syllable is set to more than one note.

Hemiola: a device where the rhythmic emphasis is shifted so that two bars of triple time sound more like three bars of duple time – for example, three minim beats across two bars of three crotchets.

Recitative: the name given to those sections of the oratorio or cantata that are declamatory rather than lyrical. Many, though by no means all, end with an instrumental perfect cadence.

Recitativo secco (literally, 'dry recitative'): here, the text is set as simply as possible, with the melodic line tending to follow the vocal inflexions and rhythms of the text and the accompaniment being slow-moving chords with a sustaining bass instrument, written in the form of a figured bass. This type of recitative was used to deliver long passages of text in a short time, with no repetition.

Recitativo accompagnato/recitativo stromentato ('accompanied recitative'): the accompaniment is orchestral and a more dramatic situation is the result: the text covered rapidly changing emotions and the orchestra both reinforced this, through its accompaniment, and added brief instrumental passages, punctuating the text.

Things to do

Compare the given figured bass with the editor's realisation of 14a in the Watkins Shaw Novello edition.

As usual with Handel, there are many examples of word painting (reflecting the meaning of the words in the music used to set them). Some examples are:

- the long sustained note on 'sound'
- the rising phrase on 'dead shall be raised' (bars 33–34 and 37–39²)
- the transformation and extension of the quaver phrase for 'changed' (bars 60–65 and elsewhere)
- the long, almost interminable phrase to set the word 'immortality' (bars 186–194 and 199–209).

Melismatic word-setting can be found at 'changed' and 'immortality' (bars as above).

The contrasting section of this aria begins at bar 156³: the music moves to B minor, the relative minor, and the trumpet is silenced, further underlining the change. There is much use of the **hemiola** rhythm, including this example from the end of the first phrase of this section:

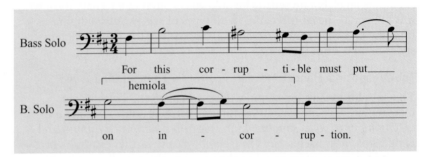

Each section of this aria ends with a short *Adagio* section: in the first section it occurs at the end of the vocal setting (the final 'We shall be changed', bars 139–140), while in the central section it takes up the final three bars ('immortality', bars 211–213²).

A contrasting style can be found in the soprano aria *He shall feed His flock*, no. 20 in Handel's *Messiah*. This is in a pastoral style with a ¹²⁄₈ time signature and marked *Larghetto e piano* (Quite slowly and quietly). It is in simple binary form, starting in B♭ major, modulating to F major (the dominant) and from there to C minor (the relative minor of the subdominant) before returning to B♭ major. The whole of the music is then repeated with different words, virtually as the second stanza of a strophic setting.

Recitative

A good starting point to compare these two types of recitative (*recitativo secco* and *recitativo accompagnato*) is Nos. 14a–16 of Handel's *Messiah* (using here the edition published by Novello, edited by Watkins Shaw).

14a: There were shepherds abiding in the field

Over a simple sustained C bass and chords of C, G⁷ and C, the soprano sings a simple, syllabic setting of the text, the melodic line following the natural inflection of the words.

14b: And lo, the angel of the Lord came upon them

This starts in F major, and the main feature of the accompaniment is the rising broken chord figuration:

This is maintained over a regular, pulsing quaver chord progression of I–I^7–IV–V^7–I–Ib–IV and then the final perfect cadence:

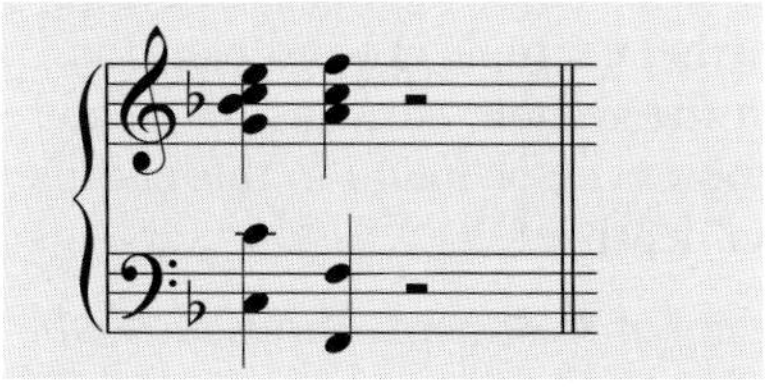

A rising fourth, G to C, attracts our attention at the words 'And lo'. The first climax is at the word 'Lord', set to high F while the word 'glory' reaches even higher – to G. The final 'and they were sore afraid' steps down from the F to the dominant, C.

15: And the angel said unto them

Returning to *recitativo secco*, sustained chords support the mainly triadic melody which, again, derives its melodic shape and rhythmic impulse from the text. The setting is in two distinct sections, each ending with a perfect cadence: the first starts on a first inversion of A and ends on E major. From there, Handel shifts the key towards F♯ minor, which is where this recitative ends.

16: And suddenly there was with the angel

The feeling of joy associated with these words is underlined by the move to a bright D major and a high register:

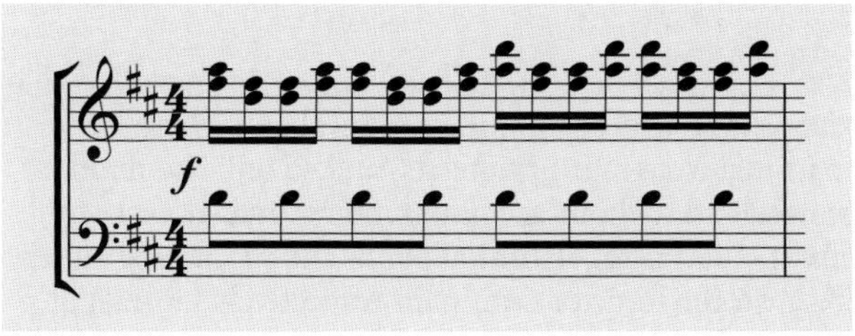

A three-bar introduction sets the mood of rejoicing before the soprano enters with a fanfare-like dotted rhythm and rise from A to repeated Ds. The Watkins Shaw edition shows some of the vocal variations that might be used to decorate the given melody and, certainly, the repetition of the high A at the end on 'say' is generally used, highlighting the ending on the dominant and preparing for the entry of the **chorus**.

Chorus

Within an oratorio, the chorus had a major part to play: see Handel's *Israel in Egypt, Judas Maccabeus* or *Messiah*, and Bach's *Christmas Oratorio* (in which they also sing chorale settings). Within music for the chorus can come homophonic and polyphonic settings. Homophonic literally means 'one sound' or 'same-sounding' from the Greek. This is where all the parts move together, presenting a melody line with chordal accompaniment. Polyphonic means 'many sounds', or contrapuntal. This is where many different melodic lines combine and interweave.

Key terms

Chorus: music sung by the choir, traditionally in four parts: SATB – soprano, alto, tenor and bass.

Did you know?

In the Baroque period, nearly all choral works were written for all-male groups using both boys and men.

These two distinct types of settings can be readily seen in no. 26 of Handel's *Messiah – All we like sheep have gone astray –* where the opening setting of 'All we like sheep' is an example of homophonic writing while 'have gone astray' is set in a polyphonic style. This is also a good example of the use of word-painting (where the music reflects the meaning of the words) in spite of the fact that the music was originally set to a different Italian text. Thus, the chorus sings as one to represent the flock of sheep but follows separate lines to reflect taking separate routes or paths. A little later comes a further example of word-painting, with the use of the semiquaver figure on the syllable 'turn', as the music turns around on itself. Many other examples can be found in this chorus and others, and will be studied in greater depth later.

You should choose some which give variety of treatment – from *Messiah*, for example, you might also study:

- no. 12 *For unto us a child is born* (here there is a good balance between homophonic writing and some *coloratura* passages for voices)
- no. 25 *And with his stripes* and no. 28 *He was despised* (largely contrapuntal/fugal)
- the sequence of choruses nos. 24–6
- no. 17 *Glory to God* and no. 33 *Lift up your heads* (antiphonal effects between high and low voices) and
- no. 46 *Since by man came death* (with its contrast of tempi and key).

In Bach's *Mass in B minor*, there are few examples of extended homophonic choral writing. Instead, Bach favours contrapuntal textures:

- no. 1: Kyrie from bar 30, with the fugal subject presented instrumentally from bar 5
- no. 3: Kyrie
- no. 20: Sanctus: the *Pleni sunt coeli et terra* section.

Fugue

This is a type of contrapuntal composition for a set number of voices or parts, giving 'a three-part fugue', 'a four-part fugue', and so on. The main theme, or 'subject', is presented without accompaniment, and successive voices imitate this subject, alternating its initial pitch, and presenting either the subject or its 'answer' in the tonic or dominant respectively (at least at first). The answer can be 'real', which is to say it maintains exactly the same intervals as the original and, therefore, is in the new key (dominant), or 'tonal', where pitches are slightly adjusted, having started on the dominant, to retain the original key. The answer is combined with a 'countersubject', voices presenting the subject/answer followed by the countersubject.

The fugue then has no set form but usually alternates 'episodes' with 'middle' and 'final' entries of the subject.

Techniques include:

- 'augmentation' and 'diminution' of the fugue subject: making the notes all longer or all shorter than the original subject
- 'stretto': overlapping entries
- pedal: where entries are heard over a sustained note.

Here is the opening of chorus no. 25 *And with His stripes* to show how the opening works. You will notice that Handel, like Bach, does not slavishly follow rules in that entries of the subject, answer and countersubject are varied, though always recognisable.

Simple homophonic settings are to be found in the chorales that feature in the cantatas: in Part I of Bach's *Christmas Oratorio,* nos. 5 and 10 set chorales *How shall I fitly meet Thee* and *Ah! Dearest Jesus* respectively.

No. 5: How shall I fitly meet Thee

Marked *Adagio* and really in A minor although it starts and ends on chords of E major, this chorale falls into regular phrases, each of which ends with a recognisable cadence and modulates frequently to closely related keys, including C major, D minor and G major. Bach adds many decorated passing notes to the lower parts.

No. 10: Ah! Dearest Jesus

In this setting, the final number in Part I, Bach separates each phrase of the chorale melody with an instrumental section, based on a simple rhythmic idea (shown alongside):

In Part II of the *Christmas Oratorio*, no. 11 is a *recitativo secco* for tenor voice, The Evangelist (*And there were shepherds*), which serves as an introduction to no. 12, the chorale *Break forth, O beauteous, heavenly light*. The recitative is in E minor and ends with a perfect cadence into B minor. The ensuing chorale is in G major, the change from minor to major emphasising the move from being 'sore afraid' to the comfort of 'the beauteous, heavenly light' that ushers in the morning. Each phrase ends with a clear cadence into G, D, A minor or E minor, and Bach maintains continuous movement in one or more of the lower voice parts. These moving parts often add passing dissonance to the harmony, and such stylistic features should be noted when moving to A2 and the study of Bach chorale-style harmony.

For example, in this extract, after an opening chord of G major, the move to the subdominant (C) is delayed by the tenor's repetition of B, with the same process being applied to the following chord. On the third beat, the chord of G moves first to A^7d and then to the 1st inversion of D major, before a suspended D in the soprano (bar 2^1) resolves to V^7–I in D major (the dominant):

In this second extract:

The phrase starts in E minor and, as the soprano sings repeated Bs (an inverted pedal), the underlying harmony is I–V⁷c–Ib before the introduction of a G♯ in the bass heralds a passing modulation to A minor. A sequential modulation to B minor ensues before a perfect cadence in E minor, which follows the pattern of the perfect cadence at the end of the first phrase. The quavers G to F♯ in the alto (last beat, bar 2, a note of anticipation) move the harmony from an A♯ diminished seventh to the dominant seventh (1st inversion) in B minor. The rising chromatic bass is often found in Bach's harmonic progressions.

In the final phrase of this chorale, you might also notice the consecutive dissonances caused by the tenor's quaver movement in the penultimate bar and the tenor's decoration of the final cadence. (Note that the F♯ doesn't resolve to the G but leaps to the B to complete the tonic chord.)

In common with several other cantatas, Part II of Bach's work starts (no. 10) with an instrumental symphony, a pastoral *Larghetto* in ¹²/₈ and G major. There is an obvious parallel with the *Pastoral Symphony* (no. 13), which comes virtually midway through Part I of Handel's *Messiah* and, as in Bach's *Christmas Oratorio*, leads into the passage about the shepherds (the sequence of recitatives already mentioned).

The mass

'Mass' in music refers to the setting of the main sections of the church service of that name. There are five main sections:

- *Kyrie*
- *Gloria*
- *Credo*
- *Sanctus* with *Benedictus*
- *Agnus Dei*.

Examples include the *Mass in B minor* by J.S. Bach, though works on this scale were not intended for liturgical use. There were also settings of single movements, such as the *Gloria*, set by Charpentier and Vivaldi, among others. The choruses in Bach's *Mass* are mostly in five parts and take up a large proportion of the work, which was written over a period of time. It is thought unlikely he ever heard it performed in its entirety, although parts were sung at Leipzig. Donald Jay Grout (in *A History of Western Music, 2005*) describes the *Mass* in this way:

> It is too long and too elaborate to be used in any church service. It is, rather, a work which . . transcends denominational limits and rises to the height of a universal statement of Christian faith.

For example, Bach divides the *Kyrie* (just six words of text) into three separate, substantial movements: the opening and closing movements are choral numbers, while the middle movement is a duet for two sopranos. The opening of the first movement serves several purposes:

1   Its strong, instrumental opening clearly establishes the tonic key of B minor.

2   The fugue subject, when transferred to the choir (here representing all of God's people), sounds like a collective cry for mercy.

3   The initial choice of timbre, melodic line and tonality sets the solemn tone of the *Kyrie*.

The ensuing *Christe Eleison* is for soprano duet and is, perhaps, a plea for mercy on a more personal level. The return of the text *Kyrie Eleison* gives rise to another fugal movement for chorus.

The *Gloria* is primarily in the major: D major as the tonic plus its related keys of A major and G major. The relative minor is used for the sections relating to 'sin' – *Qui tollis peccata mundi* – and a plea for 'mercy' – *Qui sedes ad dexteram Patris*.

Many sections of the Vivaldi *Gloria* might be studied, including the opening chorus and the famous soprano duet *Laudamus Te*.

The anthem

There are two main types of anthems:

■   The full anthem: written for chorus/choir throughout, usually in a contrapuntal style.

■   The verse anthem: written for one or more solo voices with organ or viol accompaniment and including brief passages for chorus/choir. This was extremely popular in England in the 17th century.

Henry Purcell (1659–95) wrote many fine anthems. In the verse anthem, contrasting sections of text are set as both solos and choruses. Earlier composers such as Byrd, and his successors Orlando Gibbons and Thomas Weelkes, developed the potential of this form in the period leading up to the Commonwealth (during which church music was suppressed). After the Restoration, further important developments were made to the form. In 1662 the king's enlarged violin band, modelled on *Les 24 violons* of the French court of Louis XIV, was introduced into the Chapel Royal to play symphonies and ritornellos between the verses of the anthem. This prompted the development of the 'orchestral' anthem such as Locke's *Be thou exalted, Lord*, which is written for three four-part choirs with soloists, five-part string band, a consort of viols and two theorbos.

Purcell drew together the work of his predecessors and wrote the most effective anthems of his generation; again some of them with orchestral accompaniment, such as *Rejoice in the Lord alway*. Most of his anthems were written during the reign of King Charles II (1660–85), in other words, from the late 70s to about 1685. *Rejoice in the Lord alway* is also known as *The bell anthem* because of the falling scalic figure that is a major feature of the introduction. It was written for three soloists (ATB), SATB choir and orchestra.

Did you know?

A theorbo is a stringed instrument, rather like a large lute. It was popular in the 17th century and part of the 18th.

The 16-bar introduction is written over the descending major scale, heard ten times and, on its last appearance, continued downwards to the subdominant in preparation for the dominant pedal approach to the final cadence. This coincides with a change of time signature, from $^4/_4$ to $^3/_4$, for the initial homophonic entry of the soloists:

Imitative entries begin at bar 45 ('Let your moderation be known unto all men'). The choir takes up the soloists' opening homophony, re-scored and modulating to A minor before a further modulation to D minor helps effect a return to C major. Further statements are interrupted by brief interjections by the soloists, giving an antiphonal effect (bars 65–70).

The bass soloist enters at bar 79³ ('Be careful for nothing') to music that constantly shifts tonality, reaching G major (the dominant) for the imitative entries at bar 88³, which becomes another largely homophonic passage for the soloists. The time signature of $^4/_4$ or common time returns at bar 102 as the music turns briefly to the key of A major for this beautiful passage:

The orchestra takes up this passage from the end of bar 117, starting in C major, and emphasises the descending scalic figure heard in the alto soloist from bar 113³, bringing back memories of the opening 'bell' motif. The rest of the anthem consists of earlier passages repeated: bars 16³–28² at 133³–145² and bars 55³–76² at 145³ until the end.

You could refer, at this point, to Handel's *Chandos* anthems and/or his *Coronation* anthems, in particular *The king shall rejoice* (1727). Many centres may still have copies of this work as it was set by AQA at AS as part of the previous specification.

This anthem is one of four written for the coronation of King George II and Queen Caroline, the others, equally worthy of study, being *Zadok the priest*, *My heart is inditing* and *Let thy hand be strengthened*. *Zadok the priest* has been sung at every coronation since its first performance in 1727. Coronation anthems are written on a much larger scale than those anthems designed for use during the service of Evensong and Matins.

The king shall rejoice is written for strings, oboes, trumpets, drums and SAATTB (the distribution of the choir of the Chapel Royal). The orchestration is typical of this period, with the strings and continuo providing the core of the accompaniment, while the brass are introduced for the more regal effect they provide. The choral writing shows Handel's intuition for setting words; something that had made him so successful as a composer of operas and oratorios. He sensed just when it was appropriate to use a declamatory, homophonic style for maximum impact or a polyphonic style to generate tension and excitement: this shows great dramatic talent and can be seen throughout the work, from the opening choral homophony of *The king shall rejoice* to the contrapuntal excitement and climax of the long closing *Allelujah*.

The anthem consists of five movements, beginning with an orchestral introduction (in *ritornello* form) to the first chorus: *The king shall rejoice*. The texture is mainly chordal and is largely based on primary harmonies. D major is a characteristically 'royal' key and, of course, well suited to the trumpets. The chorus' entry is chordal, a powerful homophonic texture. There follows a chain of suspensions in bars 36–38 before a modulation to the dominant.

Key terms

Notes inégales: French for 'unequal notes'.

The massive sound of this first movement gives way to 'Exceeding glad shall he be': the dotted rhythm is often played as **notes inégales**. These are characteristic of music of the French Baroque style and would often be performed as if the music were in ⁹⁄₈ rather than ³⁄₄. Thus, the opening

would be played:

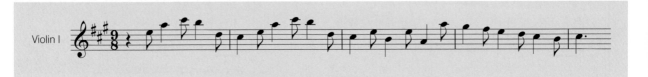

The trumpets and drums are silent while the other instruments are reduced to a three-part texture. Imitative entries from bars 31 and 41 give rise to chains of suspensions; interestingly, the first entries are a falling triadic figure, while the second are rising. Notice also the use of the hemiola rhythm in bars 45–46. In a further variation on imitative entries, Handel uses pairs of voices from bar 51. The falling triad figure returns at bar 60, rising at figure 70 to complete this binary form movement prior to the coda, which begins with a chain of suspensions over a descending bass line (bars 76–82). This chorus ends with a return to a homophonic texture (from bar 94), including two further examples of the hemiola rhythm. The opening orchestral section returns as a postlude, cadencing firmly in A major.

The short chorus *Glory and great worship* is in D major and links into the relative minor tonality of movement 4; the first of two fugal choruses, the final chorus being a double fugue. No. 4 begins with the fugue subject stated in unison by both altos and tenors, and linked to the second entry – the 'answer' – by a sequential phrase/codetta. Altos then continue with the countersubject, while the tenors and basses start the answer on the dominant.

Here is the opening of the double fugue of the final chorus:

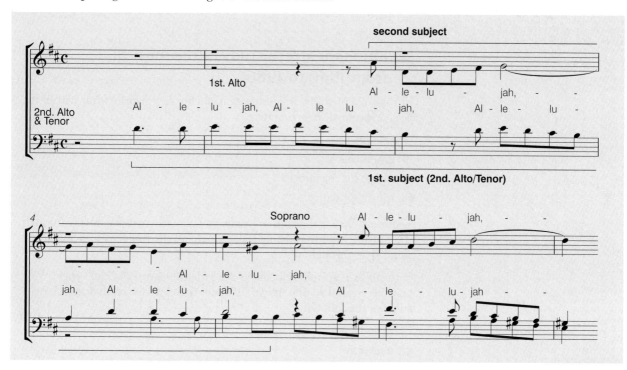

Handel uses these subjects freely and imaginatively and exploits various motifs from within them, notably as found at the 2nd alto/tenor's second 'Allelujah', the rising quavers to the minim at the start of the second subject and the three cadential notes.

Notice the antiphonal effects from letter N (bar 17), later joined to a chain of suspensions, further underlining Handel's contrapuntal skills. This great paean on 'Allelujah' closes with massive homophony before a typical Handelian silence and final, *Adagio* cadence (compare this with the ending of the *Hallelujah chorus* in *Messiah*).

AQA Examination-style questions

3 How did Baroque composers create a mood of celebration in their music? Refer to at least **two** different pieces of music in your answer.

■ Choose music for celebration such as Coronation anthems or settings of passages such as the *Gloria* from the mass.

■ Appropriate pieces include any of Handel's Coronation anthems – such as *The king shall rejoice* or *Zadok the priest* – plus the *Gloria* by Vivaldi, the *Gloria* or *Hosanna* from Bach's *B minor Mass* or choruses from *Messiah* by Handel, such as *Hallelujah*.

■ Reference should be made to the use of key, instrumentation, nature of the vocal writing (often large-scale homophonic) and structure.

4 Describe the different ways in which Baroque composers used recitative in their music. Refer to at least two different pieces of music in your answer.

■ Start by identifying/explaining the different types of recitative.

■ Locate examples in at least two works. These might include Handel's *Messiah*, Bach's *Christmas Oratorio* or Purcell's *Ode for St Cecilia's day (1692)*.

■ Look at their location and role within these works – find examples that precede a chorus and others that precede an aria.

■ Describe their vocal line and style of accompaniment, including instrumentation.

■ Music theatre: a study of the musical from 1940 to 1980

In this area of study, it is important to choose musicals from within the period specified, referring to:

■ solo songs

■ ensembles

■ music for the chorus

■ music for dance.

You must ensure that the musicals you choose create character through the music rather than being those where all the music is basically in the same style throughout.

You will be required to focus on the musical features of the songs, ensembles, and so on, and you should, therefore, be ready to discuss some of the following:

■ melody

■ harmony

- rhythm
- writing for voices: solos, duets, ensembles
- the relationship between voices and accompaniment
- word setting
- the role of the chorus
- how characters are developed through the music
- how musical techniques are used to enhance the story and project the drama
- dance movements – with and without singing.

The composers identified within the specification are Richard Rodgers (1902–79) of Rodgers and Hammerstein, Leonard Bernstein (1918–90) and Andrew Lloyd Webber (1948–). There are, of course, many others and you might want to include one or more of the musicals of Stephen Sondheim (1930–) such as *Sweeney Todd*; Claude-Michel Schönberg (1944–), such as *Les Misérables*; Lionel Bart (1930–99), such as *Oliver!*; Jerry Bock (1928–), such as *Fiddler on the Roof*; or Alan Jay Lerner (1918–86) and Frederick Loewe (1901–88), such as *My Fair Lady*.

In effect, your study of musicals can cover *Oklahoma!* (1943) to *Les Misérables* (1980). In the course of this section, various features will be highlighted, but the final choice of musical to study is yours. You will need to be selective but should cover a range of different styles of solo song, chorus, ensemble and dance sequence. You should be able to compare *two from any one musical* or *one from each of two different musicals*. Thus, for example, you could choose to study two ensembles from *West Side Story*, such as *Tonight* and *One Hand, One Heart* but also look at *Who will buy?* from *Oliver!*

Oklahoma! (1943)

Oklahoma! by Rodgers and Hammerstein ran for a then unprecedented 2,248 performances on Broadway and won the prestigious Pulitzer Prize in 1944; a prize also won by *South Pacific* (1950). *South Pacific* was unusual in its treatment of racial prejudice and it skilfully matched music to character. It included the songs *Younger than springtime, Some enchanted evening*, and *I'm gonna wash that man right outa my hair*. There followed the exotic *The King and I* (1951) and *The Sound of Music* (1959).

Oklahoma! opened on 31 March 1943 and the title song – first heard in Act II – was a showstopper. In December of that year, Decca Records released a recording of the show sung by the original Broadway cast – the first time this had been done.

The characters are exemplified through the music written for them and the context of the action is also well represented in song and dance. Hammerstein's **lyrics** were of a romantic, poetic style and enabled Rodgers to compose music that amplified their feelings and added greatly to the creation of individuals and locations within a dramatically cohesive structure – a 'musical play'. Its structure is to present three scenes that develop characters, followed by three scenes that further the plot. This enabled the creation of 'real' characters – even the 'villain', Jud Fry, can arouse sympathy because the songs *Lonely room* and *Pore Jud is daid* have revealed just how miserable he is. The plot contains two love triangles: Laurey, Curly and Jud, as well as Ado Annie, Will Parker and Ali Hakim.

Did you know?

Carousel, by Rodgers and Hammerstein, gave the world of football its famous anthem *You'll never walk alone* after the fans of Liverpool FC adopted it from the hit record by local group, Gerry and the Pacemakers.

AQA Examiner's tip

Whatever pieces you choose, make sure that they contrast well so that you will have plenty to write about.

Did you know?

During the original London run of *South Pacific*, Sean Connery was a member of the chorus at one point.

Key terms

Lyrics: the words of the song.

Ado Annie is the lively, irrepressible character who 'cain't say no!'

The lightly sprung rhythms of this song are infectious and reflect her innate joy in life and all it offers – especially the men! Its varying rhythms and tempi epitomise how she flits from one thing to another.

The opening song, *Oh, what a beautiful morning,* is first heard from off-stage while Aunt Eller churns butter on-stage. The repeating of lines helps to portray and encapsulate the hushed serenity of early morning in the countryside when life was simple and before the noises of modern civilisation encroached. There is a sense of satisfaction in the balanced rise and fall of:

The rhythm of the lyrics for *Surrey with the fringe on top* reflects the regular trotting of the horse and the clip-clop of its hooves:

Key terms

Reprise: the repetition of a song at a different stage in the musical where its new position means that its dramatic significance has changed, casting new light on a character and/or a situation.

This song appears twice: Curly first sings this to Laurey as a way of trying to conjure up his idea of the wonderful romantic evening they will have together when he uses it to take her to the dance. However, Laurey thinks that the surrey is just in Curly's imagination and has already agreed to go to the dance with Jud Fry. When it is **reprised**, Curly is telling Laurey what she has missed and prompts her to think again about her feelings for him.

Songs such as these deserve careful attention and study to form part of a response to a question on word-setting. *Oh, what a beautiful morning* uses the regular flow of a waltz-like melody, balanced in its rise and fall; *Surrey with the fringe on top*, again virtually exclusively syllabic, depends a lot on its rhythm to convey its character – the pattern of six regular, repeated crotchets followed by a closing four quavers, which is heard three times before its extension into a cadence featuring longer notes.

The waltz rhythm is captured in the accompaniment to the first; the regular motion of the horses and the surrey in the second.

A contrast of song style can be found in Jud Fry's *Lonely room,* where the slower tempo, minor tonality and often static nature of the melody line all add to the overwhelming sense of isolation and sadness as he dreams of what might be:

There are many dissonant intervals – the second is prominent – in the accompaniment: this underlines the pain of his existence and his inability to relate to the society around him. It is just so different from the happy, carefree music that pervades much of this musical.

Study should really also include the song and dance sequence which is *The farmer and the cowman,* recreating the traditional square-dance style, captured in the opening instrumental bars:

Did you know?

The choreographer chosen for *Oklahoma!* was Agnes de Mille, who had choreographed Copland's *Rodeo* for the Ballets Russes in 1942.

The song falls naturally into four-bar phrases, in line with dance music, and is well worth close attention as an example of this particular feature of the musical; parallels to which can be readily found elsewhere to enable comparison. Examples include *To life* in *Fiddler on the Roof, Who will buy?* in *Oliver!* and many more.

The sheer exuberance of the title song, the climax to the show and to the storyline, as Oklahoma becomes a state, ensured that this song would ring in the audience's memory long after seeing the show. The music is propelled forward on an infectious accompanying rhythm and the intrinsic shout of joy and triumph in the setting of the word 'Oklahoma!':

Did you know?

The title song *Oklahoma!* was adopted as the 'national anthem' by the state of that name.

West Side Story (1957)

West Side Story was based on the **book** by Arthur Laurents, with lyrics by Stephen Sondheim and music by Leonard Bernstein. The musical was directed and choreographed by Jerome Robbins, marking the arrival of this type of figure in the Broadway musical. In the mid-1950s, gang warfare was rife in the Mexican neighbourhood of Los Angeles and in Manhattan's Upper West Side. *Romeo and Juliet* gradually evolved into *West Side Story*, with the young lovers becoming a native-born Polish-American boy and a Puerto Rican girl recently arrived in New York. Instead of the noble Capulet and Montague families of Verona, there would be rival gangs, fighting over territory, and there was no room for love amid the prejudice and the violence.

Bernstein greatly admired a musical called *Regina*, written by Mark Blitzstein, referring to it as a 'musical play' because of the sheer number and variety of songs and dances it contained. *West Side Story* contains bebop (*Cool*), vaudeville (*Gee, Officer Krupke*), Latin (*America*), more complicated music and chromatic fugues (*Cool*), sprung rhythms (*Scherzo*), a beguine rhythm (*Tonight*), dissonant countermelodies, the rather unconventional *Tonight* ensemble, the non-standard structure of the songs (which don't fall into a 'traditional' 32-bar form), and so on (observations and comments derived from Larry Stempel in *Sennets and Tuckets: a Bernstein Celebration*, ed. Steven Ledbetter, publ. Boston 1988).

Dance rhythms seemed to flow effortlessly from Bernstein's pen: the mambo in *Dance at the gym*; the cool jazz references in the song *Cool*; the *Maria cha-cha* in *Dance at the gym* (the melody heard there before Tony sings it). *Somewhere* is used within dance passages, linking the dream sequence between Tony and Maria to the show's storyline.

You could choose a range of song styles from this musical, as described above.

The simplicity of the changing rhythms, alternating two groups of three quavers (as if in compound time) with three crotchets (as if in triple time), known as a hemiola (see page 44), in *America*, is also its most immediately recognisable feature, especially when allied to its constantly shifting harmonic basis: after an apparently conventional start using tonic and dominant, Bernstein sidesteps via Cm⁷ into B♭ before using A♭ as a flat submediant approach to the tonic (A♭–C)!

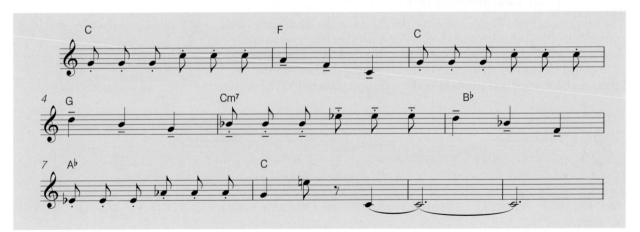

This could be contrasted with *Somewhere*, with its yearning upward phrases and its gentle use of dissonance; *One hand, one heart*, with its almost prayer-like quality; or *Maria*, with its heartfelt and rhapsodic repetition of the name, after the hushed, intoned opening. The upward tritone, which forms the appoggiatura to the G, hints at the pain and anguish, both within Tony's love for her, and in the inevitable outcome of such love:

Looking closely at two choruses such as the *Tonight* ensemble and *One hand, one heart* could give rise to many comparisons. Here are a few points about each chorus:

Tonight

- There is an unusual $^4/_4$ + $^2/_4$ time signature.
- The tonality gives the sense of A minor.
- The Puerto Ricans are represented by a rhythmic/syncopated figure.
- Anita sings a 'slinky' version of the opening music in triplets – there is an element of characterisation here (the tonality returns to A minor).
- After the modulation to A major for *Tonight* – Tony's reprise of earlier music – the opening music comes back and Bernstein begins to layer different themes.

Look closely at how the climax is achieved.

One hand, one heart

- This opens in G♭ major.
- It has a lazy, waltz-like tempo.
- It has a simple structure: four-bar phrases. Notice the use of chromatic colouring in the last phrase – C♭ for 'only death… '
- The song has a strophic setting: in any answer where this chorus is used, you should be sure to point out the differences of voice, orchestration, key, as appropriate for each strophe.
- It builds up to a big climax, but the ending is hushed and light – give reasons why this is appropriate/dramatically relevant.
- Point out the use of the celesta at the end: what is its effect/why was it used?

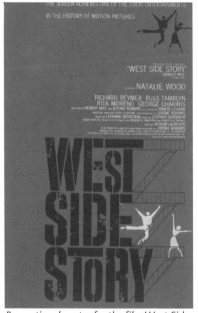

Promotional poster for the film West Side Story, *1961*

Oliver! (1960)

Lionel Bart wrote the music and lyrics for *Oliver!*, adapting the story from the Charles Dickens's novel *Oliver Twist* (1838). As well as the character songs, such as Fagin's *Reviewing the situation* and the music-hall sing-along style of *Oom pah pah*, Lionel Bart wrote songs of great tenderness in *Where is love?* and *As long as he needs me*. Any of these is worthy of study and could be used to compare song styles and characterisation.

The ensemble *Who will buy?* takes the form of a gradual assemblage of street cries before Oliver joins them to sing 'Who will buy this wonderful morning?' At this point, the previous prevailing C minor tonality is retained, but the tempo is increased. The scene temporarily is 'put on hold' for dialogue and resumes with the street sellers' cumulative 'Who will buy?'

The tempo now picks up to ♩ = 150 for an upbeat, lavishly orchestrated version of the song, sung in octaves. The minor tonality points to an undercurrent of sadness, despite the lively tempo and upbeat, almost dance-like, accompaniment style. The crowd scene is held in a dramatic tableau as the tempo slackens and, finally, Oliver sings the final line.

As the crowd begins to disperse, the individual cry of one of the street sellers returns and the chorus ends as it began with:

The descending bass line to the simple harmony has a resigned feel, reinforced by the instrumental echo of its cadence. The ensemble has a clear structure and remains firmly in C minor for the greater part, its variety coming from textural changes and a range of tempi.

Looking closely at two choruses from *Oliver!*, such as *Consider yourself* and *Who will buy?* could give rise to many comparisons. Here are some points that could be included:

Consider yourself

- 6/8 time signature
- lively tempo (♩ = 120)
- short introduction
- basically for different solo voices or in unison
- opens in G major
- modulation to C major (subdominant)
- melody line broken between Artful Dodger and Oliver in verse two
- use of contrast between 6/8 and a 3/4 *l'istesso tempo* – in other words between two and three beats in a bar
- climactic long note on 'self' and then 'us' to finish
- immediately reprised.

Who will buy?

- opening in C minor
- a gentle song for the most part
- steady tempo initially
- starts with the different cries of the various street sellers, building up the texture

- Oliver's entry changes the tempo – *Poco più mosso* (a little more movement) – and the time signature is altered to split common time (¢; basically two beats in a bar)
- the lines that Oliver sings – *Who will buy?* – alternate with the cries of the street sellers
- an accumulation of four street cries brings this chorus to a temporary pause while a spoken scene is acted out
- a repeat of the cries heralds the restart of the main song, this time sung by everybody
- a final 'frozen tableau' effect as first, Oliver, and then the Rose Seller, sing a line to conclude the song.

Given the opportunity, further comparison could be made with, for example:

- *I'll do anything* from Lionel Bart's *Oliver!* or
- *Tradition* and/or *To life* from Jerry Bock's and Stephen Harnick's *Fiddler on the Roof*
- *Tonight* and/or *One hand, one heart* from Bernstein's *West Side Story*.

Things to do

The use of the 'reprise' in musicals is also very important in establishing the overall storyline and, as songs are presented in different contexts, it is worth exploring what fresh light is thrown on the character and situation of the singer(s) when a particular song is reprised (when compared with its original position).

Fiddler on the Roof (1964)

Jerry Bock's *Fiddler on the Roof*, based on the stories of Yiddish writer Sholem Aleichem, was described by the theatre historian Gerald Borman as 'the last of the great masterworks of the era' (in *American Musical Theatre*). It tells the story of a Jewish family in Russia, around 1905, as they try to survive poverty and religious persecution in a world that is changing all too quickly around them. There is some genuine humour, there are several love stories, and the story mirrored genuine experiences. Several of its songs became standards virtually overnight. These include:

- the opening *Tradition* wherein the roles of the various members of the community are explained
- the song that highlights one of the community's main traditions – *Matchmaker*
- Tevye's wry but amusing *If I were a rich man* (a song of changing tempi, as is Fagin's *Reviewing the situation* in *Oliver!*), and
- the set piece wedding song *Sunrise, sunset*.

There are touches of Jewish harmonies in the move from C to D♭ in the opening ensemble and in the ensuing title song *Fiddler on the Roof*, which is based on some of the same musical material. This harmonic device is summed up in the phrase first heard when the daughters sing about the role of 'the momma': 'And who does momma teach to mend and tend and fix, preparing me to marry whoever poppa picks' and at the end of the title song (C minor but with a flattened second):

Again, Jerome Robbins directed and choreographed this show on its inaugural run. The drama unfolds at an intelligent pace, interweaving its various strands; the songs are beautifully written and grow naturally out of the action, contributing also to delineation and development of character. The element of sentimentality is genuine: the audience can relate to the characters and become involved in the ways in which the plot unfolds on its varied levels. There are two memorable dance sequences, which are well worth close investigation (and possible comparison with dances from other musicals such as *West Side Story*): these are the Dance in the Inn, which combines elements of Jewish and Russian dance, and the Bottle Dance at the wedding.

It is very easy to empathise with Tevye as he sees traditions collapsing around him and becomes more and more lost, deprived of the regulated social structure that has been so much of his life. We can smile with him in *If I were a rich man*; we can sympathise with his use of a fictional dream-sequence to persuade his wife, Golde, that their daughter, Tzeitel, should marry Motel, the penniless tailor whom she loves, rather than Lazar Wolf, the rich butcher whom she doesn't but who has been put forward by the Matchmaker.

Rock musicals

During the 1960s, a type of musical known as the 'rock musical' gradually emerged. The important element here is that the basic musical style is 'rock', though few were ever marketed as such. Musicals that fall into this broad category include *Godspell*, *Jesus Christ Superstar*, *Hair* and *Grease*.

Andrew Lloyd Webber

One of the more recent successes in the world of the musical has been Andrew Lloyd Webber (1948–). Since early success (1968) with a short musical based on the story of *Joseph and his Amazing Technicolour Dreamcoat* (lyrics by Tim Rice), Lloyd Webber went on to write a wide range of musicals. He cites the American musical and its composers as early influences and once stated 'Musical theatre is the only thing that's ever made me tick' (Mark Steyn in *Broadway Babies say Goodnight: Musicals then and now*, New York, 1999).

His musicals are theatrical, operatic and imaginative; they combine sound and spectacle, and songs from many of them have passed into standard repertoire, gaining a life and existence independent of their source. His songs move between rock and 'classical' in style with many other influences brought to bear as befits a particular situation. Some of his choices of subject-matter for his musicals seemed especially bold at the time:

Joseph and his Amazing Technicolour Dreamcoat *in production*

- ■ *Jesus Christ Superstar* was deemed blasphemous by some
- ■ *Evita* dealt with a South American dictator
- ■ *Cats* seemed as unlikely a topic as anything imaginable.

Songs from Lloyd Webber musicals

From *Jesus Christ Superstar* (1971) came the impassioned *I don't know how to love him*. The scenario is the last week of Jesus' life and deals with his betrayal and Passion, seen through those around him such as Pontius Pilate, Judas Iscariot and Mary Magdalene. There are many musical highlights, from the fanfare-like title song through Mary Magdalene's outpouring of emotion, to the comic number in ragtime style that is *King Herod's Song* (reminiscent of *The Pharoah's song* in *Joseph and his Amazing Technicolor Dreamcoat*).

I don't know how to love him is marked to be sung 'slowly, tenderly and very expressively'. Its opening melodic phrase is presaged in the introduction. The song's opening verse falls into two sections, each ten bars long, comprising phrases of two bars, though varied by some use of anacrusis and the subdivision at 'I've been changed, yes really changed'. The first ends with an imperfect cadence (I–Vsus–V), the second with a plagal cadence below the repeated Ds on 'He's just one more'.

The middle section modulates to B minor, returning to D before a sudden chord of C major (the flattened seventh in D major) helping to highlight the phrase 'I never thought I'd come to this', the disbelief underlined by the sudden shift of tonal centre. After nine bars, the verse returns with just its second ten-bar version. The 'middle eight' is recapitulated instrumentally before the final verse and its resigned postlude; expressing her love and fear, tinged with regret.

The song conveys character in a simple but extremely effective manner; it is simple, both harmonically and structurally, though its ten-bar verse and nine-bar middle section are both slightly unusual.

Another strong song for female voice is, of course, *Don't cry for me, Argentina* from *Evita* (1978). Lloyd Webber again teamed up with the lyricist Tim Rice, albeit for the last time, as it turned out. This is a song on a grand scale and opens with a 15-bar introduction, nine bars of which set out the melody line that is to come and one of the main musical devices – the use of a pedal. Its structure is instrumental introduction – verse – verse – chorus – verse – chorus – chorus – postlude.

The verse is, unusually, 15 bars long with its first 10 bars over a tonic pedal, above which the melody unfolds. Most of its phrases consist of repeated notes and then movement at the end of the phrase. The harmony is initially tonic, subdominant and dominant seventh over the pedal before a modulation to A♭ major, the dominant, from the eleventh bar of the verse. Verse two repeats this, though with a different accompaniment, including a warm sound from the horns.

The chorus/refrain is marked to be played with a 'slow tango feel'; Lloyd Webber uses a Latin American dance rhythm, epitomised in the use of triplets and these rhythms:

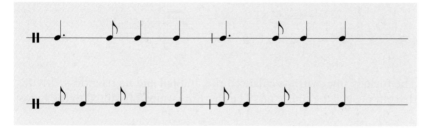

As in *I don't know how to love him*, this section is nine bars long; this ninth being a linking instrumental bar. Again, harmonically it is straightforward, using primary chords plus the submediant. The scoring is quite lush and full, lightening texturally for the return to verse three. However, Lloyd Webber never simply restates things: there are subtle alterations to accompaniment patterns and rhythms, especially in the bass. The ensuing chorus, with a slower tempo, uses an opera-derived device where, the voice being so charged with emotion, it finds it difficult to continue singing, instruments take over: here, the voice hums the melody line, while the instruments help build towards the climax. Having composed herself, Evita sings the words of the chorus one last time at the original tempo.

Unexpectedly, there is a postlude: the chorus ends and the accompaniment is marked *colla voce* (with the voice). In a quasi-recitative manner, there is a moment of introspection as the tonality moves to G♭; the harmony alternating G♭ with F minor before finally closing on the tonic, D♭.

The closing instrumental section is marked *Refrain grandioso*: the overall structure of the song is completed by this return to the instrumental statement and the triumphant statement affirms the truth of Evita's final comment: 'ev'ry word is true'.

Claude-Michel Schönberg and Alain Boublil

Continuing the tradition of many French operas, musicals by Schönberg and Boublil have war settings. *La Révolution Française* (1973) and *Les Misérables* (1980) fall within the period covered by this area of study. In the latter, the over-riding message is the power of forgiveness. The music often has the flavour of folk-melody given lavish orchestral treatment. The use of the pentatonic scale is prevalent. Numbers for chorus are central to the musical and dramatic structure of each musical and are often linked to specific choreography.

Songs from Les Misérables

Chorus songs from *Les Misérables* include *At the end of the day* (sung by the unemployed and the factory workers), *Do you hear the people sing?* and *One day more*.

Do you hear the people sing? is sung by Enjolras, the students and the citizens.

The steady tread of the accompaniment, plus the drum beat reference at the end of the bar, unite to give a military feel to this song, and a sense of the gradual upsurge of the force of the crowd:

The melody line, with its balanced rise and fall and its relentless, driving rhythm pushes the music on. The rhythm is superbly suited to the lyrics:

The triplet element comes into its own in the final line of the first verse:

Then join in the fight That will give you the right to be free!

Its overall construction is simple but its power comes from its cumulative effect; its context and the use of such large numbers of singers.

Study of songs from this musical could additionally include the duets:

- *In my life*   Cosette and Marius
- *A heart full of love*   Marius and Cosette
- *A little fall of rain*   Eponine and Marius

and the solos:

- *I dreamed a dream*   Fantine
- *Castle on a cloud*   Little Cosette
- *Stars*   Javert
- *On my own*   Eponine
- *Bring him home*   Valjean
- *Empty chairs at empty tables*   Marius

Each has its own particular features.

I dreamed a dream

Fantine, a worker in Valjean's factory, has a secret – an illegitimate child (Cosette). When the other workers find out, they demand that she be dismissed. She is thrown out by the foreman, whose advances she has rejected. She sings of the dreams and hopes she has had, dreams and hopes that have gradually been taken away and destroyed, ending 'Now life has killed the dream I dreamed'.

The song starts in a major tonality (F), which suggests hope, with strong rhythmic drive, falling into balanced two-bar phrases. The contrast is a more angular melody and a simultaneous move to G minor:

But the ti - gers come at night

The climax of this section arrives over an F pedal leading to a dominant chord (in F):

As they turn your dream to shame,

The warmth of F major returns as she remembers her lover and the joy he brought; but he left and only gradually has she come to realise that her dreams of his return, and all the other dreams of the life for which she had hoped, will never come to pass. Tonality is shifted one tone up and the song's melody climbs inexorably higher, often over a descending bass line until all dies away for the final line of resignation and despair in the recognition of her current situation:

The ending of the 'dream' is underlined by the simple expedient of the pause on the dominant seventh: it is as if Fantine is trying desperately to hang on to her hopes and dreams, while the push of the harmony indicates that this is not possible.

The song ends, as has been noted earlier, with an instrumental postlude used where the voice/character is so highly charged with emotion that she can sing no more. Here, the music tries twice to create hope through repetition, only to end by slowing down and resolving downwards to a final tonic:

Castle on a cloud

Little Cosette has been housed with the Thénardiers, and is being used as a servant. She dreams of a better life. The music conveys the fantasy aspect, partly through the constantly changing rhythm:

Harmonically, the music is simple and repetitive, always returning to the reality of the minor chord. After two verses, there is a contrast: chords of F and C (but with Bs in the accompaniment) give the music a plagal feel while the major tonality brings a brightness and (temporary) respite from the lowliness of little Cosette's present life. She sings of the things she doesn't experience – being sung a lullaby, being told she is loved, being held:

On my own

Eponine sings this song as she decides, despite her earlier promise, to rejoin Marius at the barricade. Schönberg's accompaniment to this song weaves a delicate tracery:

After three balanced four-bar phrases, Schönberg inserts a $^2/_4$ and a $^3/_4$ bar, returning to $^4/_4$ to give the verse its rhythmic climax:

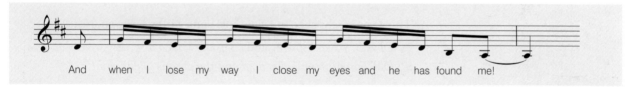

The second part of the song moves from the verse's close on A major (the dominant) to B♭ major, the flat submediant, resulting in an interrupted cadence. The accompaniment is now predominantly repeated crotchets in direct contrast to the opening. Its second phrase ends on E♭ major, being wrenched up to E minor for the third phrase: this harmonic unease reflects the tensions and anxiety within Eponine. A half-close on C^7 moves the music into F major for the return of the verse, and the semiquaver broken-chord-based pattern. The second part of the melody returns in a confident F major as she proclaims: 'I love him' – but she immediately realises that his life can go on without her, but not hers without him, and the song ends reflectively, using D minor, B♭ minor and the final F major beneath; the semiquaver patterns finishing at 'only…', to be replaced by sustained chords, giving a prayer-like ending:

Things to do

■ Study a wide range of song, ensemble, chorus and dance.

■ Make notes in such a way that you will be able to make comparisons between two examples from one musical or between musicals.

■ Be aware of the context of the musical item.

■ Be aware of the use of 'reprise' and the different function of the musical number in its new context.

■ Look at the ways in which composers have used their music to present and develop character.

Bring him home

The main characteristics here are the gentle but anguished dissonance of the accompaniment, the slow tempo, the yearning upward leaps in the melody, and the prayer-like quality of much of the song as Valjean beseeches God to save Marius from the forthcoming battle.

This outline is not intended to be either inclusive or exclusive, simply to give suggestions as to range and possible directions for study.

AQA Examination-style questions

5 Choose **two** contrasting passages from one musical you have studied and show how the composer has used the elements of music (melody, harmony, use of instruments, and so on) to enhance the drama.

Start by identifying two contrasting passages.

You can choose the area(s) of contrast with the musical elements in mind and select numbers or passages that contrast in dramatic terms and/or in simply numerical terms.

Musical elements:

■ dynamics
■ rhythm
■ structure and form
■ melody
■ metre
■ instruments (timbre)
■ texture
■ tonality
■ harmony.

Thus, you might choose a slow solo song with a lively chorus:

■ *Oliver!*: *Where is love?* and *Consider yourself*
■ *Oklahoma!*: *Pore Jud is daid* and the chorus *Oklahoma!*

Either of these choices would give plenty of scope for comparison. Here are some following points that could be included:

Pore Jud is daid

■ slow
■ for two singers (Jud and Curly)
■ simple structure
■ almost hymn-like quality
■ religious nature of song and its performance
■ some use of chromaticism
■ contrast of dotted rhythms with repeated, simple quavers
■ a 'scene within a scene' – Curly leads into the 'chanted' section ('Folks! We are gathered here to moan and groan over our brother Jud Fry').

Oklahoma!

- large-scale number
- major key
- preponderance of tonic–subdominant–dominant harmonies
- sense of excitement
- climactic song
- lively $^2/_4$ rhythm after a steady start
- stepwise ascent to the long, drawn-out *O - --– - klahoma!*
- repetition of the title word to build to final statement of the chorus
- triumphant sound: full company, full orchestra.

6 Choose two contrasting ensembles from one musical you have studied and write an illustrated programme note on each. Your choice of ensemble can be based on numbers involved, tempo, timbre, tonality and so on.

From *Les Misérables*, you might choose *Master of the house* and *Do you hear the people sing?*

Master of the house

- sung by Thénardier the innkeeper, his wife and the customers
- A minor contrasting with A major
- syncopated rhythms contrasting with repeated semiquavers
- repetitive rhythms
- harmonically quite simple.

Do you hear the people sing?

- Sung by Enjolras, the students and the citizens
- slow march rhythm
- 'swung' quavers
- opening major key changes to minor
- higher pitch
- further change of key and even higher pitch at entry of chorus
- gradual dramatic build-up.

■ British popular music from 1960 to the present day

In this area of study you will examine the development of British popular music since 1960, and your work must include the consideration of:

■ the use of voices and instruments

■ the use of melody, harmony and texture

■ the move away from a traditional backing group (lead, rhythm and bass guitars, plus drum kit) to the use of synthesised sounds and other instrumental effects

■ the increase in the use of popular song for social comment

■ the use of multi-tracking, mixing, and other studio techniques to enhance recording.

You are referred to singers/groups from this period with an initial list of suggestions:

■ the Beatles

■ the Rolling Stones

■ Pink Floyd

■ Oasis

■ Blur.

However, this just covers groups (and there are many others – The Who, Queen, and so on). You might want to look at the contribution of individual singers, such as Elton John, but better guidance would be threefold (while ensuring that the initial five bullet points are covered):

■ to look at British popular music under more general headings, such as 'folk pop/rock', 'mods and rockers', 'punk rock', 'progressive rock', 'Britpop', 'the 1980s and the use of technology in British popular music'

■ to look at recent trends in popular music

■ to look at bands/singers who interest *you*.

Questions will focus on the use of the musical elements, how the text is expressed through musical means, changes in British popular music across the period, how popular music has been used for social comment, and so on.

British bands of the 60s

The Beatles

No study of British popular music since 1960 can omit the music of the Beatles. They dominated the 1960s through the sheer variety of their work and influenced the direction taken by others as they constantly absorbed influences from elsewhere – be it America or India – and always sought new effects. In this aim, they were ably assisted and encouraged by their musical producer, George Martin. A survey of some of their songs across their output will serve to point up some of the developments and changes they brought to pop music. In fact, the songs contained on their CD of number one hits provides a useful cross-section of their output and development.

Their earliest songs were very much a product of Liverpool and its maritime links. Songs were simple, relying on fairly basic chords and with a straightforward structure. Apart from the standard line-up of three guitars (lead, rhythm and bass) plus drum kit, the Beatles added little more than basic vocal harmonies and the occasional use of harmonica.

Their first recording was *Love me do*: a song based really on the 'three-chord-trick' of using I, IV and V with a simple harmonica riff to open and a 'middle eight'. The use of these three chords (part of the heritage of 'the blues' that was so important in popular music) had been – and remained – the basis of so many pop songs, including many more to be written by the Beatles. The flattened third also features in this first recorded song. Although this early song only hinted at the rich seam of songwriting splendour that was to follow, there were already strong clues to basic elements of the Beatles' vocal harmonies:

- the way in which open fifths were so regularly used, in contrast to the usual thirds and sixths
- the use of a repeated pitch or sustained note against a moving melodic line.

In *Love me do*, we hear:

while *Please please me* opens with a mix of dissonance and consonance:

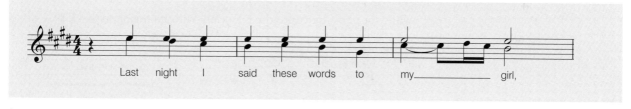

(For further investigation of this topic, you could refer to 'Vocal harmony as a structural device in the commercial recordings of The Beatles 1962–1970' by Steven Valdez (2001) (*Beatlesstudies 3*) copyright © 1997–2004 Soundscapes.)

From me to you, also from 1963, took these three chords and added the submediant plus the occasional use of a flattened ('bluesy') third. The 'middle eight' modulated to the subdominant before moving sequentially to C⁷ to return to the tonic for verse three. The use of the submediant is a device also found in *Eight days a week*, from 1964.

A more obvious and direct link to the 12-bar blues is *Can't buy me love* (1964), its verse following the standard blues pattern, its 'middle eight' using both chords III and VI before a return to the dominant seventh for the verse.

Also from 1964 comes the theme song to their first film *A Hard Day's Night*. Its opening is one of the most famous discords in pop music and, for its time, quite daring. It is a basic F chord (F–A–C) with an added ninth, played using the top four strings (so the top four pairs of strings) on a 12-string guitar. Because of the effect of the octave and unison pitches the 12-string guitar produces, a much fuller sound results than if these four notes were played on a standard six-string guitar. However, there is also the low D on the bass guitar, adding a further dimension to this chord and turning it into a Dm^7/add^{11}.

The song itself follows a fairly standard song structure and relies on three chords, though coloured by the occasional flattened third. The 'middle eight' moves initially to the mediant minor before returning, via II and V^7, to the tonic. The coda/outro is plagal in feel, though the final tonic chord is approached from the flattened seventh, B♭.

There are early signs in this song of the Beatles' willingness to experiment with chords and harmonic effects – something that stays with them throughout their careers and is encouraged by their record producer, George Martin.

There was a marked change in the lyrics of songs by the Beatles following their first trip to America in 1964: there is a wider range of subject matter (for example, *And your bird can sing*, *Doctor Robert* and *Taxman*), and some of the first intimations of their views on 'loneliness' and 'isolation' as manifest in *Eleanor Rigby* (1966). Quite apart from featuring a novel backing sound, the tonality of this song combines elements of E minor with the transposed Aeolian and Dorian modes. The opening phrase, using chords of C and Em can be seen as utilising the Aeolian mode (minor sixth – C♯) transposed to E:

while the verse moves to the E Dorian (with its major sixth – C♯):

The use of string instruments gave rise to the stabbing chords that are so much a feature of the accompaniment, identifying the song immediately as inhabiting a new sound world. On the same album (*Revolver*, 1966), came further use of the Eastern-influenced drone, heard already in songs such as *Eight days a week* and *You've got to hide your love away*.

Paul McCartney's pensive ballad *Yesterday* (1965) opens with two bars of gently strummed chords on guitar, which continue beneath the first verse. At the word 'Suddenly', lower string sounds enter, also underlining the ensuing words 'There's a shadow hanging over me'. This style of accompaniment is continued throughout the rest of the song save for a high, sustained note over the repetition of 'Love was such an easy game to play'. The close is hummed and features a plagal cadence. It was very unusual at the time in that it did not seem to have been written for dancing and there was a total absence of percussion.

You could look at the Beatles' use of melody and syllabic accentuation, perhaps ranging from the straightforward narrative strong-beat stress on important syllables of *She's leaving home* (from *Sergeant Pepper's Lonely Hearts Club Band*):

to the almost total syncopation of *If I needed someone:*

There are many other songs by the Beatles that could be included in any study of their musical development and their contribution to popular music during the 1960s, but no study would be complete without reference to their concept album *Sergeant Pepper's Lonely Hearts Club Band*. This entire album was conceived as a progression of songs, the order of which was considered extremely important. The entire album is devoted to various aspects of the theme of loneliness, sometimes treated with real tenderness, sometimes with bitter irony. Many of the recording techniques were pioneering for the time, and no previous album had taken as many studio hours as this. The use of snippets of fairground organ recordings spliced together in a random way underlines the 'circus' nature of the song *Being for the benefit of Mr Kite* as surely as the use of three tonal centres takes us through different 'acts'.

There is the unique *A day in the life* and the Eastern-influenced *Within you, without you* (with its tritonal opening phrase of E–F–G–B♭, and laughter at the end). There is the fact that a song is actually reprised within an album (the title song). There is the unbroken transition from the opening song into *With a little help from my friends*. There is the 1920s-inspired *When I'm 64 …*

In their early days, whichever of the Beatles had the initial idea for the song tended to be lead vocalist on the recording – mostly, of course, John or Paul. The contrasting timbres of their voices are well featured on *A day in the life*: it is John who starts the song. At the end of the first verse, at the words 'Nobody was really sure if he was from the House of Lords', the piano, not a feature since the introduction, is heard again, but only briefly at this stage.

The first climax comes at 'I'd love to turn you on', where the oscillating vocal line gives way to the ever-more-prominent instrumental part, which gradually increases in pitch and dynamic but, on this occasion, stopping just as quickly. The voice returns – this time Paul's – for a rather more matter-of-fact section of the lyrics. The 'dream sequence' was one of several passages on this album that gave rise to increased speculation about the use of drugs by the Beatles. Certainly, it is quite a different soundscape that is conjured up at this juncture, including the special effects and vocal harmonies.

A strong bass line leads into the third verse: 'I read the news today, oh boy: ten thousand holes in Blackburn, Lancashire'. This leads to the return of the line 'I'd love to turn you on' and the second and more prolonged crescendo. Nothing like this had ever happened in a pop song before: the build-up seems to go on forever, before silence and then a major chord on piano, which is just allowed to fade away in its own, apparently interminable, fashion.

The album dates from 1967, a massively important year for the Beatles: the album was preceded by the double-sided hit *Strawberry fields forever* and *Penny Lane*, and followed by the live public broadcast performance of *All you need is love*, which reportedly reached some 400 million people worldwide. However, it was also the year of the death of their manager and mentor, Brian Epstein.

The Rolling Stones

Other groups from this period worthy of study include the Rolling Stones and the Kinks, although there was a very important 'Liverpool' sound, which dominated much music of this period.

The Rolling Stones – comprising Mick Jagger, Brian Jones, Keith Richards, Bill Wyman and Charlie Watts – was a British rock group formed in 1962. Their rough, raucous rock-and-roll sound was heavily dependent on US rhythm-and-blues music. The group's exuberant performances, centred largely around the pouting figure of Mick Jagger, contrasted with the Beatles' softer style and won the Rolling Stones a large following. Records such as *Time is on my side, Mother's little helper, Heart of stone, Ruby Tuesday, Get off my cloud, (I can't get no) Satisfaction* and *Little red rooster* are typical of the Rolling Stones' uninhibited style.

Sounds of the 70s

Pink Floyd

Pink Floyd was a progressive rock band; their concept album *The Dark Side of the Moon* was released in 1973. It is notable for its use of philosophical lyrics and for embracing some of the features of *musique concrète* – taking music from 'real' sounds, everyday sounds – something that would become a key characteristic of Pink Floyd's style. The album was a landmark in rock music: it featured songs such as *Money, Time* and *Us and them*. The album explores the nature of human experience:

- *Time:* this deals with growing older and the approach of death.
- *Money:* a song about materialism, with tongue-in-cheek lyrics and appropriate sound effects to reflect wealth (created by Roger Waters dropping coins).
- *Us and them:* deals with conflict.

The album was recorded at the famous Abbey Road Studios in 1972–73, making use of the most advanced techniques available at that time. Standard rock band instruments were augmented by synthesisers, as well as some rather less conventional sounds – an assistant engineer running around the studio's echo chamber (*On the run*), antique clocks chiming in the introduction to *Time,* and a bass drum sound altered to imitate a human heartbeat (heard clearly at the beginning and end of the album, but is present virtually throughout as a low thudding).

Pink Floyd also perfected the use of studio techniques such as the double tracking of voices and guitars (David Gilmour harmonising with himself), the use of flanging, trickery with reverb and the use of panning.

On most CDs, a barely audible orchestral version of *Ticket to ride* by the Beatles can be heard after *Eclipse*, as the heartbeats are heard ending the album. No definitive explanation has ever been given for this.

Snippets of dialogue between and over songs are also featured on the recording.

In 1979, Pink Floyd released their concept album *The Wall*, featuring the song *Another brick in the wall*, which appears as Parts I, II and III. This was written by the band's bassist, Roger Waters. Part II, which was also released as a single, includes the words 'We don't need no education'. It provided the band's only no. 1 hit. It is a protest song against rigid schooling in general and boarding schools in particular, and has faced bans in various countries.

> We don't need no education
>
> We don't need no thought control
>
> No dark sarcasm in the classroom
>
> Teachers leave them kids alone.
>
> Hey! Teachers! Leave them kids alone!
>
> All in all it's just another brick in the wall.
>
> All in all you're just another brick in the wall.

It underlines the changing role of many pop songs with their increasing emphasis on social comment.

Genesis

Genesis had a long career, albeit with a changing line-up. They played virtually continuously from 1967 to 1999 and then briefly reformed from 2006 to 2007. Having started by playing simple, keyboard-driven songs, they evolved, during the 1970s, into a progressive rock band and their songs became much more complex; the instrumentation much more elaborate. Concerts became major theatrical events. They pioneered songs of extreme length such as a 23-minute performance of *Supper's ready*. The band built a following through live performances which featured their hypnotic, dark and haunting melodies.

Foxtrot was released in 1972. The epic *Supper's ready* is seen by many as one of the group's most accomplished works. Original lead singer Peter Gabriel's flamboyant, theatrical presence on stage made the band a popular live act. In 1974, they released their concept album *The Lamb Lies Down on Broadway*. In contrast to earlier albums with their lengthy tracks, *The Lamb Lies Down on Broadway* is a collection of shorter tracks and tells the story of a Puerto Rican, Rael, living in New York City.

Special effects feature in *The waiting room* (sequenced synthesised sounds and loops of shattering glass), while special vocal effects can be heard in *The grand parade of lifeless packaging*.

Folk rock

As the name suggests, folk rock fuses characteristics of these two styles. The genre developed in the 1960s in North America and Canada. It was taken up by British bands, such as Pentangle and Fairport Convention, in the late 1960s, who deliberately incorporated elements of traditional British folk music into their works.

Steeleye Span

Steeleye Span was formed by Ashley Hutchings (of Fairport Convention) and traditional British folk musicians such as Maddy Prior, who wished to add electric amplification and, later, more obvious rock elements, into their music. Their music is based strongly on English and Celtic folk traditions and albums often intersperse jigs or reels with the songs. The vocal talents of Maddy Prior have always been one of the group's strongest assets.

Hits have included *All around my hat* and *Gaudete*, though this second song (a hit at Christmas, 1973) is not really typical of their style. *All around my hat* was the title song from the album released in 1975.

The song opens *a cappella* before the instruments join in, to emphasise the 'folk-rock' characteristics of their music.

The band's overall style has changed with its line-up; a stronger folk basis giving way, for a time, to a greater emphasis on self-penned songs. Traditional folk musicians, Martin Carthy and John Kirkpatrick, gave a distinctive sound during their brief spell together in the band between 1977 and 1980.

After a seven-year absence, Maddy Prior rejoined the band in 2002 and the band has continued to record and tour in their original style.

Punk rock

Punk rock is a movement that emerged in the mid-1970s: it was a strongly anti-establishment form of rock music, with groups such as the Sex Pistols one of the early manifestations. Punk songs were loud and fast, used minimal instrumentation and often had lyrics with a political message. The movement epitomised an extreme youthful rebellion and was characterised by excessive behaviour on stage, lyrics often intended to shock and a distinctive style of clothing.

Punk rock quickly, though briefly, became a major cultural phenomenon in the United Kingdom. For the most part, punk took root in local scenes that tended to reject association with the mainstream. By the beginning of the 1980s, even faster, more aggressive styles such as 'hardcore' had taken over. This, in turn, gradually led to the emergence of new 'pop punk bands' such as Green Day.

The Sex Pistols came to fame with songs such as *Anarchy in the UK* and *God save the Queen*, whose lyrics are openly critical of the British political system. Other lyrics are, typically, frank and confrontational.

For a slightly different style of punk you might want to explore the music of the Pogues, the Anglo-Irish folk-rock band, best known for their punk-influenced, raucous versions of traditional Irish reels and ballads, as well as their collaboration with Kirsty MacColl on *Fairytale of New York* – a tender, rueful, and bitter ballad that became a huge hit in 1988. Their debut album *Red Roses for Me* (1984) hinted at the potential of the cultural collision of folk music and punk rock styles, which was fully realised in *Rum, Sodomy and the Lash* (1985) and *If I Should Fall from Grace with God* (1988). Lead singer Shane MacGowan's songs combined attractive melodies, eclectic borrowings from traditional and rock sources, and acutely observed lyrics.

Other bands you might care to study are the Clash, the Buzzcocks, the Stranglers and/or the Damned. Alternatively (or additionally), you might want to look at New Wave bands and artists.

Another, often overlapping area which is worthy of investigation, is the increasing use of technology during the 1980s.

1980s technology

Depeche Mode

Formed in 1980, Depeche Mode was typical of the reliance on technology of groups at the time. The use of synthesisers was central to the band's sound. For their third album, *Construction Time Again*, the band added Synclavier and Emulator samplers to their analogue synthesisers, thus being able to add everyday sounds, through samples, to their songs. Lyrics increasingly focused on social and political issues.

In 1984, they released *People are people* on the topic of racism and had an international hit. The band continued to experiment with and develop their range of sounds and textures and, in 1993, *Songs of Faith and Devotion* placed increased emphasis on heavily distorted guitars. In addition, in this album they made use of live drums and strings, uillean pipes, and gospel-style vocals.

Duran Duran

Duran Duran was one of the first 80s bands to produce multiple versions of their songs by remixing them on studio mixing desks. Their arrangements often had many layers of multi-tracked sound. The name 'night versions' for many of these perhaps suggests the length of time they took to develop. They were often grouped in a 'synth-pop' category and considered part of the New Romantic trend, which included 'style-and-dance' bands such as Japan and Spandau Ballet.

Their first really big hit was *Girls on film*, later accompanied by a (then) notorious video, banned by the BBC and edited elsewhere. In 1982 came the album *Rio*, featuring songs such as the title song itself and *Hungry like the wolf*. Other hits followed, and a rivalry was seen to exist with other bands such as Culture Club and Wham! Further number one hits followed – *Union of the snake* and *The reflex* – and at the end of 1984 Duran Duran were involved in the Band Aid recording of *Do they know it's Christmas?* In 1985, however, the band became more and more unsettled and stopped working together for a time, although that year they did get together to record the theme song for the James Bond movie *A View to a Kill*.

Spandau Ballet

Spandau Ballet was one of the leading New Romantic bands of the 1980s. Their music combined synthesiser pop and funk but gradually changed in style, becoming much more mellow and giving them wider appeal. They moved on from the cossack outfits and make-up of the New Romantic movement they had helped establish, to smart, 1940s-inspired suits and well-scrubbed faces.

Soft Cell

Marc Almond joined David Ball to form this duo: the latter musician a multi-instrumentalist who experimented with analogue-synthesised sounds and techniques.

Their world-wide hit was a cover version of *Tainted love* (1981). In his book *Tainted Life*, Marc Almond wrote that, apart from the unmistakeable vocals, his only contribution was to suggest that the song start with a 'bink bink' sound that would recur periodically.

Eurythmics

Eurythmics was formed in 1980 by Annie Lennox and Dave Stewart to experiment with electronics and the avant-garde. Lennox and Stewart were the only permanent members and songwriters, involving others in the collaboration as they saw fit 'on the basis of mutual compatibility and availability'.

Success was hard to come by until the 1983 release of *Sweet dreams (are made of this)*. The single of that name was an instant hit and featured a dark, powerfully sequenced synth bass line. Stewart later explained that this bass line was discovered by accident when he inadvertently played a track backwards. The earlier *Love is a stranger* was re-released and became a hit in its own right.

The 1986 album *Revenge* developed their increasing predilection for a 'band' sound with the track *Thorn in my side* being especially popular in the UK, while *Savage* (1987) was based much more around drum loops combined with synthesiser and guitars, all rather low in the mix. Lyrically the songs showed an even darker, more obsessive side to Lennox's writing.

Pet Shop Boys

The Pet Shop Boys are an English duo, though initially based in America. Their sound relies heavily on keyboards and electronics with hits including *West End girls*, *It's a sin* and *Always on my mind*. Listen carefully to the opening of *West End girls*, to the traffic sounds and the distant voice, to the repeated chords and then to the entry of the bass guitar. The verses are spoken over alternating minor and major chords. The chorus uses minor seventh harmonies and a chromatic approach to a major chord – the dominant or the tonic? A really 'big' sound is created, but at the heart of it are a strong beat, a prominent riff and a rising chromatic final phrase on the title words 'West End girls'. The song, having started with a strong E minor feel now reinforces E major, the tonic major, through the use of the G♯, producing a *tierce de Picardie*.

It's a sin has a very dramatic start but it is founded upon a strong disco beat with this as its basis:

Other easily recognisable features include the repeated 'It's a, It's a, It's a - - - , It's a sin' and the basic chord sequence that revolves around the tonic minor, dominant seventh and subdominant (another minor chord), best thought of as C minor, G^7 and F minor respectively.

Things to do

- Listen carefully to the end of the chorus of *West End girls*.
- Try to decide whether this major chord is indeed the tonic (in a song which seems to move between major and minor fonalifies) or the dominant of another, related key.

Always on my mind opens with more sampled sounds before the rhythm is gradually introduced:

The main chord sequence is G–D–D^6–Em–Bm/D–C–D but there are some effective extensions to this, such as the ends of the verses, turning from the dominant, D, not to the expected tonic but first to B♭^{6} (the flat submediant with added sixth) and C (the subdominant), giving almost a plagal effect.

Britpop

Oasis

Oasis are obviously indebted to the styles of the Beatles, the Rolling Stones, The Who and possibly the Stone Roses. At first, they were criticised by some as relying too much on trying to recreate the sounds of the Beatles.

Their first number one hit was *Some might say* in 1995 and, from their second album – *(What's the Story) Morning Glory?* – came two of their most enduring tracks: *Wonderwall* and *Don't look back in anger*, as well as *Champagne supernova*. After the success of their album *Be Here Now* in 1997, their popularity slid for a while and the initial fervour for Britpop abated.

Their music blends some sonic experimentation with a basic rock style and is often based on simple but effective chord progressions (most guitarists play the sequence from *Wonderwall*, and it is immediately recognisable). Throughout their career, the band has been dogged by controversy, mostly stemming from outspoken comments by Noel Gallagher.

In 2005, their album *Don't Believe the Truth* was released to widespread critical acclaim, often being cited as their best since the heady days of *(What's the story) Morning Glory?* From it came two number one hits – *The importance of being idle* and *Lyla*.

Blur

The band was formed in 1995 and was a major part of the 1990s Britpop scene. The increasing influence of the music of groups such as the Beatles and the Kinks brought a different edge to their style and they became more and more popular, partly fuelled by a rivalry with Oasis.

It was in 1994 that their breakthrough came with the album *Parklife*, from which the dance-pop single *Girls and boys* was their biggest hit and they won Best Band at the Brit Awards in 1995.

Recent trends

There have been so many different styles/genres of pop music since the 1990s that this is the period in which your own interests should hold sway. It is important to consider the continuing development of trends as well as the appearance of new styles and interests.

Many groups and singers could be studied in this section. A few examples could be:

■ girl bands, such as the Spice Girls

■ female singers, such as Kate Rusby and Amy Winehouse

■ groups such as The Kaiser Chiefs and Razorlight (although they are an Anglo-Swedish group)

■ Radiohead.

You will have your own favourites, and individual research into these could take up this part of the Area of Study, sharing your findings with the rest of the group so that all benefit.

You could profitably look at the role that the independent ('indie') labels have had on the development of popular music, enabling groups to have greater freedom to pursue, perhaps, a more individual style outside the influence and market-force dominance of the bigger labels.

Undoubtedly, the internet is playing an increasing role, not only in the distribution of music – via downloads – but in the publicity of new artists, with many now using that medium either to attract initial interest (acts such as the Arctic Monkeys, for example) or make exclusive recordings available (including media-catching ploys such as making albums/singles available free or leaving it to the individual to decide just how much to pay).

The current availability of digital recording techniques has also had a major impact on pop music and would form both an interesting area for study in its own right, as well as pointing up many comparisons with techniques earlier in the period covered by this area of study.

AQA Examination-style questions

7 Music technology has become increasingly important in the popular musical world during this period. Choose two songs that use technology in different ways and write in detail about each.

Start by identifying or explaining the different types of ways in which technology can be used, such as:

- multi-tracking
- use of a sequencer
- technological manipulation of sound, including the addition of effects such as reverb
- use of sampling
- use of synthesised sounds
- distortion
- pitch bend.

Then identify the two songs you are to deal with. There are many possibilities ranging from the Beatles onwards, including:

- the Beatles: *Being for the benefit of Mr Kite, A day in the life*
- tracks from Pink Floyd's album *The Dark Side of the Moon*
- tracks from Depeche Mode's album *Construction Time Again*
- *Tainted love* by Soft Cell.

Look in detail at the chosen songs and research the precise ways in which technology was used.

8 Choose *two* contrasting songs by different groups/artists during this period and write an essay showing how each is a product of its time.

This is a 'wide-open' question!

One of the main thrusts of focus within this AoS should be how the style of popular music has changed since the 1960s.

One main aspect is, of course, the use of instruments, starting with an almost universal line-up of three guitars (lead, rhythm and bass) plus drum kit, and developing into the use of a much wider range of instruments; be it the use of strings in *Eleanor Rigby*, the fairground organ in *Being for the benefit of Mr Kite*, the specific choices of instruments in Y*ellow submarine* or *When I'm 64*, to the use of synthesisers, multi-track recorders, voice-sampling, and so on, of music in the 1970s and especially the 1980s.

A different aspect to investigate and use as a means of comparison might be the rise of punk music in the late 1970s or the New Romantics of the 1980s.

More recently, one might focus on the various combinations of traditional instruments and electronic 'wizardry' that is so much a part of current popular music.

The final approach will very much depend on the choice of the two contrasting songs, but attention should obviously be paid most closely to the nature of the recording and the extent to which technology is used, or the extent to which the lyrics have a more or less social impact, and how this affects the musical style.

4 Introduction to composing and arranging

◼ to learn about the activity of composition and its importance through history

◼ to appreciate the relevance of studying composition for performers and listeners as well as composers

◼ to understand the approach to composition in the following chapters.

◼ Creating musical ideas

A musician's life has always involved creating new ideas in music. Far back in history, when music was transmitted aurally and only preserved by memory, every performance was fresh and open to re-interpretation or re-composition. Notation is first found associated with church music, partly because monks were literate, but also because it was important to preserve the words of the liturgy and to ensure that nothing was omitted. Although we have a vast repertory of church music from the Renaissance period, in manuscript and early prints, there is no way of estimating how much has been lost in the secular field, and how many outstanding composers have been forgotten.

Even in the Baroque and Classical periods composition was taken for granted in the employment of church and court musicians and it was not expected that a composition, once performed, would be preserved and used again. J.S. Bach was known in his lifetime as an organist, teacher and expert on organ construction, and his compositions were taken for granted. Handel probably spent more time hiring theatres, auditioning singers and directing performances than he did in the act of composition. Beethoven is the first composer we know of who was financially supported so that he could devote himself to writing music. It is interesting to speculate whether this would have happened had his deafness not prevented a growing career as a pianist, conductor and teacher. The image of the isolated composer, writing music for publication and for performers he might never meet, belongs to the 19th and 20th centuries, and is principally confined to 'classical' music.

More recently, and especially in jazz and popular music, composer and performer have come together again. Duke Ellington, Lennon and McCartney, and groups like Genesis have equal respect as composers and performers. Highly regarded composers in other fields such as Peter Maxwell Davies and James Macmillan are very much involved with performance, conducting, community projects and workshops.

Computer software and home studios make the creation of musical ideas available to anyone with a passion for music, and the internet solves problems of distribution. It is becoming increasingly difficult for a composer to maintain personal ownership of his or her work, even with copyright protection, as it becomes easier to download, sample and manipulate music. Mozart would have recognised this, as he worked through the night to produce wind band arrangements of his opera 'hits' in case someone else reached the market first.

Musicians need an understanding of the processes of composition, whether their eventual aim is performance, music production or creating their own works. The structures, skills and knowledge on which composers have always relied need to become familiar and available at will. It will then become possible to let the individual voice of each composer speak with clarity, power and penetration.

The following chapters on composition (Chapters 5–7) give a basic guide to the musical language every composer needs, and some advice on how to use it. There are examples from various sources, and some activities to help you understand how to learn from the music that you perform and study. Remember that the same language underlies the most traditional and the most experimental compositions. Once you have learned a language you can use it to speak in your own style.

The original score of Wedding Cantata BWV216 *by Johann Sebastian Bach, 1728*

Developing your composing skills for AS

- to become familiar with the basic musical language required for this unit
- to gain confidence in using melody, harmony and rhythm to build a well-structured piece
- to understand how to use instruments, voices and sound sources to good effect
- to learn how to notate your composition clearly and accurately.

Key terms

Cadence: the end of a phrase where the music comes to rest. The final chords in the phrase can be chosen to make the moment of rest seem partial or complete, natural or unexpected. See pages 3 and 88 for more information about cadences.

Mode: a particular scale pattern. The most familiar are the major and minor modes. Other scale patterns are found in music of the Renaissance period and earlier, and in folk music. Each mode creates its own mood or sound in the music.

The vocabulary of musical language

Writing music is like writing in any other language. Before you can begin you need to know some vocabulary – words that other speakers of the language understand – and the different forms in which they appear. To put these words into a sentence you must know how they work together to form a connected thought. A good piece of writing will also have a logical line of argument that keeps the reader interested, and points of emphasis or rest shown by punctuation. If the writing is poetic, it may choose individual words for their sounds and inner meanings and arrange them carefully to create atmosphere or provoke thought. Longer pieces of writing need structure – headings, changes, contrasts and development of ideas. The reader will lose interest if the writer has little to say, becomes repetitive, or introduces many fresh ideas without explaining their connection.

In Western music, chords are our vocabulary, together with the scales or keys to which they belong. The progression of chords and melody are the grammar, and **cadences** provide punctuation. Harmonies are described as functional when they work together to develop a line of thought, and non-functional when they are used as splashes of colour or moments of atmosphere.

Literature has established forms, small and large, such as the sonnet and the novel. Music has a similar variety of forms, from 12-bar blues, or binary form, to the symphony. Hundreds of composers have used these forms; not as a restriction to which they must conform, but as a sound foundation on which they can build their own ideas. The choice of form should match the style of the piece. Light and entertaining finales are often written in rondo form, with regular returns of an instantly recognisable theme and clear contrasts in the episodes. A more concentrated, reflective piece might develop a single theme, imitating it in different voices or structuring it formally as a fugue.

The specification for MUSC2 lists the harmonic vocabulary you need to understand and use, and the musical elements that are essential in creating a composition. Whatever style of composition or arrangement you choose, the same features will need to be considered to make it coherent, interesting and satisfying.

Melody: building a phrase from a series of notes

The effect of a melodic idea depends upon:

- the key or **mode** in which it is written – major, minor or another mode
- its range and tessitura – whether it lies high or low for its instrument or voice
- conjunct or disjunct movement – stepwise or leaping
- the length of the phrases – short, long or irregular
- its rhythm patterns.

Compare two melodies by Handel. *He shall feed his flock* is a solo aria from the oratorio *Messiah*. In the Baroque period, pastoral music describing countryside scenes and shepherds is commonly in compound time, and the lulling movement of the rhythms here creates the atmosphere of gentleness called for by the words. Much of the movement is conjunct, but Handel allows the voice a range of a ninth. The melody is based upon two-bar phrases, but it is prevented from becoming mechanical by one-bar extensions in two of the phrases. The use of sequence in bars 21–23 extends the melody naturally, without disturbing the effect.

The consistent style of the melody needs variety in another form to maintain its interest, and this is provided by cadences and **modulations**. The first phrase stays in the tonic (B♭ major) and ends in an imperfect cadence. The second moves to a perfect cadence in the dominant (F major). The third balances this by turning to the flat side of the key and cadencing in C minor. The final phrase passes through G minor (the relative minor) and returns to a perfect cadence in B♭ major.

Key terms

Modulation: a move from one key to another. See page 91 for more information about modulations.

The melody is very different when Handel is in war-like mood, as in the anthem *Let God arise* (see excerpt on previous page). There is more variety of rhythm and the melody strides down in leaps, or tumbles down in a **melisma**, to illustrate the words. When this melody is passed to the basses its range is a 13th from low G to high E♭. Patterns are strong and distinctive, and the theme is designed to allow easy imitation (at the octave after two bars). The melody also contains three short motifs that Handel later uses separately. All of these features help to create the force, excitement and confusion of battle.

Creating an interesting sequence of chords

Some of your compositions may begin with a rhythmic or melodic idea, but you can also work out an interesting sequence of two or three chords and build upon them. Many hit singles from the 1960s began like this. Try playing the chord sequences yourself and you'll soon discover whether the composer was working at the piano or the guitar at the time. Get used to their individual sounds and the effect of moving from one to another. MUSC2 requires knowledge and use of the basic harmonies that underlie Western classical music. Working with them in your composition will help you to recognise them in the listening questions of MUSC1, and in analysing your chosen set works. Chords and procedures needed for MUSC2 are summarised here; more advanced harmonies are required in MUSC5, and these can be found in Chapter 15 (see page 207).

Types of triads

The most common type of chord is formed by adding two intervals of a third to a fundamental note or root. This three-note chord is known as a **triad**. Play these examples:

- A major third plus a minor third forms a major triad.
- A minor third plus a major third forms a minor triad.

Less commonly:

- Two minor thirds form a diminished triad.
- Two major thirds form an augmented triad.

If a third is added to a major chord a seventh chord is formed (the new note is an interval of a seventh above the root). You will find these frequently in your listening but you are only required to use one type, known as the dominant seventh, at this level.

How to find the chords in a key

The chords available in a particular key are found by building a triad on each note of the scale, using only the notes of the key. In a major key this produces three major triads (I, IV and V), three minor triads (II, III and VI) and one diminished triad (VII). The triads of the key of D major are shown as an example, but the pattern is true in every major key. Note that chords are indicated by Roman numerals in this system, to avoid any confusion with another harmonic description, the **figured bass**.

Key terms

Figured bass: a notation used for the keyboard continuo part in music of the Baroque period. The bass line was written on a stave, with numbers to indicate the harmonies. The player improvised a part from this skeleton.

The three major chords are the strongest chords and are called the primary triads. They have an important function in establishing the key. Their technical names are the tonic chord (I), the dominant (V – five notes above the tonic) and the subdominant (IV – named because it is five notes below the tonic). Chords II (supertonic), III (mediant) and VI (submediant) are minor, and VII (the chord on the leading note) is diminished. The interplay of the sounds of these chords gives variety in a passage of harmony, and can be chosen to make the music sound strong, sad, or uncertain.

The sound of a chord changes if a note other than the **root** is used in the bass. Using the root as a bass note makes the chord firm and secure, which is useful for emphasis or to end a piece. With the third in the bass (known as **first inversion**) the sound is less stable, but this may be ideal for a gentler effect and for movement within a phrase. If the fifth is in the bass (**second inversion**) the chord is even less secure and demands immediate resolution, although this can be delayed to create tension. Second inversion chords therefore need careful use and are usually found in particular progressions where they can **resolve** rather than in free use during a phrase.

Key terms

Root: the note on which a chord is built, usually by the addition of intervals of a third and a fifth.

First inversion: a chord with the third in the bass part.

Second inversion: a chord with the fifth in the bass part.

Resolution: moving from a dissonant harmony to a consonant harmony, i.e. from tension to rest.

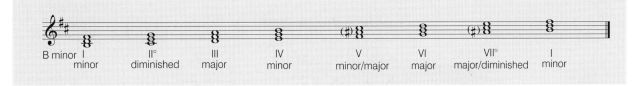

As you can see from the example above, the major, minor and diminished chords fall on different notes of the scale in a minor key. Chord I is, of course, minor in a minor key, and so is chord IV. Chords III and VI are major. Chord V would be minor in this numbering but the dominant has to play a strong part in the key and it is usually made major by raising the third of the chord by a semitone. This is the reason for the sharpened leading note in the harmonic form of a minor scale. Chord VII will become diminished if the leading note is raised.

The key signature gives an indication of the key of a piece of music, but it is the choice of chords that truly establishes the key. It's important to listen to the sound of a passage, as the same key signature can indicate a major or a minor key.

Hint

To judge whether a passage is major or minor:

■ listen to the sound

■ look for altered notes that would indicate the minor key

■ check which chords are used at important points such as the beginning, the end and other cadences.

■ Structure

Using cadences to end a phrase

A phrase in music is like a clause in writing. It is a thought that makes sense by itself, but that may or may not be complete. The chord or chords chosen to end a phrase indicate the end of an idea, and are known as a cadence.

■ A phrase that ends with chord V comes to rest naturally; but not finally as if at a comma in writing. This is known as an imperfect cadence.

■ A phrase that ends with chord IV followed by chord I sounds complete, often with a gentle release of energy. This is a plagal cadence, used as 'Amen' at the end of a hymn, and at the end of the Lennon and McCartney song *Yesterday*. Here are some examples by Handel:

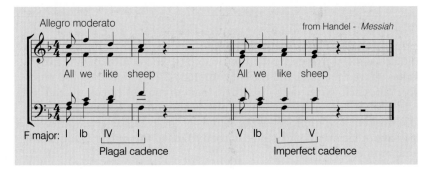

■ The ending V–I is a perfect cadence and is also complete. It uses the strongest chords of the key and forms a decisive ending, or establishes a change of key. Perfect and plagal cadences act as a full stop in writing.

■ An interrupted cadence moves from chord V to chord VI. The ear expects V to be followed by I and is surprised by the move to a minor chord. It has the effect of a question mark or an exclamation mark. Sometimes an interrupted cadence prepares the way for a perfect cadence, as in the Handel aria below.

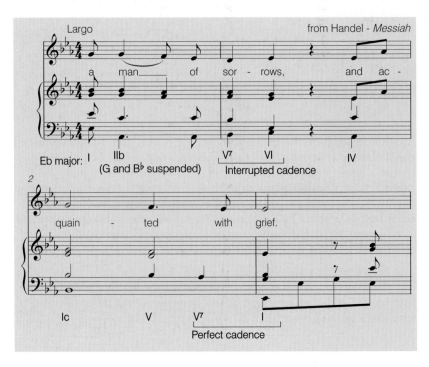

Moving well between chords

There is much to learn about moving from one chord to another within a phrase, but some general principles can guide your experiments.

Technique	Result
It is easy to move between different inversions of the same chord.	The bass line becomes more interesting without changing the chord fundamentally.
Chords whose roots are a third apart are closely related. Chords II and IV are often interchangeable, as are I and VI.	A wider vocabulary of chords is more interesting.
Chords whose roots are a fourth or a fifth apart make good progressions. Examples are III–VI, II–V, and the perfect and plagal cadences (V–I and IV–I)	The bass line gains momentum and a strong sequence can be formed, as in the Vivaldi example below.
Chord Ic can be used as a strong preparation to chord V at a perfect cadence (Ic–V–I), imperfect cadence (Ic–V) or interrupted cadence (Ic–V–VI). Chords Ic and V have the same bass note.	The second inversion chord (Ic) creates tension that is released by chord V. The cadenza of a classical concerto is usually prepared by a Ic chord. The cadenza delays the move to chord V, when the orchestra re-enters and this makes it more dramatic.
Second inversion chords can make a smooth progression in the middle of a phrase between two positions of the same chord, such as I–Vc–Ib, IV–Ic–IVb. Both progressions can be reversed.	The bass line moves by step and all parts can progress smoothly.
The dominant seventh is very common from the Classical period onwards and can be seen in the Handel example on page 96. The seventh must fall to resolve, so V^7 must be followed by chord I or chord VI.	The seventh softens the sound of the dominant chord. Because it is a dissonance it creates a moment of tension and the resolution is very satisfying.
Intervals of an octave or a fifth between parts sound strong. If octaves or fifths occur consecutively between the same two parts at a chord change they may sound unduly prominent.	These intervals can be used for emphasis. Consecutive octaves or fifths between the same two parts at a chord change should be removed.

Here is a passage by Vivaldi that has great energy because of the strong intervals in the bass line. Play the bass line alone, and then with the soprano part.

This list of harmonic principles may seem daunting, but it will help you to plan and direct your phrases, and to analyse passages where the sound is unsatisfactory. It will begin to make sense when you apply it to music you have written or are studying, and with practice the principles will become natural and need little thought.

Using chord changes to create harmonic rhythm

Changes of chord create the harmonic rhythm of the music. They help us to judge the metre or time signature of an extract because the move to a new chord creates some degree of emphasis or beat. Frequent changes within a phrase produce energy and impetus; infrequent changes suit a more peaceful mood. Handel's *He shall feed His flock* has a bass line that consists of movement by step and of long sustained notes, suggesting the drone of a shepherd's bagpipe. The example on the previous page from Vivaldi's *Gloria* shows the strength of a bass line which leaps by fourths and fifths, with a firm perfect cadence at the end. The metre of the music (triple time in this example) is formed by the changes of chord and Vivaldi makes the strong beats very clear until the end of the phrase, where he deliberately breaks the pattern with the device known as hemiola, tying a bass note over the bar line.

Thinking vertically and horizontally

Listening to a chord sequence we may be most aware of the 'vertical' effect – the total sound at any particular moment. A chordal texture in which we are most aware of the vertical effect of the music is known as homophony. There is also a horizontal logic to a good sequence of chords. The direction of the bass line is fundamental to a sure sense of progression through a phrase. The bass should form an interesting duet with the melody if the two parts are played alone. In the Baroque period, these were often the only two parts that were fully notated. Inner parts must also make sense and contain some interest for the performer. A texture in which we are most aware of the progress of individual lines is known as *polyphony or counterpoint*.

Harmony and counterpoint can be seen as distinct skills, and are examined in this way in Brief A. In practice they merge into one another, with constant flux between the importance of the chord and the importance of the line. Purcell and Bach sometimes produced surprising harmonies, including **false relations**, because they were more concerned with the melodic direction. Later composers often favoured the harmonic effect, even if it made the individual lines difficult to sing. Ideally both the vertical and the horizontal effect should be satisfying.

■ Creating longer structures

Developing your musical ideas

Most musical ideas deserve some development, just as an interesting statement in a conversation gives rise to discussion. In development, the idea is repeated, extended, fragmented or thrown into a new light. This may be achieved by changing harmonies, extending rhythms, adjusting intervals or altering phrase lengths. Change of texture, register, mode and instrumentation are also possible. Too much change will sever the connection with the original idea; too little change will make the music sound repetitive.

You can also refresh an idea by introducing a contrast and then returning to it, creating an ABA or ternary form, as in the Minuet and Trio of

Key terms

False relation: two conflicting notes, such as F♯ and F♮, which are heard close together in different parts.

Mozart's *Jupiter* Symphony. The second A section may be repeated exactly or it may be rewritten, as in the recapitulation of a sonata form movement. Simple patterns such as AAB, ABA and AABA underlie many musical works, large or small. In the hands of a great composer these patterns are enlivened by subtle connections between the sections, and by successively developing the material when it returns. The *Laudamus te* of Vivaldi's *Gloria* has four returns of the opening ritornello, but only the last is identical to the first. One of the fascinating features of jazz is the constant re-invention of a standard repertory.

Modulation: moving from one key to another

Longer structures benefit from some variety of key. Modulations are smoothest when the two keys have most of their notes in common. A major key melody is likely to move first to its dominant (one key sharper), and balance this with a further move to the subdominant or to the relative minor before returning to the tonic. The relative minors of the dominant and the subdominant are also easily accessible. Handel's melody *He shall feed his flock* quoted on page 85 exemplifies this moving from the tonic (B♭ major) to the dominant (F major) and also visiting the relative minors of the tonic (G minor) and the subdominant (C minor). In Vivaldi's *Gloria*, the *Laudamus te* is in G major, but the opening **ritornello** can also be found in the dominant, the relative minor and the subdominant.

Modulation to a closely related key is easy because the two keys have many notes and chords in common. A smooth modulation results when the music moves from the original key to a passage where the chord or chords are common to both keys. This is called a pivot chord or pivot passage. The notes that belong to the new key can be introduced without surprise and the pivot passage left as if in the new key. For example, in moving from F major to C major the new note is B♮, so the pivot passage should avoid using B♮ or B♭. See page 92 for a modulation by Handel that shows this.

Modulation from a major key to its tonic minor (such as D major to D minor) is harmonically easy, but a melody that flows easily in the major will not always transfer directly to the minor mode, and may sound very different or lose its character.

Colour, texture and timbre

Once you have chosen the chords in a passage of music, they can be arranged in many different ways. The relationship of the different parts is known as the **texture**. This can be compared to the weave of a fabric, creating pattern and different densities. The listener may be aware of the music as a sequence of chords (**homophony**), as a layering of individual melodic lines (**polyphony**) or as one of the many variations between the two. Textures can be simple or complex, with a number of threads happening simultaneously, and the main interest or melody could be in an inner part or in the bass.

The instrumentation and spacing of chords adds colour. The same melody would sound very different played in the low register of the clarinet and the high register of the bassoon. These different qualities of tone are known as the **timbre**. Instruments sound very different when they change registers, and the quality of sound is affected when they are at extremes of their range. After a passage for a full ensemble, a solo line or a two-part phrase catches the attention. The piano has a multitude

Key terms

Ritornello: an important theme that returns several times during a movement. Many concerto movements in the Baroque period have a ritornello for full orchestra and episodes for the soloist. The pattern was also used in keyboard pieces and vocal music.

Key terms

Texture: the relationship of the different parts in a passage of music.

Homophony: a chordal texture building upon a bass line or adding chords below a melody.

Polyphony: a texture that adds one melody to another, also known as counterpoint.

Timbre: the particular quality of sound of a voice or instrument. Timbre often changes in different parts of the range: for example, low notes may be gentle and high notes more penetrating.

Adagio

from Handel -*Acis and Galatea*

Must I my A - cis still be - moan,

F major

In - glo - rious_ crush'd be - neath that

Pivot passage - notes belong to both keys

stone, in - glo - rious crush'd_____ be-neath that stone,

new accidental - B natural
begins to appear

C major confirmed
by a perfect cadence

of timbres and textures that are often ignored in student compositions. Experiment by varying the register, spacing and density of chords.

The choruses from Handel's *Messiah* are good examples of choral textures. In the short chorus *Glory to God* you can find:

- ■ three- and four-part homophony
- ■ unison and octave writing
- ■ imitation in two, three and four parts
- ■ contrast between three high and two low voices
- ■ swift antiphony between the sopranos and the rest of the choir.

The many changes are effective because of the dramatic nature of the chorus. Elsewhere, as in the *Amen* chorus, Handel sustains a single texture for an extended period.

■ Using instruments well

When writing for instruments, you need to be familiar with their sound throughout their range. Computer sound cards can be misleading here: they won't show you, for example, that notes close to middle C are naturally quiet on the flute but not on the oboe. If you are composing for live instrumentalists take every opportunity to listen to them, preferably with a score in front of you so that you are sure of the quality of sound in different octaves.

Here are some things to remember when writing for instruments. If you do not play the instrument yourself talk to a player and study scores to see what is natural and what is difficult.

- Write within the comfortable range of band and orchestral instruments.
- Some keys are difficult for particular instruments. If your ensemble includes transposing instruments such as clarinet, saxophone or brass instruments, work out the key in which they will have to play to check its suitability.
- Quick figuration may not be possible at a very swift tempo.
- Wind players need opportunities to breathe. Some instruments, such as the oboe, are particularly tiring.
- There are fingering difficulties for woodwind instruments at times, for example around the 'break' on the clarinet. Some trills and patterns are impossible.
- Strings can use double-stopping, but not all chords are possible.
- Check that chord patterns for keyboard and guitar are comfortable to play.
- Some woodwind instruments have notes that are difficult to tune accurately and it is best not to emphasise these.
- Allow percussionists time to change instrument or sticks, or to re-tune timpani if necessary.
- String and brass players adding or removing mutes need a few beats' rest to make the change.
- All instruments have special effects such as harmonics (strings, guitar), flutter-tonguing (flute), pizzicato (strings). These should not be overused.

The string section in close-up

Getting the best from voices

Voices need careful handling if they are to be used to best effect.

- Be aware of the comfortable range of each voice part. The ranges below are used commonly in choral music, but a part that remains very high or very low for a voice may be tiring to sing, or ineffective.

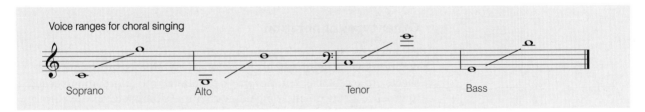

- Check the shape of line for each voice and avoid awkward leaps.
- Singers may find it difficult to locate their notes if parts cross frequently.
- Support the voices instrumentally in particularly difficult passages, and 'cue' their notes in the accompaniment for a fresh entry.
- Let the words have their natural emphasis in the rhythm of the music. Do not over-stress insignificant syllables.
- Check that there is at least one note for each syllable to be sung.
- If adjusting or repeating words for lower parts, do not leave words incomplete. The sense can be abbreviated but should not be distorted.

Hint

To find the correct time signature for the music you have written:

- listen for the regular strong beats, which usually mark the beginning of a bar
- decide whether there are two, three or four beats in a bar by counting between the strong beats
- check whether each beat sub-divides into twos (simple time) or threes (compound time). In compound time each beat is a dotted note.

■ Notation

Checklist for good staff notation

Most compositions submitted for examination are printed by computer software, although hand-written work is also acceptable. The computer playback will help to ensure that the recorded sound is as you intend, but printed scores often need editing. Here is a checklist to help with this:

At the beginning

- Be sure of the key of your music before deciding on the key signature. If the same accidental appears repeatedly it may be a sign that the key signature was incorrect or has changed.
- Similarly, listen carefully to your work before deciding on a time signature. Check that the metre is correct, and that regular strong beats fall at the beginning of a bar and not partway through, unless there is deliberate syncopation.

As you write

- For each player in an ensemble, indicate an initial dynamic, any changes, and the dynamic required after several bars' rest.
- Add articulation and phrasing to voice, wind and keyboard parts, and any necessary bowing for strings.
- Remember to cancel indications such as *ritardando* and *pizzicato* when they are no longer applicable.
- Write in lyrics for all vocal lines, showing how the words are underlaid to the music. Ensure that there is at least one note for every syllable.

Finishing off

- Check that pages or bars are numbered.
- Delete redundant staves.
- By default, scores are printed with large staves, suitable for performance. A score submitted to an examiner may be 'shrunk' to a study-score size provided that it is clearly legible.
- If possible, print scores double-sided to reduce page-turns.

Other types of notation

If you choose Brief B or C you may prefer to write in an alternative notation that is more suitable for your style. Guitar tablature and lead sheets are acceptable, but they must contain all the information needed to produce a performance; including rhythm patterns, tempo, dynamics and how the melody fits the words. If improvisation is included, indicate its duration in time or numbers of bars. Show the chord sequence, scale or rhythm pattern on which the improvisation is based.

Electronic compositions that have no score need a detailed description or annotation. The specification lists the topics that should be covered. More details are given at the end of Chapter 7 (see page 109).

Things to do

As soon as you begin to practise the knowledge and skills described in this chapter you will notice their use in the music that you listen to or perform. Keep a note of common patterns and idioms so that you can look for opportunities to include them in your work. Here are three extracts to study that show different ways of using a simple harmonic vocabulary.

Play or listen to the following three extracts and answer the questions that follow each one:

Extract 1   Bach, Menuet from *French Suite No. 3*

- What is the key at the beginning and at the end of the extract?
- Which cadence is used at bars 7–8? What about bars 15–16?
- Where is a sequence used in the extract?
- What are the chords used in bars 1–2, and in bars 5–6?
- Which notes are passing notes in the treble of bar 7, and in the bass of bar 8?

Things to do

Extract 2

Handel, Chorus See the conqu'ring hero from the oratorio *Judas Maccabaeus*

- What is the key at bar 1, bar 12 and bar 16?
- Where can you find an imperfect cadence and two perfect cadences? In each case, name the chord before chord V.
- What are the chords used in bar 2 and bar 15?
- Where can you find the progressions V^7–I and V^7–VI? Note how the dominant seventh resolves.
- How would you describe the texture of this extract?

Extract 3

Mozart, Opening of first movement, *Piano Sonata in G major K.189h.*

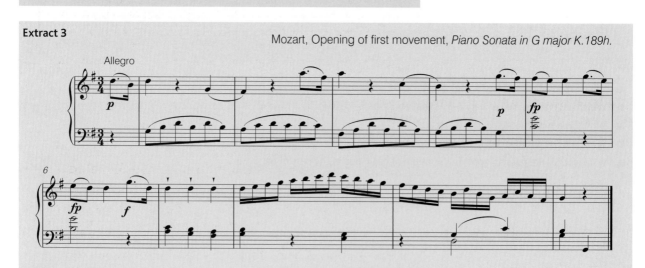

- What are the chords used from bar 6 to the end? You should find two second inversion chords.
- What are the two progressions that contain second inversion chords?
- How can you describe the harmonic rhythm (the speed of chord change) throughout the extract?
- What name could be given to the rhythm pattern in the bass in bars 8–9?

6 Choosing a composing option for AS

Learning objectives:

- to understand the choices available in this unit

- to look at examples that may suggest useful ideas and techniques

- to develop checklists that will help you to monitor and improve your work.

AQA Examiner's tip

The choice you make in this unit does not have to be carried through to A2. Depending on how your compositional skills develop during the year, you could make a fresh choice for Unit 5.

Three options are available in Unit 2 (Composing). You will need to discuss the choice with your teacher, taking into account your experience of composition so far and the skills you still need to develop. Brief A will suit you if you prefer to have specific questions to answer, Brief B allows you to create a piece entirely on your own initiative, and Brief C is best if you would like to develop a piece from a given idea.

- **Brief A (Compositional techniques)** is an excellent training in fundamental skills. It is not designed to offer a lot of scope for individual expression, but helps you to practise using harmony and counterpoint, which are valuable in all styles of composition.

- **Brief B (Either free composition or pastiche in response to a given genre)** gives the greatest freedom for individual work. The duration is prescribed (three to six minutes) and a choice of four possible ensembles given – vocal, instrumental, electronic or keyboard. The music can be written in an established historical style (pastiche), or in any style chosen or devised by yourself.

- **Brief C (Arranging)** allows more freedom of style, but the basis for the arrangement will be given in the form of a set folk song and text. Any ensemble of voices, instruments or ICT sound sources may be used, and the resulting arrangement must last between three and six minutes.

All three briefs contain guidance on the technical skills to be demonstrated, which require a fundamentally tonal idiom. The requirements cannot be met by wholly atonal compositions, nor by percussion or electronic compositions which do not include pitched sounds. Because the required techniques are common to all three briefs, it will be possible to practise composing in a variety of styles before deciding which brief will be followed for the examination.

Brief A: Compositional techniques

There are two compulsory questions.

Question 1: Harmonisation of a 16-bar diatonic melody

You will be given a melody in a major or minor key and asked to harmonise it in four parts for any four melodic instruments or voices. The harmonic vocabulary described in Chapter 5 should be the basis of the composition. It will not necessarily be possible to include all the devices or chords described there, but it is important to take every opportunity for interest in chord choice, modulation and texture.

If you are unsure how to begin, you could follow this approach:

- Choose an instrument or voice that is suitable for the given melody in range and style, and match the accompanying instruments to it. It helps to write for instruments or voices with which you are familiar.

- Examine the structure of the melody to discover phrase lengths and cadence points.

- Look for opportunities to modulate to a related key. These are not always indicated by accidentals in the melody.

Key terms

Consecutive fifths and octaves: when one chord moves to another and the same two voices/instruments are a fifth apart in both chords, the consecutive intervals can sound too prominent. The same applies to consecutive octaves.

Passing note: a note that moves by step between two notes of a chord.

- Plan the chord sequence. Bear in mind that the chord or its inversion may change under a sustained or repeated note.
- Write the bass line, choosing notes that are both harmonically and melodically suitable.
- Check for **consecutive fifths and octaves** between parts and eliminate them.
- Complete the inner parts, including melodic and rhythmic interest where possible.
- Remember that it is not necessary to provide a chord for every note of the melody. If a short note moves by step between two notes of a chord it can be treated as a **passing note**, which does not affect the prevailing chord. In the Handel example (*He shall feed his flock*) in Chapter 5 (see page 85) bar 1 is harmonised by a B♭ major chord, so the E♭ and C are passing notes.
- Passing notes can be added to other parts, including the bass, if they do not create consecutive fifths or octaves.
- If the melody is in a minor key, or passes through a minor key, you will need to decide which accidentals to apply to the sixth and seventh degrees of the scale. To imply chord V at a cadence, the seventh degree must be raised. Elsewhere, choose the notes from the melodic minor scale that sound most satisfying harmonically and melodically.

Here is Handel's harmonisation of a famous melody from the *Water Music*. It modulates to the dominant key at bar 8 and passes through B♭ major and G minor in bars 9–12. The lower parts reflect the dotted rhythms of the melody so that interest and movement are maintained.

returning to F major

F major

Question 2: Controlling texture

This question is designed to develop writing in a contrapuntal style, where each instrument or voice has an interesting independent line. A keyboard accompaniment will be supplied and you will be asked to compose two melodic lines above it.

This was a very common musical texture in the Baroque period. Trio sonatas for two violins, oboes or flutes with continuo accompaniment were written by Purcell, Corelli, Handel and J.S. Bach and it would be useful to play and study these. The same texture is found in vocal duets such as the *Laudamus te* in Vivaldi's *Gloria*. Later vocal examples can be found in opera (for example the 'Letter duet' from Mozart's *The Marriage of Figaro*), in shows (such as *One hand, one heart* from *West Side Story*) and in songs by duos such as Simon and Garfunkel.

In good contrapuntal writing, each voice in turn will lead, support or accompany, as the participants in a conversation will speak, agree or listen.

- The foundation of each part will be the notes of the prevailing chord, known as the **harmony notes**. Identify the chords and keys first so that you know which harmony notes can be used.

- Look for ideas in the bass part. You may find a sequence, or a melodic phrase you can imitate.

- Decide which voices or instruments you will use, and note their ranges.

- Now begin to work melodically, choosing notes from the available harmony notes. Aim for interesting lines with a strong sense of direction.

- Remember to use rhythmic interest in the added parts and to share the interest between them. They should complement the accompaniment, being active when the bass is sustained and vice versa.

- The added parts may be similar in style and imitate each other, or each may have a distinctive character, as in the two-part Bach example in Chapter 5 (see page 95).

- Melodic lines will have more shape and variety if unessential notes, such as passing notes, are added. **Unessential notes** also produce passing dissonances that make the harmony more interesting. Various types of unessential note are illustrated in the following examples:

Key terms

Harmony note: a note that belongs to the prevailing chord.

Unessential note: a note that sounds against a chord without being part of it. Examples are passing notes, auxiliary notes and suspensions.

Mendelssohn, Duet 'I waited for the Lord' from *Hymn of Praise*

Some points to note:

■ The two voices are equally matched, with the main melody in the second voice and a descant line for the first soprano.

■ There is free imitation between the voices, following the same rhythm and direction, but varying the intervals.

■ Most of the notes are harmony notes derived from the accompanying chords. Two kinds of unessential notes can be found – passing notes (marked as PN on the extract) and notes of anticipation. These are marked on the score.

■ Notice how the two voices come together at the cadences to mark these strong points.

Corelli, Fourth movement from *Trio Sonata Opus 3 No. 7*

Some points to note:

- The first violin part has energetic and distinctive rhythms.
- The second violin *either* imitates it freely, *or* supports in thirds and sixths *or* becomes part of the accompaniment in line with the bass.
- There are three more types of unessential notes marked on the score in this example:

1 Suspension: A note held over from a previous chord to become a dissonance and then resolve by step.

2 Auxiliary note: A note that moves away from a harmony note by step and immediately returns.

3 Changing notes: Notes that move a step above and then a step below the harmony note.

Things to do

- Listen to, or play examples of, music in the styles you are studying.
- Begin to analyse any music you perform, looking for chords, cadences and effective musical ideas.
- Get to know, thoroughly, the instruments, voices or software you will be using.

continues overleaf

■ Brief B: Free composition or pastiche

This brief allows for composition in any style for an ensemble of your own choice. The harmonic language can be in imitation of an existing style (pastiche) or individually developed. There are guidelines covering genre, duration and content.

Choosing a genre

There are four options. These allow a multitude of choices but guide you away from large ensembles, such as full orchestra or concert band. This will help you to spend more time refining and developing your work and less time on scoring.

Vocal music

Any ensemble that includes a voice or voices can be used. Among the possibilities are:

- two or more unaccompanied voices
- solo voice with guitar or piano
- four-part choir with organ
- upper-voice choir with or without accompaniment
- folk or rock group with vocalist
- live vocals recorded with electronic accompaniment.

The examiners will be looking for sensitive handling of text, understanding of the voice and balance of voice(s) and accompaniment.

The Clan, a Scottish ceilidh band, in performance

Small ensemble

Some of the possible choices are:

- flute duet
- guitar duet
- violin and piano
- string quartet, brass quartet or saxophone quartet
- piano trio
- rock band without vocalist
- ceilidh band
- jazz ensemble
- percussion ensemble including mallet percussion such as xylophone or marimba.

Electronic music

The composition can be created from any sound sources available on the equipment used for the examination. Loops and samples may be included but you must also demonstrate the ability to create and use original ideas. Do not rely entirely upon ideas, loops and samples loaded in the software. There are many possibilities, including:

- an imaginative 'soundscape' using a mixture of standard harmonies and electronic sounds
- an album track for rock band based on a loop or sample
- a piece written for traditional instrumental sounds but using them beyond their normal capabilities, for example in range or tempo
- a piece that explores different ways of manipulating an acoustic sound.

There is no limit to the creative ideas you can explore in this area but you must include music that demonstrates your understanding of the harmonies and techniques listed in the specification.

Keyboard music

This category may include mallet percussion. Possible choices include:

■ piano, organ or harpsichord solo

■ piano duet

■ marimba, xylophone or vibraphone solo or duet.

Duration

The composition should last *between three and six minutes*. The duration is given as a guideline to ensure that there is enough interest and variety in the composition. This length should give you scope to demonstrate skills such as development and modulation, which are important to achieve higher mark bands. If the composition contains significant sections of exact repetition, measure the duration without the repetitions, or revise it to introduce more material or more variation in repeats. This could apply to rondo forms and to songs with repeated verses.

Content

The specification indicates certain features that should be included to strengthen the composition and to indicate a good grasp of compositional skills:

■ The music should have a clear *structure* and some *development of ideas*. This could involve a plan such as ternary form or 12-bar blues, the development of a single idea or mood, or following a text. Do not attempt a complex form, such as sonata form or fugue, unless it is thoroughly understood and well practised.

■ The *key or mode* should be identifiable. A movement three or more minutes long will normally benefit from some contrast of key. Transitions between keys need careful handling. Advice on this is given in Chapter 5 (see page 84).

■ *Melody* needs character, consistency of style and appropriate phrasing. It should contain sufficient interest to lead the listener's attention onwards and should not appear to 'mark time'.

■ *Rhythm and tempo* control the energy flow of the music. Aim for a balance between variety and unity of style. In some forms, such as variations, rhythm can be an important device to increase or decrease tension and excitement in the course of the piece.

■ *Harmony* should be fundamentally diatonic and use a range of chords, including inversions and dominant seventh chords. In traditional harmony, the tonic, dominant and subdominant chords will be fundamental, but secondary triads should also be explored, together with a variety of cadence patterns. In pop, rock and jazz styles, different chord relationships may emerge, but it is important to avoid restricting yourself to a small harmonic vocabulary.

■ *Timbre and texture* can be varied as described in Chapter 5 (see page 91).

■ *Phrasing, articulation and marks of expression* indicate the character of the music and contribute to its dynamic shape.

Things to do

■ Use the music you study in Unit 1 and your own performing and listening to gather ideas for composition.

■ Write short practice compositions for the voices, instruments or software you will be using.

■ If you are writing for live performers, arrange a workshop performance of your practice pieces and discuss where they are most effective.

Brief C: Arranging

For this brief you will be given a folk song melody and text to be arranged for any chosen ensemble of voices and/or instruments. When you receive the melody:

- Get to know the melody well.
- Think of different ways to harmonise it. You may wish to begin with a simple harmonisation and use more interesting chords, or a quicker harmonic rhythm when it is repeated.
- Look for melodic ideas or rhythm patterns in the melody that could be used in the accompaniment or for an introduction and interludes.
- Determine if the text suggests changes of mood or tempo in different verses. It can also suggest the shape of the arrangement. Should it end loudly or softly? Which is the most important verse? Does the mood change suddenly anywhere?
- See if the text has ideas that can be illustrated in the music, for example references to dancing, singing, running or calling.
- Decide on the ensemble you will write for, and get to know its capabilities well.
- Remember to use different textures – a single melody line, two-part writing or full harmony could all be used.
- Think of ways in which the melody can be transformed to create contrast in the arrangement. You might change the mode or key, the time signature or the tempo for one or more verses.

Choosing a genre

There is more freedom in the choice of ensemble compared to Brief B as no genres are specified. The only exclusion implied by the specification is a composition for a solo instrument or voice. In practice, it is advisable to write for an ensemble with which you are familiar or which you have studied for the purpose.

Think carefully about the size of the ensemble before you begin. Writing for two unaccompanied voices or melody instruments can be very effective in performance but it needs skilful handling to demonstrate the range of compositional skills required at this level. At the other end of the scale, this brief permits the use of a large ensemble, such as brass band or concert band, but this would entail time-consuming scoring, which might be difficult to complete in the allotted hours. Traditional ensembles, such as those listed under Brief B, are tried and tested, and existing, arrangements for these ensembles can be studied. Alternatively, you may wish to write for an ensemble in which you perform so that practice compositions can be rehearsed during the course.

Duration

The finished arrangement should last *between three and six minutes*. The given folk song will naturally be short, but various methods can be used to build a longer structure:

- State the melody several times, giving fresh interest at each repetition. Change of key, harmony, tempo, instrumentation and texture are possible. Aim to support and illuminate the melody rather than to contradict its character.

Hint

There is an example question to help you practise this in the related online materials.

Key terms

Pentatonic: a five-note mode common in Scottish folk music, negro spirituals and music from Eastern Europe and the Far East. It can be found easily by playing the black notes on a keyboard.

Things to do

- Listen to arrangements of folk songs in many different styles.
- Practise writing short arrangements, concentrating each time on a different element such as harmony, texture or rhythm.
- If you are writing for live performers, arrange a workshop performance of your practice pieces and discuss where they are most effective.

- The song is likely to have more than one verse of words giving you the opportunity to illustrate their moods. Some folk songs tell a story, which can be mirrored in the music.
- Write a countermelody. This could become the foreground, with the original melody in the background.
- Develop motifs from the melody as features of the accompaniment or to provide prelude, interludes and postlude.

Content

The harmonic vocabulary required is the same as for Brief B, so the advice on Content under Brief B also applies here. Much will depend on the nature of the given melody, as folk songs may be in a major or minor key, but could also be modal or **pentatonic**. It is important not to distort the melody, but this does not limit the overall harmonic language of the arrangement. Rock, jazz and folk styles can be explored, provided they are in sympathy with the original. There is a wealth of existing material to study. Some examples are:

- album tracks by groups such as Steeleye Span and Pentangle
- Britten: folk song arrangements for voice and piano
- Vaughan Williams: folk song arrangements for upper voice choir
- Vaughan Williams: *English Folk Song Suite* for concert band
- Tippett: *Suite for the Birthday of Prince Charles* for orchestra
- Copland: *Appalachian Spring* (contains five variations on folk song *'Tis the gift to be simple*)
- Tippett: *Five spirituals* from *A Child of our Time* for mixed choir
- Fats Waller: *Swing low, sweet chariot* and *Deep river* for organ.

7 Managing your time

Learning objectives:

- to learn how to prepare for the examination, which will be in controlled time
- to plan your method of working during the controlled time
- to understand how to complete your submission with the necessary documents and recording.

The composition briefs and instructions will be available in good time, but all the work you submit for this unit must be written under examination conditions towards the end of the course. A maximum of 20 hours of 'controlled time' is allowed, in sessions planned and supervised within your centre. You will not be able to submit any work that has not been supervised in the controlled time, so you must not begin work on a brief or start your final composition for Brief B at home or outside the examination sessions.

Preparation

To prepare for the examination you will need to:

- learn the harmonic language you plan to use in the composition
- study the distinctive features of the style to be used, and the characteristics of the voices, instruments or software
- practise the mode of working needed for the examination sessions.

The basic harmonic language is described in Chapter 5. It is also required for the listening questions and analysis of works in Unit 1, so that work on one unit will help with another. Remember to listen with the ear of a composer, investigating the language and construction of set works for your own use. Extensions to the basic language may be needed according to the brief chosen; for example, to write in a jazz style or to arrange a modal folk song.

> **Hint**
>
> You will find information about the musical style of jazz in the section on jazz in Chapter 13 (see page 187).

It is not necessary to decide which brief to choose immediately as exercises can be devised which are useful for all options. The skill of harmonising a melody may be applied later to a given question in Brief A, to a folk song in Brief C, or to an original melody in Brief B.

Brief A can be studied practically by examining the harmonies and counterpoint in works you listen to or perform. It is particularly valuable to become aware of the interweaving of melodies needed for Question 2 by singing or playing in an ensemble.

For Briefs B and C, experience in writing for the intended ensemble or software is necessary. Short, practice compositions tried out in performance will teach you about balance, technique and effective use of equipment. Aim to complete two or more compositions in the style of your brief during the course so that any arising issues can be discussed at this stage.

> **Hint**
>
> There are practice questions for harmonising a melody, controlling texture (Brief A) and arranging (Brief C) in the related online materials.

Speed and fluency of writing will increase with practice. Because the final composition is written without consultation or assistance, the ability to translate musical ideas into notation is vital in all compositions where a score is produced.

The length of the supervised examination sessions will be decided by your centre. If you are unaccustomed to working at composition for sustained periods it will help to practise timed sessions of increasing length, for example starting at 45 minutes and increasing gradually to 90 minutes or two hours. In this way, the examination duration will become familiar before the controlled time begins.

Using the controlled time effectively

The composition submitted for the examination must be completed entirely within the controlled time. Discussion and consultation are not allowed within the supervised hours. You will not have access to your work between sessions, and no written material may be taken into a supervised session. It will be possible to consult reference books, scores, or a teacher between sessions, on matters of fact and technique, but your teacher will not be able to comment on the examination composition. This emphasises the need to develop confidence and well-practised skills during the course.

If you choose Brief A you may find that you will not need the full allocation of 20 hours to complete your work, but would benefit from more practice of sample questions before beginning the final brief. Preparatory exercises will give a clear indication of the length of time needed. You are not required to attend further sessions once you are satisfied with your work.

Briefs B and C leave more decision-making to you, and it is to be expected that you will delete and re-write or re-structure parts of the composition in the process. The following hints may help during the composition time:

- Always save deleted material. You may find you want to return to it later.
- Plan your time carefully. It is sometimes tempting to spend a long time perfecting a passage when it is more important to move on to new material.
- If you are making little progress in one passage, leave it and return later. It may be more productive to work on a new section or to undertake some scoring.
- Do not expect all work sessions to be equally productive. It is easy to become dispirited through lack of progress, but a difficult session is often followed by a more successful one.
- Avoid beginning one brief or composition and changing to another, as lost time cannot be reclaimed.

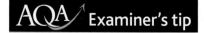

AQA Examiner's tip

Leave time within the 20 hours to check your score for accuracy. Give attention to detailed editing, such as phrasing, dynamics, articulation and underlay of text.

Recording session in progress

Completion: recording and annotating

When the controlled time is completed you will no longer be able to alter your composition, and a copy will be taken for submission to the examiner. If the composition has no score, for example an electronic composition for Brief B or C, you will need to write an annotation. An annotation is a written document taking the place of a score, giving as much detail as possible about the composition. You should include the following points:

- Information about the melodic and rhythmic ideas, notating or describing them clearly.
- A description of the structure and development of the composition, and its overall plan.
- A plan of the keys and chord sequences used.
- Comment on textures, timbres and dynamics.
- A written copy of any text, may be used where relevant, which as a basis for a plan of the composition.
- In an electronic composition, information on the sound sources used, distinguishing between loops, samples and original material. Give an account of the processes by which the composition was created.

It is also possible to make a recording of the composition after the controlled time, especially if you intend to make a live recording. The recording must represent the composition as completed in the examination: it is not possible to make further refinements at this stage.

Things to do

- Listen to as much music as possible in the style of your composition.
- Practise writing short compositions at first, with a clear aim for each one: for example, to experiment with harmony, rhythm or texture.
- Discuss your compositions with your teacher and your friends so that you learn to assess your own work.

8 Introduction to performing

There is a wide choice of performance options within this unit and you must, therefore, work to your strengths and spend time weighing up the possibilities. The options are as follows:

Acoustic options	Technology-based options
Solo performance on an instrument	Performance 1 – sequencing
Solo performance on voice	Performance 2 – multi-track close microphone recording
Solo performance on a second instrument	
Ensemble performance	

You are required to choose *two* performance options from the six available. Each must last between five and eight minutes. You are not necessarily expected to choose just one work which lasts that long: it will obviously be possible to do that with some pieces but it is more likely that you will put together a short programme of pieces which will, in total, last between five and eight minutes for each of your chosen performances. The actual specification states, regarding each option:

> For each performance, candidates may submit a single piece or a programme of shorter pieces.

For all options, you can perform one or more of your own compositions if the standard of technical expertise and expressive control is considered suitable: always consult your teacher about this before deciding.

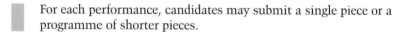 What you need to submit

In each case, your performances are to be submitted on CD or minidisk and there will be a candidate record form to complete.

You must also be able to submit either:

- a score of the music you have played; or
- a detailed annotation/lead sheet; or
- a recording of the original work (this is a useful option if you have learnt the piece by listening to the recording rather than using notated music/TAB);
- any additional information required by the technology-based options.

However, you must still make it clear what your role is in the performance so that your part can be identified by using your annotation/ lead sheet and listening to the recording of your performance.

The recordings can be made at any time during the course.

How the performing options are assessed

Performing is one of the three assessment objectives for all Music specifications. At AS, it carries the highest weighting of the three components at 40 per cent (or 20 per cent if considered as part of the overall A Level assessment).

This weighting has been given to reflect its importance, but also to acknowledge that this area tends to be the strength of most AS students. It is hoped and anticipated that you will do well and, with 40 per cent of the marks available, it is crucial that you prepare thoroughly and take full account of the requirements of your chosen options.

Assessment objective 1 (performing/realising) requires you to:

interpret musical ideas with technical and expressive control and a sense of style and awareness of occasion and/or ensemble.

These requirements are reflected in the assessment criteria, and you should read these carefully as you choose your programme and prepare your performance(s).

Assessment criteria for acoustic performances

Acoustic performances are assessed in terms of:

- *Level of demand:* The examining board establishes a certain level of playing competence as its basic measure for AS standard. This area of marking reflects the difficulty of the music selected for performance out of a maximum mark of 4.

- *Accuracy:* This refers to how closely you stick to the actual pitches and rhythms of the music. Attention to the composer's instructions for dynamics, phrasing and articulation are also taken into account.

- *Communication:* This reflects the extent to which you project the music in your performance. Do you sound confident? Is your performance committed and convincing?

- *Interpretation:* How well do you understand the conventions of how to play the music you have chosen? Does your playing reflect the period and style of the music? These are the issues marked in this section.

- *Sense of ensemble (where applicable):* Where you play as part of an ensemble, or group of performers, you will be assessed on how well your playing is integrated with that of the others to produce a cohesive, balanced result wherein each player is responsive to the others and can, if necessary, accommodate problems encountered.

Assessment criteria for technology-based performances

The technology-based options have different sets of assessment criteria:

Technology-based performance 1: sequencing

This option does, in fact, cover sequencing *and* multi-track recording. It is assessed on your response to the following five requirements:

■ *Accuracy of pitch and rhythm:* This measures the extent to which the performance is an accurate reflection of the pitch/intonation and rhythmic demands of the music.

■ *Use of timbre, balance and panning techniques:* Within this section, your ability to choose and manipulate sounds appropriate to the genre of the music being performed is assessed. The mark will also reflect your success in achieving a good balance between the various parts and using panning, or the effect of spatial separation, to ensure that the parts are heard clearly.

■ *Evidence of close attention to performing and expressive detail:* Attention to phrasing, dynamics and issues of articulation will be assessed here.

■ *Awareness of style required:* Given the genre of music chosen, credit will be given for the extent to which your technology-based performance shows understanding of its style.

■ *Ability to use the facilities available within the software and hardware to produce a valid result:* As part of your submission, you will be required to state the facilities available within the software package(s) and the hardware (amplifiers, mixers, effects boxes, and so on). You are then assessed as to how well you have used these.

Technology-based performance 2: multi-track/close microphone recording

This is assessed on the following:

■ *Balance:* You need to ensure that the four (or more) parts that make up your recording are balanced in such a way that no one part overpowers the others, or is drowned out by the others. The extent of your success in achieving this is measured here.

■ *Dynamic range, including use of compression:* It is expected that your recording will demonstrate a range of dynamics in keeping with its style. Where necessary, you will need to show your ability to handle compression, thus ensuring that sudden loud or quiet passages are automatically adjusted.

■ *Manipulation of mixing desk:* The mixing desk is the hub of your activity for this performance and where you ensure that all the detail you require is audible and effective so that each part can be clearly identified.

■ *Use of effects such as reverb, delay, and so on:* The use of effects is an important aspect of this performance option but such use must be in keeping with the style of the music being performed.

■ *Quality of the recording across a wide range of frequencies:* Your music must maintain clarity across a wide range of frequencies and your success, or otherwise, in achieving this is assessed here.

■ **Did you know?**

Daniel Barenboim (1942–), pianist and conductor, gives this advice to young musicians: 'Live life to the full and become more curious every day. The more you find out about life, the richer your music-making will be.'

9   Acoustic performances

Learning objectives:

- to appreciate the level of demand required at AS

- to understand some ways in which additional skills can be gained for the acoustic performances

- to be in a position to choose between the acoustic options

- to know how to prepare acoustic performances

- to understand how to record and annotate acoustic performances.

Developing the skills you need

You need many skills to give good acoustic performances, and you will probably have started acquiring these before you embarked on your AS Music course. Performing skills are built up and honed over time, and you may have received instrumental and/or vocal tuition at some point, or still be receiving tuition as part of your overall musical studies and activities.

Your teaching and your previous experience of performing will have introduced you to a wide range of musical experiences and genres and you may prefer a particular approach to performing.

Improvisation can form a part of your performances but, whenever this occurs, you must make clear the basis of that improvisation, be it a chord sequence, a specific scale, a melodic or rhythmic fragment, a melody or a riff.

How your performance will be assessed

Your performance will be assessed on:

- *accuracy:* technical accuracy, fluency and security and the extent to which you have observed the composer's performing and expressive directions
- *communication:* your ability to communicate the music to the audience in a committed, convincing and assured manner
- *interpretation:* demonstration that you understand the requirements of the music in terms of its period and style.

Working at the right level

The general level of demand expected at AS is that of music which matches the Grade 5 standards of the main examining boards: the Associated Board of the Royal Schools of Music, Trinity/Guildhall, Thames Valley University (also known as London College of Music) and Rock School. However, you should be sure that your choice of repertoire falls well within your technical and expressive abilities so that you will be able to produce a fluent and convincing performance: it is better to sacrifice a mark or two for level of demand, if necessary, and then be in a better position to score well in the other areas of assessment.

Developing your skills

There is no substitute for regular performance of a wide range of music to help you develop your technical, communicative and interpretative skills. If you are receiving instrumental and/or vocal tuition, your teacher will be working to a programme that will result in the gradual acquisition of additional skills and a steady improvement in your overall confidence. It is, therefore, important that your instrumental/vocal teacher is aware of the requirements of this unit and can recommend a range of pieces for you to work at to consolidate or gain skills and then provide a practice schedule to ensure that you learn the piece(s) and will be able to fulfil the assessment criteria.

Acquiring the technical skills necessary for any piece of music will involve exercises in addition to merely playing/singing the chosen pieces. You should never stop practising scales, arpeggios, breath control, tone and dynamic gradation, or the various types of articulation relevant to your instrument. There is a substantial difference, for example, between playing or singing a phrase of music and carefully shaping that phrase with overall attention to dynamics and tone. Even remembering the simple principle that a long sustained note should not be all at one dynamic, or use just one tone, can make a major contribution to the improvement of a performance.

Choosing acoustic options

Acoustic performance options

a   Solo performance on an instrument

b   Solo performance on voice

c   Solo performance on a second instrument

d   Ensemble performance

Choosing acoustic-only routes through the options

Good on two instruments?

If you are equally good on two instruments and are at Grade 5 standard or higher, then the most sensible and straightforward options could be simply to choose programmes for each of your acoustic instruments: options **a** and **c**.

Good on one instrument and have a good singing voice?

If you play an instrument well and have a good singing voice, then options **a** and **b** could be the ones for you.

Regularly play or sing with others?

Perhaps you sing or play an instrument well, but also regularly play or sing with a small group of others – in other words in an ensemble. In this case, options **a** and **d** or **b** and **d** are possible. The specification defines an ensemble as normally consisting of three or more performers where the demands of the parts are of roughly equal difficulty. It also points out that 'duets at an appropriate standard for, e.g. pianists, will enable them to demonstrate the necessary *ensemble* skills if the part chosen contains passages where the candidate fulfils the roles of both melody player and accompanist in the course of the piece'.

Good at accompanying others?

You can also demonstrate your ensemble skills by accompanying one or more other performers. However, do appreciate the fundamental difference between 'accompanying' and, for example, 'playing the piano part while one or two others play and/or sing'. In a true accompaniment, you, as accompanist, will be fully aware of what the other performers are doing and will be constantly adjusting tempo, dynamics and phrasing to coincide with them; thus providing a complementary and supporting role. If just playing, you will be concentrating on your part to the virtual exclusion of the needs and problems of others.

All programmes should be discussed with your instrumental teacher and/or subject teacher and with any other people who will be involved in the performance(s) with you, such as accompanists, duettist, or other members of a group/ensemble.

Within each of the ensemble options, it is permissible for you to be assessed 'holistically' – for example, playing the piano *and* singing, or playing guitar *and* singing – as long as, for the ensemble option, you combine with other players to meet its requirements.

These are the acoustic-only routes through the options. However, there are also two technology-based performance options (described on page 124) if your interests lie in technology.

Suggestions for acoustic solo performances

We cannot suggest programmes for every instrument here, but, as an initial guide, here are some possibilities around which to build a programme. Remember that these are just suggestions and that all are based on music at Grade 5 standard:

Flute	Grieg: *Anitra's dance* from *Peer Gynt Suite* (ABRSM Gd. 5) Stephen Dodgson: *Circus Pony* (ABRSM Gd. 5) Rutter: *Chanson* from *Suite Antique* (Trinity/Guildhall Gd. 5)
Clarinet	Paul Reade: *Summer* from Suite from *The Victorian Kitchen Garden* (ABRSM Gd. 5; Trinity/Guildhall Gd. 5) Malcolm Arnold: *Andantino*: 2nd movt from *Sonatina for Clarinet* (ABRSM Gd. 5) Debussy: *La fille aux cheveux de lin* (Trinity/Guildhall Gd. 5)
Violin	Granados: *Andaluza* from *12 Danzas Españolas* (ABRSM Gd. 5) Howard Blake: *Dance of the snowmen* No. 3 from *The Snowman* suite for violin & piano (ABRSM Gd. 5) Mascagni: *Intermezzo* (Trinity/Guildhall Gd. 5)
Cello	Borodin: *Nocturne* from *String Quartet No. 2* (ABRSM Gd. 5) Gershwin: *Summertime* from *Porgy and Bess* (ABRSM Gd. 5) Strauss: *Radetzky March* (Trinity/Guildhall Gd. 5)
Trumpet	Gershwin: *I got rhythm* from *Girl Crazy* (ABRSM Gd. 5) Franck: *Panis angelicus* (ABRSM Gd. 5) Wedgewood: *Tequila Sunrise* (Trinity/Guildhall Gd. 5)
Trombone	Purcell: *Rondo* from *Abdelazar* (ABRSM Gd. 5) Gershwin: *Let's call the whole thing off* from *Shall We Dance* (ABRSM Gd. 5) Purcell: *Rondo* from *Abdelazar* (Trinity/Guildhall Gd. 5)
Xylophone	Bartlett: *Clownin' around* No. 45 from *Play Percussion* (Trinity/Guildhall Gd. 5) Weijmans: *Rock* No. 23 from *Mallet Minded* (Trinity/Guildhall Gd. 5) Dvořák: *Humoresque* Op. 101, No. 7 (ABRSM Gd. 5)

Electric guitar	Dave Barnard: *Rock Steady* (Rockschool Gd. 5)
	Deirdre Cartwright: *Queen for a Day* (Rockschool Gd. 5)
	Hussein Boon: *Downtime* (Rockschool Gd. 5)

Voice	Lerner & Loewe: *I could have danced all night* from *My Fair Lady* (ABRSM Gd. 5)
	Rodgers & Hammerstein: *People will say we're in love* from *Oklahoma!* (ABRSM Gd. 5; Trinity/Guildhall Gd. 5)
	Schönberg: *I dreamed a dream* from *Les Misérables* (Trinity/Guildhall Gd. 5)

Suggestions for ensemble performances

ABRSM lists several pieces for a range of small ensembles that would be useful here, and peripatetic teachers will also be able to recommend pieces of a suitable standard. It may, at times, be preferable to arrange music for a specific group rather than risk that a candidate will be let down by the performance of one of the other players within a chosen ensemble.

| Piano duets | Moszkowski: *Spanish Dance in G minor*, Op. 12 No. 2 (ABRSM Intermediate) |
| | Warlock: *No. 1 Basse-Danse* and *No. 5 Tordion* from *Capriol Suite* (ABRSM Intermediate) |

Piano as accompanist

To voice	Schönberg: *On my own* from *Les Misérables*
	Lloyd Webber: *Tell me on a Sunday* from *Song and Dance*
	Schubert: *Du bist die Ruh*

| To flute | Rutter: *Chanson* from *Suite Antique* |

| To clarinet | Finzi: *Carol* from *Five Bagatelles* |

The suggestions given here should not imply that your repertoire need be taken only from those pieces listed by ABRSM, Trinity/Guildhall or Rock School, although the grades assigned to pieces by these boards will be accepted by AQA and equated to level of demand marks. A coursework adviser will be appointed to your centre by AQA and, through your teacher, you will be able to receive advice as to the level of demand of a specific programme.

Playing within your limits

As there are only four marks out of the possible 40 given for the level of difficulty of the piece(s) you perform, it might be better to opt for music slightly easier than Grade 5, if that is your limit of achievement, and play comfortably within your means rather than risk stretching your abilities and losing marks in other assessment areas.

Addressing the demands of your programme

Practice is essential

For the solo acoustic options, arrange regular practices with your accompanist: as well as your own part, there will be sections in the music where you are not playing or, perhaps, sections where your line and the accompaniment need special attention in order to achieve good synchronisation. As soon as possible, try to set aside a regular session and always remember that there is no need to perform your entire programme at the same time (though, of course, you may prefer to do this).

For the ensemble option, you must be careful to work with other players/ singers who will be able to perform the chosen music and attend regular rehearsals. It would be a great advantage, if you were able, either to work with a group that is already established, or to form an ensemble from among members of the examination group.

Preparing your acoustic performances

Take time to warm up

For all acoustic performances, take sufficient time to warm up and to tune the instrument carefully; whether it be to your accompanist or to other members of the ensemble. If one instrument is of 'fixed' tuning, such as the piano, you must tune to that, otherwise you either use the pitch given by the best player or you could use one of the many electronic tuning aids available. Stringed instruments will take longer to tune, simply because of the number of strings to be checked. Time taken here will be rewarded within the context of the performance.

Focus on style, dynamics and articulation

It is during the final stages of preparation that you deal with the main characteristics of the music, focusing on its style and the composer's instructions for dynamics and/or articulation. If you are playing Baroque music, most such indications will be editorial and it is up to you, your teacher, your accompanist and/or the rest of the ensemble, to determine to what extent these are followed or adapted. Whatever you decide, make sure that the score you submit matches your intended interpretation.

During performance, dynamics should be exaggerated so that they can be heard easily (without, of course, going to absurd extremes). Articulation should equally be made obvious: very short *staccato* notes, strong accents and so on. Tempo markings, where given, should be strictly observed and changes carefully practised.

Preparing solo performances

When you have chosen your pieces, practise them thoroughly, both individually and with your accompanist. You and your accompanist must have ample opportunities to work together to appreciate how the different parts fit together and complement each other.

Get used to performing them under examination conditions. Perform to people who have not yet heard you play or practise so far: perhaps you have a relative who is musical; perhaps you can organise a performance to a group of pupils in your school, in their classroom or in an assembly; perhaps there are other teachers in your school who are interested in music and would be prepared to give up some of their time to listen to your performance.

> ### Hint
>
> As in public music examinations, you can omit repeats, unless they are an important part of the structure or add something to your performance/ interpretation. This might be, for example, when the convention of the piece allows for embellishment or other forms of improvisation during repeated sections.

Whatever you manage to arrange, try to perform your pieces as a unit on more than one occasion. You are quite likely to be nervous in this new situation, but if you find that you are having problems with passages then it is vital that you return to personal practice. You will need to decide whether any problems you encountered were minor and can, therefore, be remedied quite easily, or whether they are of a more serious nature, to the extent that a possible revision of your intended programme is necessary. This is another reason why early preparation of your pieces for acoustic performance is so important.

When you are playing, remember that you now have an audience. Let your manner of performing the music really communicate its meaning to them. You need to be confident, not only with the notes, but also with the style of the music.

Band ensemble in rehearsal

Key terms

Cantabile: literally 'song-like'; to be played in a flowing manner as one would sing.

Legato: smoothly.

Pesante: heavily.

Pitch bend: a device, usually a wheel, on a keyboard that enables the user to 'bend' the pitch of the note up and down.

Paying attention to style

Close attention to stylistic features is paramount: whatever music you choose to play falls into a particular genre and so brings with it various expectations and conventions. The scheme of assessment gives credit for your ability to convey these characteristics through your performance, so you must be clear what they are. Here are some examples:

Baroque

Music from the Baroque period will *contrast* dynamics (tiered dynamics) rather than shade them excessively; any trills will begin on the upper notes; dotted rhythms might well be played as if double-dotted, or might be played as *notes inégales* (where a dotted rhythm is played more as if in compound time) – for example, something written:

would be played like this, if *notes inégales*:

You might legitimately choose to use much less vibrato in music from this period and, if playing the piano, you would not use the sustaining pedal. Be especially careful with the interpretation of ornaments.

Classical

Music from the Classical period needs a balanced approach, with poise and a sense of elegance. There will be opportunities to include dynamic shading within phrases, as well as changes of tone quality and articulation.

Romantic

Music from the so-called Romantic period will often require a greater depth and range of emotions to be portrayed. Certainly, a wide range of dynamics will be covered and the music could need a ***cantabile*** and ***legato*** approach, a dramatic, ***pesante*** mode of playing, or styles that are shades or combinations of these. Playing techniques will be different from earlier music and your teacher will be able to advise you on the correct approach. However, there must always be evidence that you have tried to bring some of your own character and interpretation to the music.

Modern

Modern music will often call upon additional skills, such as the interpretation of **swung rhythms**, the articulation of the **stride bass**, or the use of **pitch bend**.

Preparing ensemble performances

All the comments on interpretation on page 111 apply equally to ensemble performances with the addition that all members of the ensemble must agree on the interpretative approach to be taken. Before the full ensemble meets, individual practice should be well advanced to minimise the time spent on technical problems.

Rehearsal time should be for uniting the players in a common purpose. The assessment criteria make it clear that you should be aiming for:

> a performance showing complete unity of purpose in all aspects of ensemble playing, including balance, timing, intonation and responsiveness to others, including, if necessary, the ability to react positively to any difficulties which may occur.

(AQA AS Assessment Criteria 2008)

There are several key phrases here; firstly:

- *complete unity of purpose:* the playing of all members of the ensemble will be matched in all aspects of the performance.

Key terms

Swung rhythms: in jazz and blues, where a rhythm notated as dotted quaver/semiquaver, or two quavers, is to be played as a triplet crotchet/quaver, as in these examples:

Stride bass: a bass/left-hand pattern typical of ragtime music; it consists of a single bass note followed by a chord:

These 'aspects' are then itemised as balance, timing, intonation and responsiveness to others:

■ *balance:* no one instrument should overpower the others (unless the composer's dynamics point unequivocally to that), and it may well be that players have to listen to each other very carefully to prevent this from happening, even to the extent of adjusting the volume of their own playing to maintain balance.

■ *timing:* this is mainly to do with maintaining the ensemble and ensuring that there is no miscounting that leads to late or early entries, no tendency to drag or rush a phrase or passage by one or more of the players, and so on.

■ *responsiveness to others:* the way in which players can respond to slight changes in tempo, dynamics, rhythmic interpretation, and so on.

A further important feature of good ensemble playing is:

■ the ability to react positively to any difficulties which may occur.

This aspect of the assessment criteria shows appreciation of the fact that something unexpected might happen during the performance – in other words, it doesn't have to be absolutely perfect! It takes into account the way in which other players within the ensemble respond to any such difficulties and ensure that the music continues. It may be that a member of the group loses his or her place and, albeit temporarily, affects the flow of the performance. It may be that a page turn is not executed cleanly and the player comes in slightly late. There are, of course, other possible scenarios, but the important thing is that this phrase points to the fact that it is not always necessary to stop the performance and then restart: if the group of players has responded well to the difficulty, this is a positive!

Communication: giving confident and well-projected performances

Within all acoustic performance options, there is a section of marks awarded for communication: the ability to give a committed, assured, convincing and well-projected performance of the music. In this unit, your teacher will most likely be the person doing the initial assessment before the recording; their marks and their reasons for the marks awarded are sent off to a moderator appointed by the examination board.

In any live performance, your confidence will come partly through your sense of conviction that the way you are performing the music is not only valid but also correct, and partly through your body language during that performance. An introverted player cannot communicate the meaning of the music. This is not to say that you have to be excessively physical during your playing or singing! It does mean that you must look confident and make eye-contact with members of the audience, your accompanist and/or other members of the ensemble. Do not 'hide' behind your music. If you are singing, it is invariably better to have memorised the songs, as your facial expressions are important in your interpretation and communication of the music to the audience.

Interpretation and accuracy

An equal number of marks are awarded for *interpretation* (commented on above) and *accuracy*. For accuracy, the top band of marks begins with the statement:

- At the top of this band, there will be no discernible flaws.

For full marks, you are expected to give an accurate performance. It is a three-mark band for both solo and ensemble performances, with the descriptor for the lower end of the band reading:

- at the lower end, there may be occasional slips but these will not affect the overall fluency of the programme.

In other words, it is all right to make a small number of errors as long as this does not interrupt the flow of the music. You are also expected to observe:

- the composer's expressive and performance directions.

This refers to indications of tempo (and changes of tempo), dynamics and articulation. If you are adding your own markings to the score in addition to or instead of the composer's, then these should be clearly shown, as your performance will be assessed against the score as submitted.

To reiterate, out of the total of 40 marks, a maximum of just four is available for the level of demand of your chosen programme: at AS, it is considered more important that you are able to *perform* the music to a very high standard in all areas: that is *accuracy*, *communication* and *interpretation* for the solo options **a–c**; these three plus *sense of ensemble* for the ensemble option **d**.

Recording and annotating acoustic performances

What to submit

Acoustic performances must be submitted with:

- a recording on CD or minidisk
- either a score, a lead sheet/detailed guide to the music or, if the learning process was based on this, a recording of the original work
- a candidate record form (CRF).

On the CRF, you must fill in:

- the name and number of your centre
- your full name and candidate number
- if appropriate, the track number from which your submitted recordings begin
- the options you have chosen (do this by listing the titles of the piece(s) you have played in the appropriate boxes)
- the instrument(s)/voice(s) you have performed upon and what either accompanied you or made up the rest of the ensemble
- your signature and the date (and your teacher must also sign and date the CRF).

Preparing your recording

For acoustic performances, try to arrange it so that you can play your pieces as early as is practical. They should be fully prepared, but if you have the opportunity to record them (or those for one of the options) reasonably early during the AS course it will ease pressure on you as you work at the other elements.

Your recording should be as clear and balanced as is possible. Time should be taken to ensure that microphones are positioned to optimise balance and clarity. Short passages should be recorded to test balance and dynamic levels: performances must be clear, neither too faint nor too distorted. Your teacher should make a comment on the CRF if the recorded balance is still different from that heard live and, therefore, used for the initial assessment: this is particularly crucial in the ensemble option. However, all practical steps should be taken to ensure your recorded performances match the live ones as closely as is possible.

It is not part of this examination to rely on just one 'take' of your performance. However, you should beware of attempting to play the piece(s) too often: much better to have fully prepared and be in just the right frame of mind, having warmed up and played through any passages you particularly wish to look at 'for the last time', and then approach your performance as if it was 'the big occasion' and the climax of all your careful practice and endeavour (which it is, actually).

Do not spend too long warming up or playing through the piece(s), especially if you are a brass player. Make sure that the music stand, if you are using one, is at the correct height and is carefully put together – a stand that collapses part way through your performance is the last thing you want!

Your teacher will make sure that the room set aside for the recording will not receive interruptions during the performing and recording process so, in so far as you can, when it comes to the actual examination performances, relax and enjoy yourself: you know the pieces, you are well prepared, you have played them on many previous occasions to a range of audiences and this is what it has all been leading towards. You can rest secure in the knowledge that, if the worst does happen and something totally unexpected does go wrong, all is not lost: you can have another go!

Scoring and notation

If you have played from standard music notation, then this score should be submitted. Wherever possible, you should enclose the full score, be it your part plus the piano's, or the complete ensemble score. This makes it much easier for your teacher, who does the original assessment, and the moderator (who will be listening to your *recorded* performance) to hear and appreciate how your part fits in with the rest of the musical texture.

If you do not use standard notation, there are various other options open to you, but, whichever one you choose, you must give both your teacher/ assessor and the moderator enough information to be absolutely certain what you are playing during the performance(s).

While a TAB score is fine for indicating the pitches of notes by showing their positions on the strings, it does not give a clear indication of rhythm and will rarely show any dynamics or phrasing. Wherever possible, you should add extra information and make sure that, on the recording, your part is clearly audible (do short test recordings first). Where there is possible confusion because of a similarity of timbres between your part and that of another player, give clear details to enable the listener to follow *your* part.

If you learnt your part from a recording by the original artist, you should submit this recording as a 'benchmark'; a means of comparing an original with your performance. In such cases, you must make it very clear just what your role is: your teacher will need to know for the initial assessment, and the moderator will have to be able to understand exactly what you have played.

10 Technology-based performances

Learning objectives:

- ◼ to understand the requirements of the two technology-based options

- ◼ to be in a position to choose whether to follow one or both of these options

- ◼ to understand the scheme of assessment that will be applied

- ◼ to decide on equipment to use

- ◼ to learn more about preparing technology-based performances

- ◼ to learn more about preparing and annotating technology-based performances.

◼ Developing skills for technological performances

Technology Option 1: sequencing

Technology-based option 1 requires you to demonstrate the skills of sequencing and multi-track recording. You must gradually get to know the program you are going to use, become proficient at playing the tracks in accurately and then learn how to improve alignment where necessary. You will need to ensure that all parts are well synchronised, adjust the accuracy of pitch and rhythm and deal with matters of transposition before moving further into the program to adjust velocity/dynamics, panning, tempo and so on.

A music sequencer/MIDI sequencer is software or hardware that will enable you to create music and then edit it. Many sequencers include features that make possible audio editing and processing.

Drum machines generally have a sequencer built in. Limited music notation is possible, and most can set out your work as a piano roll.

Your sequencer will record anything that you input from the keyboard and many will allow you to input up to 64 tracks – many more than you will need for this specification!

What you play is recorded as digital information, not music, and this is why you can edit it to such a great extent; even altering, adding or removing individual bars.

You need to learn how to use the sequencer's 'quantise' function so that your inputted information/music can be brought into time by the careful selection of an appropriate time value. It is very important that you can use this well, otherwise your final piece will probably not be at all satisfactory. Careful and appropriate use of the 'quantise' function will ensure that the different parts are aligned well, both in respect of the beat/pulse, and of each other.

You are advised not to use loops and samples – that is, pre-recorded sections of melody, chord pattern, bass riff and so on, as found on programs such as *Ejay* – as you will invariably have less control over the editing of these. Programs that permit the alteration or manipulation of such loops or samples can be used, but you should be careful to explain fully how you have modified the original loop and to what extent you have been able to adjust parameters.

When using a sequencer, your first action will probably be to record a click track: a simple beat that will enable you to keep the tracks in time. This can be muted or erased later. Other parts can then be added and the final input then edited, using the facilities available within the chosen software. Sequencing software, such as Cubasis VST, features an inbuilt metronome.

Using Cubasis VST

One of the most popular sequencing packages is Cubasis VST. It is operated from a 'piano roll editor' window, which enables you to add or delete tracks and view what is inputted in a linear format.

- Double-clicking on the Cubasis VST desktop icon will reveal an empty Arrangement window similar to this:

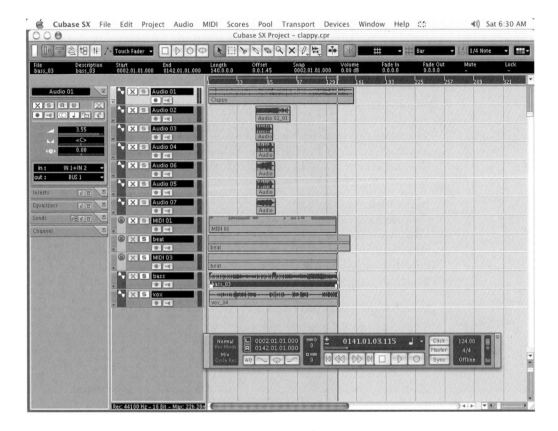

- To add or delete tracks, use the top toolbar.
- From a blank arrangement window – that is, one with no tracks – the first track added will be a MIDI track. In the blank window above, you will notice, in column C, the different icons for an audio and a MIDI track. Clicking on an audio icon will change it to a MIDI icon and vice versa. A search window might appear, at this point, to find where you want to keep any temporary audio files and then confirm it.
- To delete a track quickly, highlight the track and press the 'delete' key on your PC keyboard. If the track holds MIDI or audio information, you will be asked to confirm the action (*Yes* or *No*).
- If you find that you become happy working with a particular combination of MIDI and audio tracks, you can save this combination as your 'default' setting: Create your preferred layout of tracks (MIDI, VSTi, audio) and, before entering any information, select 'File>Save As' and search the Cubasis VST folder for a song file icon titled 'def'. A set-up can be changed at any time but it will replace any previous default setting. You can now start adding music onto your selected tracks, either in **real** or **step** time.

Key terms

'Real' time: the music is played in via a keyboard or other instrument connected to the sequencer; the sequencer records what is played in terms of pitch, rhythm and dynamic (velocity).

'Step' time: this is where each note of the music is entered from a keyboard, and you select duration as you enter.

Using Able MIDI Editor

A further program perhaps worth investigating is the Able MIDI Editor – a MIDI music editor for Windows. It enables you to compose and edit music in MIDI form. The editor is designed similarly to a piano roll: in other words, the time axis is located horizontally, and different positions on the vertical line correspond to different pitches.

Included in its basic functions are the capability to add and delete musical notes, adjust the pitch and duration of notes, and play back results. The editor also lets you arrange bar-lines manually, or by ear, with the Tapping Tool, and provides the means for working with tracks with a wide range of possibilities for grouping and combined note editing.

A useful feature is its 'precise bar-line arrangement'. Most piano-roll editors have a regular bar grid. This can sometimes lead to hardly printable notation. The Able MIDI Editor allows you to avoid these flaws by enabling you to adjust bars manually, so that the majority of notes do not cross bar lines, and the sound of the piece is not altered. In particular, this might be very useful when preparing data recorded with a MIDI keyboard for score printing.

Its Multiple Selection feature lets you select any group of notes and adjust their attributes all at once. Notes are selected according to standard Windows rules; thus it is possible to add notes one-by-one to those already selected, and use the cursor to select a section of the editing area. Not only this, the editor lets you select all notes lying within a defined time or frequency range, by choosing a section of the time-ruler or piano keyboard.

Which skills will be assessed for technology option 1 ?

The following skills will be assessed:

- accuracy of pitch and rhythm
- use of timbre, balance and panning techniques
- evidence of close attention to performing and expressive detail
- awareness of style required
- ability to use the facilities available within the software and hardware to produce a valid result.

What examiners are looking for is covered under 'Key areas to be assessed' on page 132.

These skills will be acquired over time and by working through short examples of sequencing and multi-tracking, possibly separating the activities of sequencing and recording audio tracks at first. Your final submission, however, will combine both recorded audio and MIDI sequenced tracks with a minimum of four tracks required. It is your decision just how many of each type of track is included, but both types must be present.

You will also have to set out details of the various facilities available within the hardware and software that you have used; for example, the facility to add reverb, chorus and/or delay, so that assessment can reflect how well you have used these.

Technology option 2: multi-track/close microphone recording

The main difference between this and option 1 is that, after having achieved an initial recording, it is your skill and ability to take this and, by applying various editing devices, produce a quality mixdown that will be assessed.

Which skills will be assessed for technology option 2?

The main areas that will be assessed are:

- balance
- dynamic range, including use of compression
- manipulation of mixing desk
- use of effects, such as reverb or delay
- quality of the recording across a wide range of dynamics.

What examiners are looking for is covered under 'Key areas to be assessed' on page 134.

Your preparation for this should include working with short recordings, gradually experimenting with the facilities available and improving your skills in each of the areas required for assessment.

Choosing technology-based options

Technology-based performance options

Performance 1 – Sequencing

Performance 2 – Multi-track/close microphone recording

Choosing technology option 1: sequencing

This requires you to use a combination of sequencing and multi-tracking/close microphone recording to create one or more pieces of music. It is an obvious fact – but nonetheless worth stating – that, unless your centre or you yourself can supply the necessary equipment, there is no point in even contemplating this as an option. You will need access to a device such as Cubase or Logic. Sibelius is an excellent tool for scoring and checking work, but it was never intended to be a sequencer. You also need a reputable and versatile multi-track recorder.

Although your music can be in any style, there are several conditions you must meet when embarking on this particular option:

- there must be at least four independent vocal/instrumental parts
- there must be a combination of recorded audio and MIDI sequenced tracks (though it is for you to decide the ratio of one type to the other)
- a piece must be at least 32 bars long
- pieces in a classical style must have some tempo control
- pop or jazz music should feature some use of a drum kit
- there must be at least a moderate level of dynamic variation.

You could, for example, choose a pop/rock song, sequence the drums, bass and keyboard, and then add the vocals and lead guitar as audio recordings.

When your work is submitted, you will need to give details of the equipment you have used, including the use you have made of the various facilities available within the hardware/software.

The examination specification makes it very clear where your performances will gain credit (see 'Key areas to be assessed' on page 132) and you must make sure that you meet each of these requirements to as high a standard as possible.

As this option requires the use of sequencing and multi-track/close microphone recording, you have a limitless range of music from which to choose. Your choice will be governed by:

■ your own interests
■ the performers available to you
■ the software and hardware available.

Although you can be involved, personally, in the performance of one or more of the audio tracks, or leave this to others, *you* must be the person who inputs the music into the MIDI tracks and *you* must manipulate both that aspect of the software/hardware as well as being responsible for the actual mixing.

Choosing technology option 2: multi-track/close microphone recording

This option showcases your ability to work on an initial recording of four or more independent vocal and/or instrumental parts. The recording will have been made via multi-tracking/close microphone recording. Basically, you can play one of three roles within this option. You can:

■ be one of the performers
■ perform up to all four of the tracks
■ confine yourself to the technological aspects of recording and editing.

You have to submit the original recording and also the final mix that you have achieved.

The specification requires:

■ a minimum of four independent parts
■ at least 32 bars in length (there is no real maximum except for the upper time recommendation of eight minutes)
■ demonstration of appropriate use of effects (such as reverb or delay)
■ some use of stereo field/panning at mixdown.

Your recording must be accompanied by details of the equipment used and the recording process.

For this option you could, for example, choose a piece of music for four instruments and place a microphone in front of each of them. You could then:

■ do initial sound checks to ensure that there will be no distortion or, if preferred or necessary, use some degree of compression
■ record the ensemble performance onto a multi-track recorder
■ use the panning effect on the recorder to separate the four channels into a sound pattern that would reflect that experienced at a live performance, such as arranging the four sounds as if in a semicircle
■ check the balance of the different instruments
■ check for overall dynamic level
■ add any effects, though sparingly
■ mixdown to a stereo recorder.

The examination specification makes it very clear where your performances will gain credit (see 'Key areas to be assessed' on page 134). You should make sure that you meet each of the requirements to as high a standard as possible.

The main starting point here will be your intentions in terms of the performers to be involved in the 'initial recording'. Accuracy is a vital element and you will be deciding primarily on your own role within this performance. Again, the style of music will depend on your own interests and the performers available to you.

Preparing technology-based performances

Much of the preparation here will involve gradual accumulation of the skills required – this will, of course, vary from one student to another – and the working of short recordings to hone skills in the use of MIDI, multi-track recording and the other areas which will be assessed.

Initially, you might choose to work specifically either with MIDI sequenced tracks or with audio. Ultimately, in option 1, you will have to combine these, using a minimum of four tracks overall: it is entirely your decision just how many tracks will be MIDI sequenced and how many will be audio recordings, but both must be present.

You should take note of the facilities available within the software and/or hardware you are using and ensure that you make optimum use of these. Above all, the assessment criteria will reward well-judged use of timbres, balance and panning techniques, so it will be well worth your while to experiment with these and produce several versions of the same initial recording for either self-assessment or assessment by your peers/teacher.

Basic equipment

You should ensure that at least basic equipment is available:

- a sequencing software package, such as Cubase SX or Logic Pro 7
- a mixing desk
- condenser and dynamic microphones
- all the necessary cabling and connections
- good-quality headphones and speakers
- a good system to 'back up' work in progress
- keyboard: this could be a 'controller keyboard', a 'synthesiser' with GM/XG capacity and/or a 'soft synth' – a VST instrument that operates from within the computer (VST or VSTi = virtual instrument, such as Hypersonic)
- a processor/external effects, such as provided within the Behringer series.

You might also find a notation/scoring package such as Sibelius, Garageband or Coda Finale 2005 useful.

Key recommendations for equipment to use

For the music technology assessment tasks set by AQA for Units 3 and 6 you are recommended to stick to the use of MIDI sound module/keyboard, computer sound card and virtual sound module. These are described in more detail overleaf.

You do not need to use VSTi at AS level, though it will be a requirement at A2 for technology-based performance option 1. The use of VSTi is recommended providing that the VSTi is controlled by the candidate using MIDI controllers and editing techniques. Thus, VSTis that have inherent performance characteristics within their timbres that are not directly controlled by the candidate using MIDI controllers, should not be used.

MIDI sound module/keyboard	This is a hardware unit that contains a range of electronic synthesised or sample-based sounds. It is likely that this instrument will contain a general MIDI sound set in addition to a wide range of other sounds. Common makes: Yamaha, Roland, Korg.
Computer sound card	This is a hardware sound card fitted to a computer that is likely to function as a MIDI sound module and as an audio card allowing digital recording. The range of sounds within these units is largely based around a GM sound set. Most common manufacturer would be Creative Labs.
Virtual sound module	This is a piece of software that is loaded onto a computer and provides a range of MIDI sounds through host sequencing software. The sounds are likely to include a GM sound set. The sounds respond to MIDI controllers in order to alter dynamics and so forth. These can be thought of as a software version of a hardware sound module. Common makes include Edirol Virtual Sound Module and Steinberg Hypersonic.
Virtual studio instruments – VSTi	These are specific pieces of software that comply to the VST standard. They tend to be electronic sound sources that create specific sets of sounds – either by instrument, or as a software emulation of a famous synthesiser. They do not usually contain a GM set of sounds and do not necessarily respond to all MIDI controllers in a conventional way. Some are based on synthesised technology while others rely on sampling. Most of the popular sequencing software includes some virtual instruments. Popular VSTi include Steinberg The Grand (piano), Steinberg Neon (synth), Arturia Prophet (old synth), Arturia Bass (range of bass instruments), Logic Instruments.
Sample library virtual instruments	These are libraries of samples of instruments or sounds that can be replayed using MIDI trigger notes. Some sample libraries have their own playback engine, while others make use of sample players, such as Steinberg Halio or ESX, Kontakt player. Sample libraries are increasingly common in relation to orchestral instruments, with different notes and performance styles captured for each instrument. Drum samples are also common. Many of the samples contain inherent performance characteristics, such as swell or staccato. They do not generally make use of MIDI controllers to create musical shaping. Common makes include Vienna Symphonic Library, East West, Steinberg Halion Symphonic Orchestra, ESX-24, Kontakt.
Loop-based sample instruments	This new range of software instruments contains a large amount of musical content organised into riffs, patterns and styles. The user makes use of pre-determined musical material using a pattern-based interface. It is not possible to create totally original musical compositions using these instruments. They do not generally respond to MIDI controller data since the 'content' has its own inherent performance characteristics. Common makes include Steinberg: Virtual Guitarist, Virtual Bassist, Groove Agent (drum machine).
Content-based software	The most popular version of this software is Reason. It provides the user with the ability to manipulate and create a wide range of timbres using both synth and sample techniques. It can integrate with more common sequencing software using 'Rewire' technology. Some of the 'instrument modules' can respond to MIDI controllers.

Preparing technology performance option 1: sequencing

Sequencing skills needed

For those considering this sequencing option, you will need to acquire or hone the following skills:

- Data input methods: whether inputting data in step time or real time, you must ensure that your chosen method will lead to consistently good results.
- Note accuracy: this refers to the need to ensure accuracy of pitch and rhythm.
- Articulation: you need to be able to manipulate the sequencer so that accents, staccatos, bowing (strings) and other features of articulation are realised precisely.
- Expression (dynamic) and phrasing: thorough knowledge of how to apply and alter dynamics and phrasing must be acquired and demonstrated.
- Tempo handling: the ability to set and, where necessary, vary the tempo/speed.
- Convincing drums: you must edit drum/percussion sounds to ensure that they sound realistic.
- Individual note editing: if necessary, you might need to alter a single note here and there within a sequenced passage.
- Drum and guitar parts: the basis of much popular music is an accompaniment by guitars and drums; these require careful handling in terms of balance, articulation, velocity (dynamics) and so on.
- Listen and imitate: you need to pay attention to the sound qualities of acoustic instruments and strive to reproduce these through your application of sequencing skills.

Other considerations

For this option, you will have used a combination of sequencing and multi-tracking/close microphone recording to create one or more pieces of music. Although your music can be in any style, there are certain conditions you must meet, which are outlined on page 127.

Remember, also, that your submission within this option must include 5–8 minutes of music. It is unlikely, though quite permissible, that your work for assessment will consist of just one long piece: it is much more likely that you will submit two or more shorter pieces. This will be easier for you to handle as you plan, build up and then combine and edit the tracks to produce your final version.

As you plan each piece, decide on the balance of resources you will use:

- Will the accompanying parts be MIDI-generated with a single solo audio track (a voice or solo instrument)?
- Will there be just one line, such as the percussion, generated via MIDI with the other three parts being audio tracks?
- Will your ratio be two and two?

Other questions you will have to answer include:

- What will be the best order in which to lay down the tracks?

- If your piece is in a 'classical' style, how will you ensure that it meets the requirement to have evidence of 'some tempo control'? What problems will this pose?
- If your piece is in a pop or jazz style, how will you incorporate the drum kit? What problems will this pose?
- How will you ensure that there is at least a 'moderate level of dynamic variation'?

You need to look carefully at the facilities available within the software and hardware that you will be using and decide to what extent you will be able to use them in the production of your recordings.

Key areas to be assessed

Below is some guidance on each of the five areas for assessment. It is best always to aim to meet the criteria of the top band of marks in so far as it is possible: to aim lower is to risk not even achieving at that level!

Accuracy of pitch and rhythm

Excellent accuracy of pitch and control of all rhythmic elements to produce a musically satisfying performance.

You are responsible for obtaining the various tracks that go to make up the performance. Most recording machines that are of the standard needed to tackle this option will have a facility that enables you to adjust the recorded pitch so that it will come in line with that of other instruments and MIDI channels used. Additionally, there is a 'transpose' function within most sequencing packages. Rhythmic accuracy from MIDI tracks may well involve some use of the quantising facility, while rhythmic accuracy from players/singers on audio tracks needs to be assured through careful practice and rehearsal. The degree to which you will be able to adjust such elements will depend on the software/hardware being used and this is why it is vital to give such information on the Candidate Record Form (CRF).

Use of timbre, balance and panning techniques

Judiciously chosen timbres set within a well-balanced and effective recording.

Obviously, the choice of timbres is your own, but it must be appropriate to the genre of music being performed – this is where the extent to which your choice is 'judicious' can be assessed.

Your recording must be 'well-balanced', with no track being either overpowering or unacceptably faint. This will be done through your work at the multi-track recorder and/or at the sequencer. You will, where necessary, use panning techniques to separate the tracks and produce an effective recording. Careful use of panning will enable you to produce a 'spacious' sound with the tracks being 'placed' either centrally or at different degrees to the left or right. Given the sounds and effects being used, it may even be effective to convey the sense of a sound 'moving' from one side of the aural spectrum to the other – in other words, panning across, from left to right, for example.

Your final result will be an 'effective recording': it will, within the parameters of your chosen genre, combine appropriate timbres to produce a performance where each line is clear and at an appropriate level and clearly audible because of your attention to this and to panning techniques.

Evidence of close attention to performing and expressive detail

Comprehensive evidence of close attention to all aspects of performing and expressive detail to create a musical performance.

This will credit your close attention to matters of dynamic contrast, articulation, phrasing, shading and tempo control. There will need to be aural evidence of all of these elements in your recorded performance if you are to access this top band of marks.

Awareness of style required

Complete awareness of the stylistic requirements of the music and the ability to achieve this through the careful editing of data.

Stylistic awareness is an awareness of the characteristics of the music allied to an understanding of how to interpret them. Reference should be made to some of the points under the comments on the acoustic performances above (see page 119).

Ability to use the facilities available within the software and hardware to produce a valid result

Complete understanding of the measures needed to use the facilities within the software and/or hardware to produce an authentic recording.

This assesses your ability to make full use of the chosen software and/or hardware to produce what is referred to as 'an authentic recording'. On the CRF, you have to identify just what the software and hardware can do and this is where you show your skill in utilising those properties in order to effect a final recording that reproduces the original sounds and performance situation. In other words, this measures the level of your success for whatever goal you set out to achieve in the recording.

Preparing technology performance option 2: multi-track/close microphone recording

For this option, an important feature is that you will submit the *original* recording of your chosen ensemble and also your *finished* version: it is the difference between these two that forms the basis of the assessment – in other words, what you have done with the available technology to improve on the initial recording.

Using a mixing desk in a recording studio

■ **Useful resources**

Books
- ■ Bartlett, B. and Bartlett, J. (2005) *Practical Recording Techniques: The Step by Step Approach to Professional Audio Recording.* Oxford: Focal Press.
- ■ Mellor, D. (1993) *Recording Techniques for Small Studios.* Thetford: P.C. Publishing.
- ■ White, P. (1997) *MIDI for the Technophobe.* London: Sanctuary Publishing.
- ■ White, P. (1997) *Music Technology: A Survivor's Guide.* London: Sanctuary Publishing.
- ■ White, P. (1999) *Creative Recording.* London: Sanctuary Publishing.
- ■ White, P. (2000) *Basic Mixing Techniques.* London: Sanctuary Publishing.

'In Sequence' books
- ■ Lloyd, W. and Terry, P. (1996) *Music in Sequence.* London: Musonix Publishing.
- ■ Lloyd, W. and Terry, P. (1996) *Classics in Sequence.* London: Musonix Publishing.
- ■ Lloyd, W. and Terry, P. (1996) *Rock in Sequence.* London: Musonix Publishing.

Other
- ■ *Sound on Sound* magazine: see www.soundonsound.com
- ■ *The Mix* magazine: updated info on equipment and tutorials – see http://mixonline.com

Useful websites
- ■ www.mtrs.co.uk: The Music Teacher's Resource Site (MTRS). Here you will find a useful article entitled 'The Music Teacher's Guide to Technology: A survival guide for music teachers in the 21st century'.
- ■ www.soundcraft.com: This site has some useful tutorials, which can be accessed in its 'Learning Zone'.

There are also a number of sites that are useful for information on MIDI software:
- ■ www.midi-classics.com
- ■ www.cakewalk.com
- ■ www.steinberg.net
- ■ www.synthzone.com

There must be four or more independent vocal and/or instrumental parts. Your initial planning will involve making decisions about track allocation. You will have to take care in your preparation of the music and allow sufficient setting-up and recording time. Finally, and very importantly, you must allow yourself time to do the actual mixdown.

Key areas to be assessed

Your teacher and the moderator will listen to the original recording and then to the final mix before starting the assessment. Again, there are five different areas and these are the descriptors you must meet in order to attain at the highest level:

Balance

■ Excellent sense of balance throughout the recording.

This is where you ensure that each of the parts is clear and that none overpowers or is obscured by another. Always bear in mind that the only way to 'undo' poor recording is to redo it.

Dynamic range, including use of compression

■ Excellent management of dynamics in ways completely appropriate to the music.

It will be expected that a range of dynamics will be evidenced through your final mix. As you record the individual tracks, the use of a compressor may be needed, especially if pop music instruments and/or the voice are used. (If you are recording a more 'classical' piece, there should be a wide range of dynamics anyway.) A compressor is, basically, an automatic volume control that turns down the signal level when it gets too loud and turns it up when the parts get too quiet: its judicious use is important and its level of use should be shown within the information included with your submission.

Manipulation of mixing desk

■ Excellent use of mixing desk which enables all aspects of the recording to be appreciated.

This is where you demonstrate your ability to bring together your recorded tracks into one finished, coherent musical work. You need to work on each channel separately, then in conjunction with others. Think how the instruments/voices would be grouped on a stage and apply appropriate panning. Keep logical sections of your mix, such as the drum kit, together, so that you can adjust their overall level together.

Use of effects such as reverb or delay

■ Judicious and appropriate use of effects throughout the piece.

Notice the important words 'judicious' and 'appropriate': don't overdo your use of effects, especially reverb, as this can take away the contrast you need to enhance your mix. However, you will lose marks if there are sections of your mix where the use of effects has been unsuccessful or their use would have enhanced the mix but they are missing.

Quality of the recording across a wide range of dynamics

■ An excellent recording with clear use of a wide range of frequencies.

This is where your use of equalisation or EQ is assessed: this is the function that allows you to adjust the relative balance of the frequencies present in your audio recording. EQ channels are present on even the most basic mixing desks with three sections – low, mid and high. Low and high (or bass and treble) enable you to cut or boost frequencies above or below a specific point (usually below 100Hz for the bass and above 10Hz for the treble). Bands of mid EQ control the range between these extremes. In the information you present as part of your submission, the range of frequencies used should be shown.

Recording and annotating technology-based performances

What to submit

For technology-based performances you need to submit your recordings on CD or minidisk; there should be no material included on the CD/minidisk apart from your performances for assessment. You should also submit a copy of the music performed, either in standard notation, or as a lead sheet/detailed guide or, if neither reflects accurately the way in which the music was learnt prior to performance, a separate recording of the original work.

The candidate record form (CRF) must contain:

- the name and number of your centre
- your full name and candidate number
- if appropriate, the track number from which your submitted recordings begin
- the options you have chosen (do this by listing the titles of the piece(s) you have recorded in the appropriate boxes)
- details of the equipment used
- information as to the facilities available within the chosen software and hardware (performance 1)
- details of the recording process (performance 2)
- your signature and the date.

Keeping track of your time

Make sure, whichever options you choose, that your teacher receives the materials in good time – it is in nobody's interests to leave things till the last minute!

For technology-based performances, you will need to liaise with the other performers but, in many cases, it might well be true that the performers themselves would welcome an earlier opportunity to do their recording rather than leaving everything to that period when demands on time grow ever greater.

Providing a guide for your teacher and moderator

As part of your submission, you need to provide, for your teacher and the moderator, a guide that explains how each aspect of your coursework has been created. Here are some possible approaches for each of the technology-based options:

Providing a guide for the sequencing option

It is important that your teacher and the moderator can fully appreciate and follow the steps you have taken during your work in this option. A series of headings is suggested as a framework around which to build your outline. Areas to be addressed should include:

■ identifying the hardware and software
■ explaining how the musical data was entered into the sequencer
■ explaining how the sequencing software was used to shape a musical performance and create the style of the chosen piece
■ explaining how the audio was added and blended with the sequence.

The hardware and software

Under this heading, you will need to cover areas such as:

■ make, name, model/version of hardware and software, and their capabilities/facilities
■ details of any interface used
■ details of the sound module, keyboard and microphones
■ details of the multi-track recorder, the mixing desk, and the two-track stereo mastering recorder
■ any external effects
■ the use of a digital interface (DI) box or other equipment.

Musical data entry into the sequencer

This will cover matters such as:

■ how the data was entered initially – using real time or step time? Metronome or grid/piano-roll editor?
■ any subsequent overdubbing, correcting, or use of quantise.

Use of the sequencing software to shape a musical performance or create the style of the chosen piece

This is where you will need to cover your use of controller data to manipulate elements such as:

■ dynamics, expression, articulation, panning, phrasing, sustain, velocity
■ your efforts to imitate 'live' performers through measures such as breathing (wind players), bowing (string players), strumming (guitars) and pedalling (pianists)
■ use of reverb
■ tempo, balance and choice of timbre.

How the audio was added and blended with the sequence

Finally, you need to refer to:

■ the process of integrating MIDI with audio
■ the recording method used – room, equipment, number of takes
■ the order of recording
■ the use of foldback and effects
■ the final mixdown process.

Providing a guide for the multi-track/close microphone recording option

As no sequencing is involved in this option, the guide you need to produce will cover slightly fewer areas. The main 'headings' under which to structure your response might well be:

- details about the equipment used
- the recording process used to achieve the initial recording
- the process of producing the final mix.

Details of the equipment used

Here you will need to give full information on:

- microphones, headphones and monitor speakers
- multi-track recorder and mixing desk
- effects unit and dynamic processing unit
- two-track stereo mastering recorder
- any other equipment used.

The recording process used to achieve the initial recording

Some of the main issues that need to be addressed include:

- the order of the recorded tracks: a detailed track listing, indication of the number of 'takes', and decisions as to the final choices for use
- venue
- microphones, digital interface (DI), use of foldback
- recording levels, microphone positioning (consider supplying photographs and/or diagrams)
- any initial use of compression
- the performers – how you got the best from them (and/or yourself)
- problems encountered and overcome.

The process of producing the final mix

This is where you explain how you transformed the initial recording into the final mix. Remember that this is the focus of the assessment in this unit and, therefore, it is essential that you give full details of the process you went through. You will need to cover the following, as they apply to your work:

- effects used – preferably for each track – including, where applicable, compression, EQ, reverb, and so on. Give your reasons for such use.
- the style of the piece – what did you need to address? Did you listen to any specific recordings? Did you receive any specific advice?
- use of panning and the stereo field
- balance
- refining the mix and setting the master recording levels
- transferring your mix onto a two-track stereo master.

AQA Examiner's tip

Double-check that you are submitting *everything* required for this coursework component.

11 Listening

Learning objectives:

- to understand the additional musical terms and features that may be found in Unit 4 listening questions

- to develop further the skill of identifying what you hear and describing it

- to learn more about writing in accurate staff notation.

You will find listening questions in Unit 4 to be largely familiar in format from Unit 1 at AS Level, but your answers will cover a wider range of musical features. Examiners will also expect more precision and detail. Your study of set works will introduce much of the knowledge you need, but you will need practice to recognise the same features in a fresh context. This chapter summarises the additional knowledge for Unit 4 listed in the specification. The musical features required for Unit 1 listening questions should also be revised. These are described in Chapter 1.

Rhythm and metre

Time signatures

Time signatures with five or seven beats in a bar may be included in listening questions. Quintuple and sextuple patterns occur in some folk music or may be chosen by a composer to create an unsettled atmosphere. *Mars, the bringer of war* in Holst's suite *The Planets* is in $5/4$ time, and parts of the *Dies irae* from Britten's *War Requiem* are in $7/4$ time.

You should be familiar with compound time signatures as well. Compound time has a distinctive character because the fundamental beat is not a simple note but a dotted note. This divides into three, and feels very different from a division into two. Most English nursery rhymes are in compound time: think of *Hickory dickory dock* or *Hey diddle diddle, the cat and the fiddle* and you will sense the triplets within each beat. The division into three can usually be sensed, but at a slow tempo it may be difficult to distinguish from $3/4$ time. Compound time should always be described by its main beats (such as two dotted crotchet beats in a bar), although the time signature can only be expressed with the beats subdivided (such as $6/8$ time). This remains true even if the music is counted or conducted in six in a slow tempo. The most familiar compound time signatures are shown opposite, with an example of each:

Time signature	Meaning	Rhythm example
$^6/_8$	Two dotted crotchet beats in a bar	*(rhythm notation)*
$^9/_8$	Three dotted crotchet beats in a bar	*(rhythm notation)*
$^{12}/_8$	Four dotted crotchet beats in a bar	*(rhythm notation)*
$^6/_4$	Two dotted minim beats in a bar	*(rhythm notation)*
$^9/_4$	Three dotted minim beats in a bar	*(rhythm notation)*
$^{12}/_4$	Four dotted minim beats in a bar	*(rhythm notation)*

Many examples can be found in the music of Brahms: for example, the first movement of the *Clarinet Quintet* is in $^6/_8$ time and his *String Quintet* no. 2 in G begins in $^9/_8$ time.

Polyrhythms

Sometimes composers use different metres or different time signatures simultaneously. These are called polyrhythms. There is a famous example in the finale of Act One of *Don Giovanni* by Mozart, where three different dances are played simultaneously in a ball scene. Instances can be found in 20th century music, and also in Brahms. In the second movement of his Clarinet Quintet, bars 1–14, the clarinet and violin are in $^3/_4$ time, the second violin and viola mostly move in $^9/_8$ time, and the cello alternates between the two.

Hemiola

An apparent change of metre in the approach to a cadence, for example making two bars of $^3/_4$ time into one bar of $^3/_2$ time. The effect is of a slower pulse just before the cadence. Examples are frequent in music by Handel and Vivaldi. An example is printed on page 44.

Harmony

The new harmonies that may appear in Unit 4 listening questions are described with examples in Chapter 14 (see page 200).

Pedals

A pedal is a sustained or repeated bass note over which the harmony changes, becoming dissonant with the pedal note. The first and last chords of a pedal must be consonant with the bass note. The pedal note is usually the **tonic** or **dominant** of the key. A tonic pedal helps to

Key terms

Tonic: the 'home note' of a scale – for example, the note F in F major.

Dominant: the fifth note of a scale – for example, the note C in F major.

reinforce the stability of the key note, especially when it leads up to the final chord of a movement. A dominant pedal is often used to build a climax resolved by a perfect cadence. If the sustained note is in a middle or upper part it is described as an inverted pedal.

Cycle of fifths

A succession of chords, or a succession of keys, which continually moves to the chord or the key a fifth away. As a cycle of chords it is frequently used in Baroque music to form a sequence, as in the Vivaldi example below. In the short example from Vaughan Williams' Fifth Symphony, we can see how he gives a sudden sense of forward motion to a passage that has been more static harmonically.

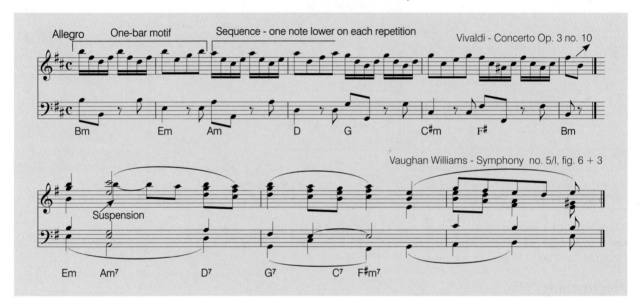

The cycle of fifths can be used to create a change of key or modulation. Any pair of chords in the sequence can be adjusted to make a perfect cadence: for example, in the Vivaldi sequence the Am chord could become A7 and the music cadence to D major. On a larger scale, composers sometimes move through a cycle of fifths as a sequence of modulations in a development section.

Suspensions

A note that begins as a harmony note and is held or repeated when the chord changes. It becomes a dissonance in the new chord and resolves by falling or rising a step. Normally, it should be possible to identify all three components of a suspension: the *preparation*, the *suspension* (the moment of dissonance) and the *resolution*. Examples in Chapter 5 show suspensions used to add strength and interest to a cadence in Baroque style (see page 88). In later music they are often chosen as an expressive dissonance. In the Vaughan Williams example above, the B in the Am[7] chord is a suspension, adding further point to the emphasis on the second beat.

Sequence

A melodic or harmonic pattern that is repeated one note higher or lower. The melody line of the Vivaldi example above is a falling sequence formed from a one-bar motif.

Hint

See the Examiner's tip on page 155 for identifying passages in the Vaughan Williams score.

Augmented and diminished intervals

Augmented intervals are one semitone larger than the major or perfect interval; diminished intervals are one semitone smaller than a minor or perfect interval. In a major scale there is an augmented fourth between the fourth and seventh notes and a diminished fifth from the fourth note down to the leading note. Augmented intervals tend to step outwards to resolve (so F–D♯ would resolve to octave Es), and diminished intervals tend to step inwards (F♯–E♭ would resolve to a perfect fifth G–D).

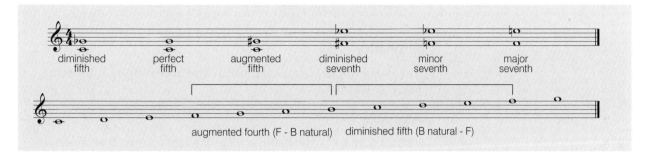

Further unessential notes

Accented passing notes are defined and illustrated in Chapter 1 (see page 6). An *appoggiatura* is an expressive note falling on the beat which is not part of the harmony. Like the accented passing note, it resolves by falling or rising by a step, but it is approached by a leap. If the expressive note is not part of the prevailing key, it is described as a chromatic *appoggiatura*.

Tonality

Modes and scales

A greater variety of modes and scales are used in 20th century music and this is reflected in the listening questions. The most common modes are major and minor and these will already be familiar. The following can now be added:

- The pentatonic scale is a five-note scale with no semitone steps. It can be found by playing a major scale with the fourth and seventh notes omitted, or by playing the black notes of the piano. It is common in folk music from Scotland, Eastern Europe and the Far East, and in spirituals. In the oratorio *A Child of our Time* by Sir Michael Tippett, the spirituals *Steal away, deep river* and *O by and by* have pentatonic melodies.

- Other modes that can be found in 20th century music have been drawn from folk music or from Renaissance church music. Vaughan Williams was an expert in both, and modal melodies are often found in his compositions. The most common patterns can be found as scales of white notes on the piano and are known as the Dorian mode (D–D), the Phrygian mode (E–E), the Lydian mode (F–F) and the Mixolydian mode (G–G). Used purely, each has a subtle atmosphere of its own, but you will not be asked to name individual modes. Modal harmony can often be distinguished from tonal harmony because it is less directional, and has softer cadences.

- The whole-tone scale has no semitone steps and six notes to the octave. It appeared in 20th century music as an influence from the far east in the music of Debussy and Ravel.

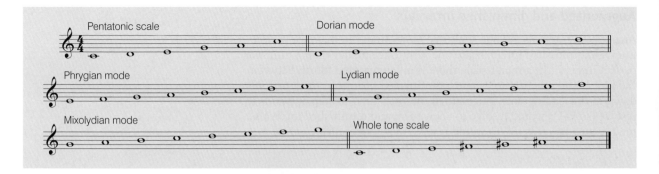

Bitonality

The use of two keys simultaneously. There are examples in the piano music of Bartók.

Atonality

The technique of writing music without a tonal centre. It is important to distinguish aurally between true atonality and music that is fundamentally tonal but in which the key may be temporarily lost or disguised by complex harmony. Music may be freely atonal or it may achieve atonality by use of the **12-note** or **serial** method of composition. It is possible to recognise atonality aurally but you cannot be sure that the method of composition is serial without studying the score. Occasionally, the 12-note series is presented as a melodic idea and then it can be recognised.

▮ Texture, timbre and techniques

Texture

Texture describes how the voices in the music are woven together. Be as precise as possible in your descriptions at this level. These questions may help to make your answers more exact:

- ▮ Is the music written in homophony (chords) or polyphony (counterpoint)?
- ▮ Is there any imitation in the counterpoint?
- ▮ Can you distinguish between a single-line melody, instruments/voices in unison or instruments/voices in octaves?
- ▮ What styles of accompaniment are being used?
- ▮ Is the melody in the treble, bass or an inner part?
- ▮ Does an ensemble have one instrument to a part (as in chamber music) or many instruments to a part (as in orchestral music)?
- ▮ Are the instruments playing independently or are they doubling one another?
- ▮ If there is antiphonal writing (call and response) how are the instruments grouped? Are the groups small and large, or high and low, or separated in space?

Timbre

The timbre of the music will indicate the differences between:

- upper voice, male voice and mixed choirs
- boys' treble voices and soprano voices
- brass band and concert band
- jazz combo and swing band
- four-part choirs and larger choirs with multiple divisions
- various types of percussion sticks.

Techniques

You will also be able to describe techniques that affect the sound of an instrument: for example, the use of mutes for bowed strings and brass, including jazz mutes; double-stopping on bowed strings; *portamenti* or *glissandi* (slides between notes) found in some vocal and violin music and in jazz solos.

Melodic dictation

A new feature at this level is that sections of melody to be completed may include chromatic notes – in other words, it may be necessary to add accidentals. Melodic dictation will improve with practice, but the following hints may be useful:

- Listen attentively to the passage all the way through at the first playing without trying to think about it or retain it. Concentration on one feature near the beginning will prevent you from hearing the remainder, and memory works best when the mind is quiet and open.
- If possible, memorise the passage to be completed so that it can be repeated mentally between playings. It may help to follow the movement of the melody silently in the voice or to imagine the feel of playing it with your fingers.
- Pay attention to the passage before and after the section you are to complete. Often you will find a similar rhythm pattern or a related note in the surrounding passage.
- If the melody to be completed is a bass line, or if an accompanying part is given, use your knowledge of harmony and intervals to identify features and to eliminate obvious errors.
- In a longer passage, use each playing to work at both the beginning and the end of the passage.
- Do not leave gaps in the melody, even if you are unsure of your answer. First impressions and intelligent guesswork are often correct.

12

Set works – Mahler's *4th* or Vaughan Williams' *5th Symphony*

Learning objectives:

- to understand the methods of study needed for a set work at this level

- to acquire detailed knowledge of the chosen work

- to consider the types of question that may be asked and how to approach them.

Methods of study

The detailed study of a set work introduced in Unit 1 is developed further in Unit 4. The set work for the 2010 examination (and for some years to follow) is a complete 20th-century symphony: either *Symphony No. 4* in G major by Gustav Mahler or *Symphony No. 5* in D by Ralph Vaughan Williams. Both are major works which repay in-depth study, but they have also stimulated conflicting views about their intentions and their success. The aim of study at this level is to know the work so thoroughly that you can form your own views from a firm basis of fact. The initial stage is to understand what happens in the symphony. Afterwards, it is possible to discuss the composer's intentions, the way in which they are carried out and whether they are successfully realised.

First impressions

Depending on your previous experience of listening to music and attending concerts, you may prefer to listen to the whole work at once or take one movement at a time. Following the score may be helpful but is not essential, especially if you are not well practised in reading a full orchestral score. First hearings often produce swift reactions of like or dislike and these should be set to one side for the time being. Note down any strong impressions and look at them again when you know the work better to see if they can be justified. It is interesting to compare our own first reactions to newspaper reviews of the early performances.

Getting to know the music

- Concentrate on one movement at a time; listen to it repeatedly and become familiar with the written notation. You should reach the stage where you can continue mentally if the recording is stopped at any point, and you can hear the sound on opening any page of the score.

- Ensure that you understand the names of instruments, tempo indications and technical instructions in the score. Mahler added many performance directions in German, as well as using common Italian terms. Important terms are translated in the analysis of Mahler's *Symphony No. 4* in this chapter, and transposing instruments are explained under 'Types of question' on page 162.

- Identify the main themes and sections of each movement. Give each theme a name or reference number and draw a plan of the movement to see an overview of its structure. Include the key at each appearance of a theme.

- Compare your overview to traditional forms: for example, compare first movements to a plan of sonata form. It is to be expected that forms will be reinterpreted afresh by 20th-century composers and it is interesting to note where a traditional plan is followed and where the music departs from expectations.

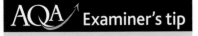

AQA Examiner's tip

It would be useful to revise the outline plan of sonata form before you begin work on this symphony. The first movement of Mozart's *Jupiter* Symphony, the set work for AS Level, is a good example.

- Consider the use and importance of the musical elements in the movement: melody, harmony, rhythm and tempo, tonality and modulation, orchestration. In each case, select passages that demonstrate typical features of the composer's style.
- Discover which themes undergo development, and what kind of development occurs.
- Note whether returning themes are affected by the intervening development or remain unchanged.

The music in context

Once the set work is familiar, look at its historical position and context. It is important to understand the effect of the music on its first audience and this may be helped by researching the context and reading contemporary accounts. You should be aware of:

- the musical activities, interests and experience of the composer
- the work's place in the composer's life
- earlier works by other composers that may have influenced it
- the time and place of its composition and first performance
- reaction to it at the time of writing and in subsequent years
- any documents which throw light on the composer's intentions.

Interpretation

Listen to more than one recording of the symphony, if possible, and note the date when each was recorded. Traditions of performance change over time and styles may also change according to the orchestra playing and the personal taste of the conductor. Some 'historic' recordings may bring us nearer to the sound expected by the composer and to his choice of tempo and playing style. Recent recordings may shed fresh light on the music. Differences in interpretation provide interesting material for discussion on which view best reveals the character of the music.

Two conductors who worked closely with Mahler, Willem Mengelberg and Bruno Walter, recorded *Symphony No. 4*, although the recordings date from many years after Mahler's death, and their interpretations could have changed in that time. Vaughan Williams was recorded conducting his Fifth Symphony in 1952 and he supervised the recording made by Sir Adrian Boult, so these should give a good guide to his intentions.

If possible, attend a live performance of the symphony you are studying. Leave the score at home and enjoy the visual experience as well as the sound. By the 20th century the symphony had become a form in which composers were expected to make their most significant and universal statements. A live performance will convey, better than any recording, the total experience that the composer intended to present.

Gustav Mahler conducting. Silhouette *by Schliessmann, 1901*

■ Mahler, *Symphony No. 4 in G major*

Background

Gustav Mahler was born in 1860 in Bohemia. He studied piano and composition at the Vienna Conservatoire and took a job as a conductor at the age of 20. From then until his early death at the age of 50, he lived a very busy life, progressing through a series of conducting posts to become Director of the Vienna Opera in 1897. He left this demanding post in 1907 and visited America to conduct the Metropolitan Opera Company and the New York Philharmonic Orchestra. An infection that damaged his heart forced him to return to Vienna in April 1911 and he died a month later.

Mahler lived in the public eye, and it is possible to obtain a very clear impression of the strains of running a major opera company from his surviving letters, minutes of meetings and press reports. There were constant debates and disagreements over budgets, repertory and the appointment of singers. In spite of these pressures, Mahler managed to devote his summer vacations to composition and completed a series of nine symphonies on an unprecedented scale, together with a number of other major works. His intimate knowledge of the orchestra is evident in his very individual orchestration and his almost obsessively detailed instructions to conductors and performers. Several symphonies include solo and choral singing, written with an opera conductor's understanding of melody and of the voice. The large-scale structures found in the symphonies may also derive from his experience of opera, where the dramatic situation often requires long musical periods of great intensity.

The Fourth Symphony

Symphony No. 4 marks a turning point in Mahler's symphonic development. It is closely linked to the first three symphonies but also looks forward to changes of style seen in the Fifth. Connections with the adjacent symphonies are easy to demonstrate: the finale of the Fourth was originally planned to end the Third Symphony, and the opening theme of the Fifth is prefigured in the first movement of the Fourth.

The Fourth Symphony was begun in the summer of 1899 after a pause in composition caused by his new duties at the Vienna Opera House.

The Vienna Opera House – the Staatsoper – where Mahler was conductor from 1897 to 1907

It was completed in the summer of 1900 and first performed in Munich in November 1901. Its composition history could be said to begin earlier, in 1892, when Mahler composed the song *Das himmlische Leben* (The Heavenly Life), which was included as a seventh movement in the original plan of the Third Symphony. He later removed it and it became the finale of the Fourth. This created the unusual situation of writing a symphony to lead up to an existing finale. The poem describes a child-like view of heaven, and Mahler matched this with a simple and attractive setting that set the tone for the whole symphony. The Fourth Symphony is his shortest and is often regarded as the most approachable, but its style was unexpected and it was greeted with incomprehension by audiences and orchestras at early performances.

After the six-movement plan of the Third Symphony, Mahler returned to the **Classical pattern of four movements** and to a slightly smaller orchestra than previously. Trombones and tuba are absent, and there is a large percussion section of bright-toned instruments including triangle, glockenspiel and sleigh bells. The scoring for three oboes, clarinets, bassoons and trumpets, and for four flutes and horns allows each instrument to play chords in its distinctive timbre. The wind section is further enriched by players doubling on piccolo, cor anglais, bass clarinet and contrabassoon.

First movement

The musical language of this movement often sounds like Haydn or Schubert, and the clear divisions of the structure point to Classical models. Mahler set out from the beginning to see the symphony through the eyes of the child who narrates the final poem. The movement's plan is based on sonata form.

Exposition

Bars 1–31 Bedächtig. Nicht eilen (Cautiously, unhurried). The first impression is of bright sounds in the key of B minor, as flutes, clarinets and jingling sleigh bells set off in cheerful fashion. This theme is an immediate reference to the finale, where it recurs throughout the song beginning in bar 40.

Key terms

The Classical pattern for a four-movement symphony was:

1. A quick movement in sonata form
2. A slow movement in binary, variation or short sonata form
3. A minuet and trio or scherzo and trio
4. A quick movement in sonata or rondo form.

The order of the second and third movements may be reversed. All movements are in the tonic key except for the slow movement, which is usually in the subdominant key.

This gives way to a graceful G major melody, simply harmonised with a pizzicato accompaniment. The dotted rhythms of bar 6 and the yodelling figure in clarinets and bassoons in bar 20 are seeds for later development.

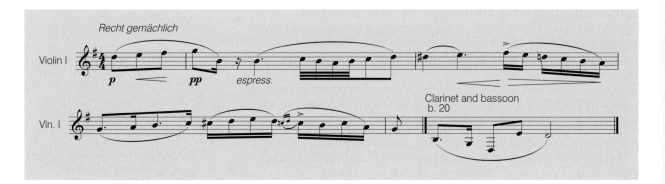

The repeat of the first theme at bar 17 has already gained an imitating cello countermelody – a hint of the many contrapuntal textures to come. The passage in bars 21–25 is one of many that would not be out of place in a Haydn symphony.

Bars 32–37 A brief and energetic transition to the dominant, again in a Classical style.

Bars 37–57 The second subject group contains two rich and lyrical melodies given to the cellos in the expected key of D major. Mahler asks for the first to be broadly sung (*Breit gesungen*).

Bars 58–72 A child-like closing theme for the exposition, still securely in D major. It darkens as it moves to bass clarinet, cor anglais and bassoon.

Bars 72–102 Unexpectedly the exposition appears to repeat as if in an 18th century sonata form. After a slightly extended 'jingling' introduction the first theme returns as it was at bar 17, with a counterpoint in the oboe. The clarinet and bassoon figure in bar 79 will soon become significant. The key of G major becomes very firmly established with a tonic pedal at bar 91, and the clarinet and bassoon figure grows into a gentle theme that subsides towards the end of the **exposition**.

The exposition follows Classical models except for its truncated repeat. This causes the exposition to end in the tonic instead of the more usual dominant, and removes the tension between two key areas that is often a feature of a sonata-form exposition. Mahler will create variety instead by rapid changes of mood and by the many abrupt tempo variations which are already apparent. As will be seen later, the key scheme of the whole symphony is more complex than in a Classical-period work.

Key terms

Exposition: the first section of a sonata-form movement, in which the main themes are announced. In the Classical period there were two themes or groups of themes in contrasting keys, known as the first and second subjects. They were linked by a bridge passage or transition. Normally the second subject was in the dominant key and the exposition was marked to be repeated in full.

Development

Bars 102–125 The sleigh bells begin again in B minor but this key does not remain for long. A solo violin appears to guide the music back to G major but it dies away rather than resolving and the key moves to E minor. Familiar fragments from the exposition appear in quick succession but they have become more disturbing, with sudden dynamic changes and threatening stopped notes in the horns. Even the first-subject melody, beginning unhurriedly in C major, becomes fragmented and anxious before dying away.

Bars 125–142 The sounds of nature often appear in Mahler's music and the next section could be seen as an example. Over an **ostinato** of A and E various 'songs' emerge, with a cheerful melody played by four flutes in unison rather bizarrely answered by the bass clarinet. Trills and semiquaver passages in the strings provide a rustling background. The bassoon joins in, making the connection with the birdsong of the flutes and the bassoon's earlier yodelling motif.

Bars 142–208 It is unusual to find such a tranquil passage in a **development section** and it is soon disturbed. Keys become transient with the minor mode predominating, and motifs are passed between sections of the orchestra. Mahler's detailed instructions on sound add to the unsettled feeling. Clarinets and oboes are made more prominent by playing with the bell of the instrument raised (*Schalltrichter auf*), and trumpets play muted chords, contrasted starkly with distant chords on the flutes in bar 160. In some bars, the string instruments are instructed to tap the strings with the wood of the bow (*col legno*). It is as if the sunny forest of the A major section has become a place of frightening shadows. A three-crotchet motif becomes insistent and it is surprising to remember that this rhythm originated in the warm second-subject melody in bar 38.

Bars 209–238 The climax comes unexpectedly as a triumphant trumpet melody over a dominant pedal in C major, again using the insistent crotchets. The sudden move from here to a crashing dissonance (bar 221) causes a collapse from which a menacing trumpet fanfare emerges. This has extra significance with hindsight, as it became the opening of the Fifth Symphony. It may be a reminiscence of the military fanfares Mahler heard from nearby barracks as a child. The music dies down without resolving its conflicts and the recapitulation arrives unannounced and in mid-sentence, as if it had begun earlier and been hidden by the confusion.

Recapitulation

Bars 239–262 Abruptly, G major is re-established at the beginning of the recapitulation, with familiar themes from the exposition, but a more complex contrapuntal texture. The triumphant theme from the development returns briefly, followed by the original transition moving to D major.

Bars 262–297 The new key is ignored and the two second subject melodies return classically in the tonic key, but with much-enriched orchestration. The powerful tone of the strings is increased by doubling and by using high register and many bow changes (*Bogen wechseln*) on long notes. The simple closing theme returns as if to bring the recapitulation to a quiet conclusion.

> **Key terms**
>
> **Ostinato:** a short phrase, persistently repeated.
>
> **Development section:** the central section of a sonata-form movement, in which the themes are fragmented, extended or otherwise developed. The music usually passes through a number of keys.
>
> **Recapitulation:** the third section of a sonata-form movement. It follows the exposition closely, but resolves the conflict of keys. Usually both subject groups are in the tonic key.

Key terms

Coda: An optional 'tail-piece' at the end of a movement. It may contain further development of the themes, and resolves any remaining conflicts of key.

Coda

Bars 298–349 The jingling bells begin again to indicate the beginning of the coda in E minor, although a timpani roll introduces a threatening note. The familiar motifs are developed further but the key becomes more settled at the return of the G major tonic pedal. It seems as though the movement will fade quietly but a final reminder of the main theme suddenly picks up energy and crashes to an ending which is part classical symphony and part military march.

Second movement

The second movement is an easy-going dance in the style of a Ländler and marked 'Leisurely, without hurrying' (*In gemächlicher Bewegung. Ohne Hast*). The Ländler was a country dance in the tempo of a slow waltz, but less sophisticated in style. Originally the movement was entitled *Freund Hein spielt auf* (Friend Hein plays up). Freund Hein was a folklore character who played the violin, appearing friendly at first but enticing those who followed to their deaths. The character is represented in the music by a solo violinist who plays a strangely wayward melody on a violin tuned a tone higher than usual. Mahler's intention was to create the sound of a rough country fiddler.

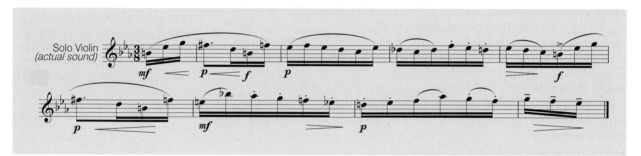

Because of the re-tuning, the music for this instrument is printed a tone lower than it sounds and this must be borne in mind when reading the score. A second solo part later in the movement is tuned normally (*natürlich bestimmt*).

The overall plan is of a slow scherzo with two trios making an ABABA pattern. It is in the key of C minor but turns towards C major at the end.

Scherzo

Bars 1–4 A short introduction for horn and woodwind. This will return as a linking passage throughout the movement. The staccato chords in the woodwind recall similar patterns in the first movement.

Bars 4–34 The main theme is announced by the solo violinist, who is gradually joined by other strings – muted solo cello and viola at first and later the full string section without mutes. The texture remains very light and the melody is answered by a small woodwind group. The melody remains uncomfortably angular and there are some unexpected outbursts, as when a solo viola is told to play boldly (*keck*).

Bars 34–45 The second idea is a flowing melody in C major played over a C pedal on horns. It is suddenly diverted by a dissonance (bar 43), and the main theme returns.

Bars 45–63 Strings are divided with Mahler's typical attention to detail. The melody is played with the bow (*arco*) and muted; accompanying chords are *pizzicato* or *col legno* without mutes. The unsteady feel of the harmony is resolved in a C minor cadence at the end of the section.

Bars 63–68 A short link to the Trio, based on bars 1–4.

Trio

Bars 68–109 The Trio begins with a brash horn but settles into a slightly slower tempo and into F major, with much of the music over a tonic pedal. There are interjections from woodwind with raised bells, but the strings introduce a leisurely dance with *portamenti* (slides) in the melody. Mahler's detailed instructions guide the diminuendo at the end, not only by dynamics (eventually *ppppp*), but also by the numbers playing. Double basses diminish from half of the section (*nur die Hälfte*) to one desk only (*1. Pult*).

Bars 109–114 The link signals the return of the Scherzo.

Scherzo

Bars 114–200 The Scherzo is re-orchestrated and extended, from an ABA pattern to ABAB. The second A is subjected to further fragmentation and more extreme dynamics. The final B section has growling additions from the horns which recall the link section.

Trio

Bars 200–246 A trumpet marked *schmetternd* (blaring) introduces the second appearance of the Trio, again in F major. It retains its graceful style and simple harmonic basis but new countermelodies are added.

Bars 246–275 The link becomes quieter and darker, combining low strings and contrabassoon, so that the return of the Trio in the new light of D major is a gentle revelation.

Bars 275–280 The link passage returns.

Scherzo

Bars 280–329 The final return of the Scherzo is substantially rewritten. It begins in D major but migrates back to C major for the second theme in bar 314.

Coda

Bars 329–362 As in the first movement, the Coda injects another burst of energy. The aim seems to be to end in C major, but D♭s persist in the bass until the final bars and the concluding woodwind flourish in C major is emphatic, but not completely convincing.

Third movement

Mahler is reported to have said '[The Scherzo is] mysterious, confused, uncanny … It will make your hair stand on end. But in the Adagio that follows everything will be unravelled and you will understand that no harm was meant after all.'

There is a world of difference between the unpredictable Scherzo that is the second movement and the carefree vision of heaven in the finale. Mahler makes this transition with an extended slow movement in a loose variation form. Although variation form has a long history, this movement does not follow a Classical pattern until a series of short, sharply contrasted variations begins at bar 222. Before that, the composer meditates on a warm and restful theme that takes a number of new directions but is firmly rooted in its opening bars. The clearest precedent for this, in Classical times, is in the variations of Beethoven. The slow movement of Beethoven's Violin Concerto has some notable similarities to this movement, and Mahler may also have been thinking of the variations of Beethoven's late piano sonatas Op. 109 and 111.

Theme A

Bars 1–61 Ruhevoll (Restful). Divided lower strings introduce a theme A of warm chords, gently urged on by a pizzicato bass line.

The music returns to this opening in bars 16, 25, 37 and 51, each time exploring a new direction by adding an instrument, redesigning the melody or venturing towards a new key. The music suggests D major at bars 14 and 34, A minor at bar 30 and C major at bar 47, but never modulates.

Bars 62–106 Theme B is a contrasting section beginning in E minor and moving to D minor. Although it is marked *Viel langsamer* (Much slower), the rhythms are more lively and there is a greater sense of forward momentum. The rhythm in the bassoon is related to the bass of Theme A (see example above) and the staccato quavers in bar 81 recall the opening of the symphony. This section is more passionate after the utter serenity of the opening. Alternating oboe and violin melodies in a lamenting, very expressive style (*klagend, sehr ausdrucksvoll*) lead to a warmer section at bar 81 and a powerful climax. The bass rhythm returns in D minor as part of a lightly scored passage leading back to Theme A.

Bars 107–178 Anmutig bewegt (Gracefully animated). A more flowing version of Theme A, which retains its distinctive bass pattern under new melodies. The bass pattern migrates to upper parts at times. There are a number of excursions but the key is never far from G major. Mahler refers back to the beginning of the movement without following it strictly, but the horn and bassoon idea from bar 31 is adapted for clarinets and bassoons in bar 137.

Bars 179–221 The return of Theme B, with its oboe melody now a duet with cor anglais in G minor. It signals a build to a new climax in C♯ minor; more powerful than before and taking the melody from bar 66 to new heights. This time, the music does not return to the bass motif, but ends undecided between F♯ major and F♯ minor chords.

Bars 222–282 The atmosphere is lightened by a quick-fire series of characteristic variations on Theme A:

- an expressive melody in 3/4 time, darkly scored for lower strings and clarinets
- an elegant dance in 3/8 adding extra countermelodies to each phrase
- a sudden burst of energy in 2/4 time and E major. Horns add a serious note but the triangle keeps the mood light
- an even faster variation, abruptly back in G major.

Mahler directs that each tempo change should be sudden and surprising.

Bars 283–314 There is an abrupt return to slow tempo, which leads to a variation based on the final section of Theme A, complete with a return of the rhythmic bass.

Bars 314–325 A brief breathing-space (*Luftpause*) leaves the listener totally unprepared for the colossal climax on a shining chord of E major – the key in which the symphony will end. Timpani connect this powerfully to the bass motif, as shown in the example on the previous page. The horns anticipate the main theme of the finale.

Bars 326–353 If the climax is a glimpse of the heaven to come, the coda is a relinquishing of earth, juxtaposing the brightest chords – E major, C major, D major and finally G major. The final instruction *Gänzlich ersterbend* (Dying away completely) could be taken as more than metaphorical as the instruments fade out from lowest to highest and the sound becomes more and more insubstantial.

Fourth movement

The text at the heart of this movement came from a collection of folk poetry called *Des Knaben Wunderhorn* (The boy's magic horn), which Mahler had known from childhood. He set nine poems from the collection for voice and piano between 1887 and 1890, and ten with orchestral accompaniment between 1892 and 1899. References to these songs appear in the fourth movement of the Second Symphony and in the third and fifth movements of the Third. The poem *Das himmlische Leben* (The heavenly life), which became the finale of the Fourth Symphony, describes a child's idea of heaven. There is dancing, singing and plenty to eat, with gardeners who encourage you to pick fruit from their trees. Biblical figures and saints appear with their traditional attributes: St Peter fishes, St Cecilia plays music and Herod is the butcher. Mahler was aware that performers and audiences might misunderstand the sweet naïvety of the poem. He instructs the singer to perform 'with childlike, serene expression; above all without parody'.

Bars 1–12 Orchestral introduction in G major, lightly scored for woodwind solos, strings and harp. The dotted quaver–semiquaver motifs look forward to the setting of the words *himmlische Freuden* (heavenly joys) and back to the first subject of the first movement.

Bars 12–39 Theme A. The soprano voice describes heaven in a folk-like melody beginning over a tonic pedal.

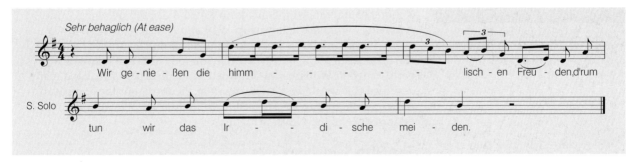

The orchestration is always delicate, featuring flowing flute and piccolo countermelodies. A chorale-like phrase with parallel harmonies strikes a suddenly austere note.

Bars 40–56 Interlude. The source of the 'jingling' opening of the symphony. Here it is quicker, more extended and more dramatic, establishing the key of E minor.

Bars 56–75 A new idea for the voice, still in E minor and darker but retaining the semiquaver countermelodies from the interlude. It concludes with the chorale-like theme in the same key.

Bars 76–80 The interlude is heard again briefly in E minor.

Bars 80–114 A reworking of section A in G major. Leisurely at first, it gradually increases in speed and acquires the staccato quavers and semiquaver countermelodies from the interlude. The chorale phrase concludes this section, in D minor.

Bars 115–121 A final appearance of the interlude, in B minor.

Bars 122–142 Coda, with E major finally secured by a long tonic pedal. The melody is fresh, but in the same spirit as the opening.

Bars 142–184 A final vocal return of section A in E major, concluding with a version of the chorale. It reduces to a chamber-sized ensemble of cor anglais, bass clarinet, horns and harp, and double basses and harp fade into inaudibility at the end.

■ Vaughan Williams, *Symphony No. 5 in D major*

Background

Ralph Vaughan Williams was born in Gloucestershire, England, in 1872. He undertook a long apprenticeship as a composer, studying at the Royal College of Music before and after taking a degree in history at Trinity College, Cambridge. He also took a BMus degree, and passed the Cambridge DMus examination in 1899. His composition teachers included some of the most prominent figures of the day: Parry and Stanford in England, Max Bruch in Germany and Maurice Ravel in France. In the early years of the 20th century he became interested in folk song and collected over 800 examples, fascinated by their modal melodies and keen to preserve them for future generations. He was a lifelong friend of the composer Gustav Holst and the two continued to meet and discuss their compositions until Holst's death in 1934.

The strongest musical tradition in England at the time was of choral music and Vaughan Williams wrote many cantatas, anthems and songs as well as editing *The English Hymnal*. His first symphony was a choral cantata in symphonic form called *A Sea Symphony* (1910). *A London Symphony* followed in 1914 and *A Pastoral Symphony* in 1922. Symphony No. 4 in F minor provoked much surprise by its harsh dissonances in 1935, but the Fifth Symphony does not follow this path. Vaughan Williams was 70 when it was first performed and many assumed this would be his final work in the form, but the composer lived to write four more. He died in 1958, four months after the first performance of the Ninth Symphony.

The Fifth Symphony

Symphony No. 5 was composed between 1938 and 1943, and was first performed with the composer conducting at a Promenade concert in London, in June 1943. It follows the traditional pattern of four

■ **Did you know?**

The composer Busoni said of Mahler, 'He had an artist's soul and a child's heart'.

Interior of the Royal Albert Hall where Vaughan Williams conducted his symphony at its first performance in 1943

movements with the scherzo lying second. The orchestra is modest for the time, with only two flutes, clarinets, bassoons, horns and trumpets; one oboe and cor anglais, and three trombones. Timpani are the only percussion instruments. Each movement has a title (*Preludio*, **Scherzo**, *Romanza*, **Passacaglia**) but there is no programme. Some of the themes, especially in the slow movement, were drawn from an unfinished opera based on John Bunyan's *Pilgrim's Progress* that had occupied Vaughan Williams over a long period. It was eventually completed and performed in 1951, but it is rarely heard today. The composer hesitated to name a key for the symphony but eventually designated it as 'in D major'. Much of the harmony is modal rather than tonal, but it begins with a contradiction of key in which D major is one element, and it resolves satisfyingly to D major at the end of the finale.

First movement: *Preludio*

The title *Preludio* (Prelude) does not imply a particular form. Each movement of the symphony has a title, and this heading may indicate that the first movement does not stand alone but leads into the following movements. It begins and ends with an uncertain sound, which is only resolved when the opening theme returns at the end of the finale. The movement is based on sonata form.

Exposition

Beginning–7 bars after fig. 3 The opening section is built from five small motifs shown below.

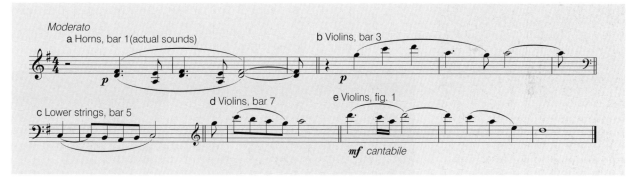

The motifs are introduced one by one and gradually assembled into longer melodies, until it is hard to find an instrument that is not using one of these patterns. They appear in imitation between instruments, and, beginning at fig. 1, there is a canon between violins and violas and cellos lasting more than five bars. The harmony is more modal than tonal: the horns appear to be in D major but this is contradicted by C♮ in the bass. Motif **a** appears alternately with F♯ and F♮, and there is ambiguity between the decorated C in the bass part and the constant return to D in the violin melody. The gentle rhythms and string textures, often in octaves, give this section an unhurried and spacious atmosphere.

Eight bars after fig. 3–fig. 5 The key signature changes and, although the same motifs are used, bass and treble become more related. Motif **c** in the bass is inverted in the melody, and the melody moves its centre to F and then to C, at last agreeing with the bass.

Key terms

Scherzo: literally, 'a joke'. In the symphony, a quick movement in triple time. Originally it followed the binary-form pattern of the minuet and trio.

Passacaglia: a movement built on a repeating chord sequence or melodic bass line. The form dates back to the Renaissance period.

AQA Examiner's tip

The score of Vaughan Williams' *Symphony No. 5* has no bar numbers. Bars will be identified in examination questions in relation to the rehearsal figures: for example, the first entry of bassoons in the symphony is at '3 bars after fig. 1' or 'the third bar of fig. 1'. If you prefer to use bar numbers you may write them into the score and use them in the examination.

Fig. 5–fig. 6a The appearance of the second subject is one of the most striking moments in the symphony, moving unexpectedly to the bright sound of E major. The melody is taken from *Pilgrim's Progress* but it is surrounded by familiar motifs from earlier in the movement. The woodwind rhythm at fig. 5 comes from motif **a**, and motif **d** appears five bars after fig. 6. The security of E major does not last for long. It begins to move onwards through a cycle of fifths three bars after fig. 6 and when it cadences to E at fig. 6a it is in the minor mode.

Fig. 6a–10 bars after 6a The coda to the exposition recalls motif **e**. The woodwind and strings are in imitation at distances of two bars and at the half-bar. One new idea is heard – a quietly emphatic falling semitone (motif **f**), which will be an important feature of the development. This idea is also taken from *Pilgrim's Progress*.

Development

Eleven bars after 6a–8 bars after fig. 8 There is a brief reference to motif **a** in the bassoons and to motif **c** in the strings, suggesting C minor. Strings weave a background texture from modal phrases, constantly imitating one another. The semitone figure E♮–E♭ is sounded in the woodwind, expanded into three notes (E♭, D♭, C) and then developed into falling woodwind phrases.

Eight bars after fig. 8–2 bars after fig. 9 The key centre moves to E♭ and woodwind phrases imitate increasingly frequently.

Three bars after fig. 9–fig. 11 The move to a key centre of F♯ introduces a more confident melody in flutes and clarinets, although motif **f** is still important. Woodwind and strings become more insistent as the key centre moves again and leads to a strong climax and pealing phrases in the wind. These die away to leave motif **f** sounding (C, B♭, A) as the energy disperses and the opening of the movement returns.

Ralph Vaughan Williams conducting the Boyd Neel Orchestra in rehearsal in July 1953

Recapitulation

Fig. 11–6 bars after fig. 12 Motifs **a** and **c** appear as before, but there is some re-working of material. The phrases of **b** are more widely recognised. The accompaniment from the second subject appears in the woodwind and the wind section echoes a new fragment developed from motif **b**.

Seven bars after fig. 12–3 bars after fig. 14 The second subject is as glorious in effect as before, but now in B♭ major, and it repeats its climax after a brief suggestion of G. This time, the true cadence to G is emphatic.

Coda

Three bars after 14–the end Motif **d** begins but it is supplanted by motif **f**, darkening the sound. The strings come to centre on F, but the horns persist with F♯s in motif **a**. The two notes alternate without either giving way. The final thought of the movement is of D major over C in the bass, as at the beginning.

Second movement: *Scherzo*

The *Scherzo* lives up to its indication of *Presto misterioso* (Fast and mysterious) and its character is eccentric rather than humorous. The triple time opening is increasingly challenged by duple rhythms and this creates a short-lived but ferocious battle between the two metres. They reach a truce at the end, but the triple time has the last word.

Beginning–fig. 1 Muted strings set up the triple metre, which achieves a momentum at the eighth bar. The harmony is modal, with emphasis on E, and with frequent fourths in the melody. This theme becomes the background against which a succession of melodies appears.

Fig. 1–7 bars before fig. 4 Theme A, sparingly scored for flute, high bassoon and pizzicato double bass.

It is clearly in triple time but has irregular phrase lengths of 2+3+2+4 bars. It centres on E at first, suggesting the Phrygian mode, and is repeated a fourth higher with small variations. At fig. 2 short falling woodwind phrases briefly contradict the bar line, and then the sections of the orchestra exchange roles, with the background theme on clarinets and bassoons and Theme A in the strings.

Seven bars before fig. 4–10 bars before fig. 8 Theme B is less good-tempered, with tart grace notes in oboe and cor anglais, and fifths in the bass which become increasingly important. Their rhythm frequently includes a **hemiola** pattern which suggests that the triple metre of the movement will not remain undisturbed.

> ### Key terms
>
> **Hemiola:** a device where the rhythmic emphasis is shifted so that two bars of triple time sound more like three bars of duple time – for example, three minim beats across two bars of three crotchets.

The key centre moves to C at the beginning of this section and then moves frequently. Several new motifs are heard, the most important being a snatch in the style of a folk song, beginning four bars before fig. 6 in the woodwind. It is later played by strings, and by clarinets and bassoons. The background has moved into quavers but the 'fifths theme' continues to appear in the bass.

Ten bars before fig. 8–10 bars after fig. 14 Trombones bring back the opening fourths in conversation with the fifths of Theme B, and these become the background to a new Theme C.

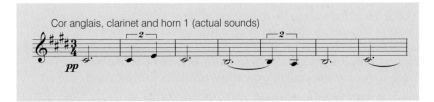

Cor anglais, clarinet and horn 1 (actual sounds)

This is a developed version of the folk-song fragment in the previous section and it sounds in duple time, although surrounded by a quick triple-time accompaniment. The theme alternates between low brass and woodwind. The conflict between duple and triple time is becoming stronger.

Eleven bars after fig. 14–fig. 16 The background theme of fourths is recapitulated at its original pitch, but played staccato. It is possible that Vaughan Williams was recalling the *pizzicato* return of the scherzo in Beethoven's fifth symphony. The same feature occurs in the fifth symphony of Shostakovich, written in 1937.

Fig. 16–fig. 21 Theme A returns on flute and piccolo, but the introduction to Theme B that begins at fig. 17 is overtaken by a new Theme D, which forces the whole orchestra into $2/4$ time.

Woodwind in octaves

The background theme makes various attempts to begin again and, at times, $2/4$ and $3/4$ time signatures appear simultaneously in different instruments.

Fig 21–end A compromise is reached in $3/2$ time and opposition to the triple metre dissolves in a gentle passage of modal harmony for strings, based on the background theme. The woodwind and muted strings pass around phrases from the background theme until it dies away with a final touch of timpani and *pizzicato* bass.

Third movement: *Romanza*

This is the slow movement of the symphony and uses several ideas from the opera *Pilgrim's Progress*. Originally, the composer headed the movement with the words accompanying the cor anglais theme but these were later deleted.

After the surprises and conflicts of the *Scherzo*, it is a serene and reflective movement. It is loosely in AABA form with a coda, and has five distinctive ideas:

- A sequence of four or six chords C–A–G minor–A (G minor–A) at their first appearance.
- The melody quoted above, which is accompanied by the chords. It begins on C but alternates between F♮ and F♯ as it proceeds.
- A string melody beginning with rising fourths. The stepwise falling fourth is later used separately.
- A pattern of parallel chords, first heard at fig. 2.
- Florid woodwind solos, again using fourths as a motif.

Beginning–9 bars before fig. 3 The five ideas are introduced in succession.

Eight bars before fig. 3–fig. 5 The same sequence of material is repeated with the chords and melody a fourth lower and a more impassioned climax.

Fig. 5–fig. 7 A more animated section begins with **diminutions** of the parallel chords and of the opening four chords, now transposed to begin on E major. The woodwind use motifs from the cor anglais melody to build a climax.

Fig. 7–4 bars before fig. 11 The recapitulation is re-ordered. The cor anglais melody returns, but with a more intense harmonisation, and there are references to all the previous ideas, including the *animato*. The pattern of four chords returns at a new pitch, but returns to its first pitch nine bars before fig. 9. The string melody again reaches an impressive climax.

> ### Key terms
>
> **Diminution:** a rhythmic feature in which note values are halved so that an idea is played at double speed.

Four bars before fig. 11–the end Four of the five original motifs return in the coda. The four chords are heard once, beginning on A, but then settle to their original pitch, ending with a plagal cadence in A major. A solo violin takes over the woodwind idea and a horn borrows from the cor anglais. The final thought is the falling fourth from the string melody, allowing a quiet close with plagal cadences to A major.

Fourth movement: *Passacaglia*

The finale re-energises the symphony after the restful slow movement. The *passacaglia* form was common in the Renaissance and Baroque periods but became rare in the Classical period. In the 19th century, Brahms used the form to conclude his *Variations on a theme of Handel* and his Fourth Symphony. Later examples are the storm interlude in *Peter Grimes* by Benjamin Britten, and the finales of Lutosławski's *Concerto for Orchestra* (1956) and William Walton's Second Symphony (1960).

Beginning–5 bars before fig. 5 The seven-bar theme (Theme A), also derived from *Pilgrim's Progress*, is announced by cellos alone, and nine variations follow.

The first of these introduces a rising countermelody in first violins (Theme B), which becomes equally important.

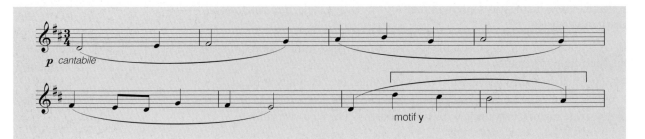

Motif **x** (the first five notes of A) and motif **y** (the falling fourth in Theme B) will be used later. There is some flexibility about the length of variations: the fifth statement is five bars long and the sixth, eight bars. Rhythms become more emphatic to lead into the Allegro section. The music is firmly in D major.

Five bars before fig. 5–fig. 6 Theme B takes over, with imitation creating a contrapuntal texture.

Fig. 6–9 bars before fig. 7 Scherzando (Playful) The opening of Theme A returns in F major with its rhythm adapted, to suggest duple time, and staccato woodwind adding to the scherzando character.

Nine bars before fig. 7–5 bars before fig. 9 The original key and tempo return for grand statements of Themes B and A.

Four bars before fig. 9–4 bars before fig 14 A dramatic change brings the minor mode, tremolo strings and woodwind solos based on Theme A. Both themes are subjected to rhythmic and tonal variations, leading to a series of loud statements of Theme A in brass and woodwind. The rising shape of Theme B is often evident and eventually there is a fortissimo statement of motif **x** with most of the orchestra playing in octaves.

Four bars before fig. 14–fig. 15 The climax dies down to an alternation between the notes C and D, which recalls the music of the *Preludio*. It is combined with motif **x** and then with three motifs from the first movement – **a**, **b** and **e**.

Fig. 15–fig. 17 Theme B leads the way to a coda in D major, originally for strings alone, but adding strands of melody for woodwind and horn.

Fig. 17–the end Final statement of Themes A and B in combination. Motif **y**, which has been a feature throughout the symphony, brings the movement to rest over a long tonic pedal.

An oboe player in the National Youth Orchestra, 2008

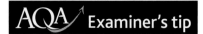

■ Types of question

The examination paper will ask two types of question on your chosen set work:

■ short questions asking for a detailed description of a passage in the score
■ longer essay questions of several different types.

The short questions will be compulsory. You will answer one essay question from a choice of two. Both types of question were set in the previous specification, so you can look at past papers to find examples given on different set works.

Answering short questions

The question will indicate two short passages in the score and you will be asked to write about a musical element in them. The musical elements listed in the specification are:

■ form
■ harmony
■ instrumentation and texture
■ melody
■ rhythm and metre
■ texture
■ tonality.

You may also be asked to identify the main themes in the extract or to explain its position in the work. The best preparation for this type of question is a thorough knowledge of the score, and the ability to hear the sound when you see the notation. If you have an unmarked score available, or can remove your notes as suggested above, you can test yourself by choosing a passage and explaining how one of the elements listed above is used.

Understanding the score

You will need to learn the meaning of the composer's marks of tempo, style and technique. These occur very frequently in Mahler's *Symphony No. 4*, but they will be easier to learn if you remember the sound of the music and the effect of instructions, such as as **col legno** and **Schalltrichter auf!**

To analyse harmony, you need to know the sounding pitch of each note. Transposing instruments sound at a different pitch from their notation, so they need particular care. The key of the instrument (e.g. Horn in F) tells you the note which *sounds* when the instrument plays what is *written* as note C. A complete table of the transposing instruments in the two set symphonies is given on the following page.

Transposing instruments

A transposing instrument sounds at a different pitch from its notation. This system is traditionally used where players may have to change instruments in the middle of a piece, such as for different sizes of clarinet. It is also used at extremes of the range to avoid writing long passages on ledger lines.

Vaughan Williams, *Symphony No. 5*

The tables below show how each instrument sounds compared to its written part.

Instrument	Sounds
Piccolo	an octave higher
Cor anglais	a perfect fifth lower
Clarinet in B♭	a tone lower
Clarinet in A	a minor third lower
Horn in F	a perfect fifth lower
Trumpet in B♭	a tone lower
Double bass	an octave lower

All other instruments used in this symphony sound as they are written.

Mahler, *Symphony No. 4*

Mahler uses all the instruments listed above, and the following additional instruments.

Instrument	Sounds
Clarinet in E♭	a minor third higher
Bass clarinet in B♭	a major ninth lower
Bass clarinet in A	a minor tenth lower
Contrabassoon	an octave lower
Trumpet in F	a perfect fifth lower
Solo violin I in the second movement	a tone higher

The Mahler score uses German instrument names, so 'in B' means 'in B♭'; 'in Es' means 'in E♭'.

Clefs

Violas use the alto clef, with middle C on the middle line.

High phrases on bassoon and cello may be written in the tenor clef, with middle C on the third line from the bottom of the stave. It is important not to confuse these two clefs.

> **Hint**
> ■ Trombones, and clarinets in C, play at written pitch.

Describing the music: points to remember

■ Describe chords as fully as possible. Remember to name the key if you are using Roman numerals: 'Chord V' can only be identified if the key is known. Chords may also be described individually, without reference to a key (e.g. D^7, A min). This may be advisable in the Vaughan Williams symphony as the harmony is often modal and reference to a key may be difficult. Whatever notation you use, indicate the position of the chord (root position, or first, second or third inversion), added notes (e.g. 7ths, 9ths) and unessential notes (e.g. passing notes, suspensions).

■ The key signature alone may not indicate the current key, nor whether the mode is major or minor. Look for added accidentals and the context of the passage to establish the key. Try to remember how it sounds.

■ Pedal notes in the bass, or elsewhere, can be described separately from the chords associated with them (e.g. 'C♯ diminished seventh over a G pedal').

■ If you identify a theme by name (e.g. Theme B) give a bar reference when you first use the term. There are many different ways of analysing the music and the examiner must be able to understand the terms you are using.

Answering longer questions

Understanding the question

Essay questions will be of different types. Here are some examples:

■ Description of a long section, such as a complete movement, in the form of a programme note. This is usually straightforward to answer. Balance the answer so that all parts of the movement are covered according to their importance. For example: 'Write a detailed programme note on the fourth movement (Passacaglia) of Vaughan Williams' *Symphony No. 5.*'

■ Comparison of two passages, such as two appearances of the same theme. For example: 'Explain how the first three bars of Mahler's *Symphony No. 4* are used and developed later in the symphony, and how they contribute to its structure.'

■ Discussion of a musical element, such as rhythm, orchestration or form. In this case you may be asked to select interesting passages to discuss. Prepare for this by studying suitable extracts chosen to demonstrate the composer's style. For example: 'Choose *three* passages from Mahler's *Symphony No. 4* that illustrate his techniques of orchestration and comment on their effectiveness.'

■ Questions which relate the set work to its context or the composer's life. These need a broader knowledge but it is important to support your answer by detailed reference to the symphony. For example: 'Why were audiences surprised at the first performance of either Mahler's *Symphony No. 4 or* Vaughan Williams' *Symphony No. 5*? Explain how the symphony you have studied differed from the composer's previous symphonies. Identify passages in the set work that illustrate these changes.'

■ Discussion of an opinion about the work. Take some time to understand the point of the opinion given, and develop a balanced argument showing how far you agree or disagree with the writer. For example: '"Vaughan Williams was sincere. His works, large and small, did grow out of his life" (William Austin). What features of the Fifth Symphony could be said to "grow out of his life" and reflect the composer's other works, interests and activities? You should refer in detail to selected passages from the score in your answer.'

Planning your answer

Essay questions need careful planning. The quality of language, grammatical accuracy, use of technical terms and clarity of expression will be taken into consideration by the examiner. Read the question carefully and make notes on the main points before you begin. You will save time if you have a clear structure for your answer, and a plan will also help you to allocate your time effectively.

Because you will have the score in the examination, there is no need to write out quotations. Make detailed reference to the score, by instrument and by bar or figure number, in your answer, such as 'horn, bar 5'.

It is important to keep the question in mind at all times, and to avoid introducing irrelevant material.

13

Historical study for A2

Learning objectives:

- to learn how to select representative examples from the chosen area of study
- to understand how to investigate the chosen works and record your findings
- to develop study and revision techniques
- to understand the types of question which may be set and how to approach them.

Areas of study

For this section of the examination you will choose one of the following AoS:

- English choral music in the 20th century *or*
- Chamber music from Mendelssohn to Debussy *or*
- Four decades of jazz and blues 1910–1950.

Performing

You will need to use the same techniques of analysis for your chosen area of study as for the set work (Chapter 12), but there are some differences of approach. You will choose a selection of works to study from the period and the choice can be guided, to some extent, by your interests, your performing experience and the availability of scores and recordings. Questions will be written in general terms, asking about the musical elements but without requiring knowledge of specified composers or works. AQA publishes a list of 'core works' for guidance, but these are not compulsory. You may wish to include works that you have performed or heard live, or composers who are already familiar to you. It is very valuable to take part in a performance of a work from your area of study. For example, clarinettists may be able to play part of a Brahms clarinet sonata, and choral singers join a performance of works by Benjamin Britten, John Rutter or John Tavener. Jazz players could compare their performances of standards from the early 20th century with recordings from the period.

Listening

At the beginning of the course, draw up a list of the composers and works that fall into your area of study. Look out for recordings and performances so that you gain experience of the styles of the time. Find out the date of composition of each piece so that you begin to understand lines of development and relationships between works. There is a wealth of music performed every week on BBC Radio 3. Look ahead at the schedules to find relevant examples.

Taking notes

No scores are allowed for this part of the examination paper. Aim to adopt a method of study that will make it easy to remember and select material for the essay questions. You should also build up a collection of musical quotations to illustrate important points from your study.

The methods of study for the set work, described in Chapter 12, can be applied to works from the area of study, but the way in which you keep notes may vary. When you first study a chosen piece you will probably make notes of your findings movement by movement. The notes on the Schumann *Piano Quintet* in this chapter are in this form, as an example. Develop abbreviations and tables to make your notes more concise and easier to revise. Because questions will centre on the musical elements, you should also record your findings under the headings of form, melody, harmony and so on. This method has been used for the analysis of the Stanford and Parry anthems, *Belshazzar's Feast*, the Mendelssohn *Piano Trio* and Louis Armstrong's *West End Blues*. It is a good idea to produce notes in both styles on each work so that you can select elements easily for an essay, or give an overview of a whole movement or a complete work.

English choral music in the 20th century

This area of study dates from 1900 to 1999, but the title 'English' can be interpreted in different ways. If the choice is limited strictly to composers born in England it will exclude Sir Charles Stanford at the beginning of the century and Karl Jenkins and James MacMillan at the end. All of these composers have made important contributions to the English choral tradition, although they were born respectively in Ireland, Wales and Scotland. As the English choral tradition was so strongly influenced by Handel, who was born in Germany and trained in Italy, it seems appropriate to include composers who are (or were) English-speaking, in the British Isles and have written significant works for English choirs.

The field of choral music in this period is very large. In this chapter it has been divided into two categories:

- short works for church or chamber choirs
- larger works, **sacred** or **secular**, which are commonly performed in the concert hall.

You will need to select works of both types to study, but you should aim to include any that you have performed and know well. In a long work, choose short sections for detailed study as in the examples below. If you chose to study choral music in the Baroque period at AS Level you will already have a good background for this period. If you are studying Vaughan Williams' *Symphony No. 5* in Unit 4 you could include one of his choral works so that the two units will support one another.

Short choral works

This category includes:

- Settings of texts required in worship. In the Roman Catholic Church these are the movements of the Mass (e.g. Kyrie, Gloria, Credo, Sanctus, Agnus Dei). In the Church of England these are the canticles which make up a service (e.g. Te Deum, Jubilate, Magnificat, Nunc Dimittis).
- Settings of other texts suitable for use in church. These are often called anthems if written in English and motets if written in Latin.
- Secular part-songs, usually intended for small choirs.

The early 20th century

Two composers helped to revive English choral music at the beginning of the century. Sir Charles Stanford (1852–1924) was born in Dublin but studied in Cambridge and was Professor of Music there from 1887 until his death in 1924. He was also Professor of Composition at the newly founded Royal College of Music. Sir Hubert Parry (1848–1918) was Professor of Music at Oxford University from 1900 to 1908 and Director of the Royal College of Music from 1894.

> **Key terms**
>
> **Sacred:** written with a religious or devotional purpose.
>
> **Secular:** non-religious.

> **Hint**
>
> The works on the following pages are treated in different styles to demonstrate ways of recording and revising your notes. Stanford's *Magnificat in G* and Parry's *I was glad* are analysed under the headings given in the specification. Examination questions may focus on one or more of these elements.

Stanford, *Magnificat in G major* (1902)

Form

English church music written in the late 19th century is sometimes criticised because the only organising factor is the text. The effect can be sectional with no overall sense of unity. In contrast this canticle, which is part of the Evening Service, has a logical key structure, a persistent accompaniment figure and a returning theme for the soloist, as in rondo form. It is linked to other parts of the G major Service by a shared theme in the final section *Glory be to the Father*.

Harmony

The harmony is expressive but largely consonant, in keeping with the joyful mood of the text. The opening figure is supported by a tonic pedal, and diminished seventh chords are reserved to emphasise words such as 'holy' and 'empty'. Another version of the diminished seventh leads to an unexpected modulation to E♭ major. Each appearance of the soloist's striking top G is differently harmonised. It is originally heard over a root-position G major chord, but later it appears as part of a C major chord, and over V⁷b in E♭ major on the word 'holpen'.

Instrumentation and timbre

The Magnificat is set for four-part choir with a treble soloist and organ accompaniment. The treble solo represents the voice of Mary, the speaker of the text in the Bible. There are some delicate touches of **word-painting**: low voices sing the word 'lowly'; 'Holy is His name' is set to quiet chords with a pause in the arpeggio movement; and there is a strong fanfare style for 'He hath shewed strength'.

Melody

Stanford was renowned for his ability to write attractive melodies. The opening solo of this canticle is wonderfully uplifting, matching the mood of the words 'My soul doth magnify the Lord'. The rise to a high G is an important characteristic of the whole work.

Key terms

Word-painting: illustrating the words by the sound or look of the music: for example, using a rising phrase for 'he ascended' or a long note on the words 'for ever'.

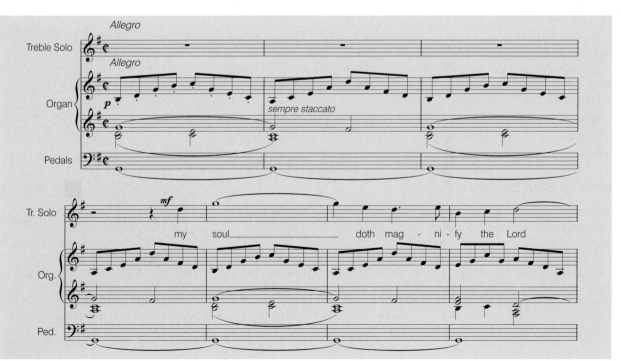

The melodic phrase for the words 'Holy is his name' returns later to the words 'for ever'.

Rhythm and metre

Choral rhythms are mostly even, although 'He hath scattered the proud' has a dotted rhythm. The most important rhythmic feature is the staccato arpeggio pattern of quavers in the organ part. It is made more effective by brief pauses to emphasise words, and it is also varied a little in the section beginning 'and the rich'. The Magnificat is in $^2/_2$ time but changes to $^3/_2$ for the Gloria.

Texture

The choral parts are almost entirely homophonic and often doubled by the organ. Other choral textures appear briefly: there is occasional imitation between the soloist and a choral part, and the Gloria begins with the voices in octaves. The organ has an accompanying arpeggio pattern in the treble or tenor range which characterises the entire canticle.

Tonality

The Magnificat begins in G major and returns to this key four times. The three intervening episodes move to B minor and D major ('For behold'), E minor and B major ('Holy is His name') and C and E♭ majors ('and the rich'). Of these keys, B major and E♭ major are more distant and add extra colour. The final return of the opening theme begins in C major and moves back to G major as it proceeds. The final 'Gloria' is in G major but passes through several of the earlier keys before its final plagal cadence.

Performers, audience, occasion

The Magnificat was written for church and cathedral choirs, as part of the Evening Service of the Anglican church. It was originally intended for all-male choirs with boy trebles and **male altos**.

Your personal view

All these details have still not said everything about the Magnificat. Your personal view of the piece is important, and the examiners will be looking for evidence that you have heard and remembered the sound of the music. Make a note of your own impressions. These may change as your study progresses, so add to them when you hear the piece again later in the course.

Parry, *I was glad when they said unto me* (1902)

Form

Six sections, divided according to text. The rising third is a persistent motif as shown below. Interlude at B returns at C, D, bar before G, Alla Marcia after G in choir at K. The 'Vivat' section is needed for a coronation ceremony but can be omitted in other performances.

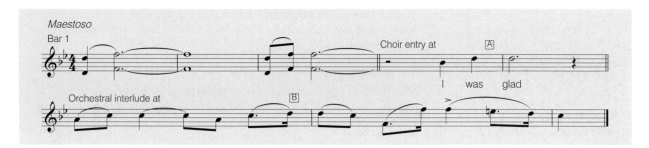

Harmony

Richer than Stanford: more appoggs, suspensions, dim. 7ths for colour in intro and for modulation three bars before C. Striking change of chord from Bb to G major on 'I was glad'. Impressive inverted dom. 7ths beneath 'Vivats'. Contrast with warm chords, passing notes and expressive appoggs. in 'O pray for the peace'. Strong dom. pedal at final *Allargando*.

Instrumentation and timbre

Originally for a choir of 430 voices (all male) and an orchestra of 65 plus 10 fanfare trumpeters. Opening sung by Westminster Abbey choir; remaining voices joined for double choir sections and the climax. Can also be performed with organ accompt. Brass used to give dignity and ceremonial atmosphere, especially before 'Vivats'. Strings and woodwind provide gentler contrast at 'O pray for the peace'.

Melody

Strongly influenced by rising third figure and fanfare patterns. 'O pray for the peace' more conjunct and flowing.

Rhythm and metre

Written in $^4/_4$ and in dignified march style – intended to accompany processions of the King and Queen into Westminster Abbey. Dotted rhythms for fanfare style, and smoother movement when required by words. No change in pulse until final *allargando*.

Texture

Many different choral arrangements. SSATTB at first, then imitation between SSA and TTB. Double choir at 'Jerusalem' in antiphony, comes together after the word 'unity'. 'Vivats' by trebles alone – whole choir responds in octaves. Small semichorus SATB sings 'O pray for the peace'. Final section SATB with some divisions.

Tonality

'I was glad' Bb maj, modulating to F. 'Our feet shall stand' F maj to D min. 'Jerusalem' G min to Bb maj Vivat implies Eb, C, D, G majors without settling; moves to Gb at end. 'O pray' Gb maj. (surprising, effective) 'Peace' Bb major, with brief reference to Gb again.

Performers, audience, occasion

Composed for the coronation of King Edward VII and Queen Alexandra. Planned for 26 June 1902 and postponed to 9 Aug with shortened ceremony because of King's illness. Choirs of Westminster Abbey, St George's Windsor, Chapel Royal and St Paul's Cathedral, plus representatives from other London churches. Queen's Scholars of Westminster School had the right to acclaim the King – Parry wrote this into the anthem to make it more dignified. Choir in specially erected galleries in north and south choir aisles with sub-conductors. 'Vivats' and final section had to be repeated because processions were delayed.

Your personal view

Remember to add your impression of the piece to your notes. It is particularly valuable if you have experience of hearing it or performing it live.

The mid-20th century

Here is a selection of short works written from the 1930s onwards that are suitable for study. There are many other possibilities.

- William Walton, *Set me as a seal* (1938)
- Benjamin Britten, *A Ceremony of Carols* (1942)
- Herbert Howells, Evening Service *Collegium Regale* (1945)
- Ralph Vaughan Williams, *O taste and see* (1952)
- John Joubert, *O Lorde, the maker of al thing* (1952)
- Kenneth Leighton, *Give me the wings of faith* (1962)

William Walton, *Set me as a seal* (1938)

Who was the composer, and what else did he or she write in this genre?

William Walton (1902–1983) composer of symphonies, concertos, operas and the 'entertainment' *Façade*. Wrote occasional church music. Walton was a boy chorister at Christ Church, Oxford.

When and why was this piece written?

Walton was introduced to Alice, Viscountess of Wimborne in 1935 and they became lovers and constant companions until her death in 1948. This anthem was written for the wedding of her son in 1938.

What instruments and voices does it use?

SATB choir unaccompanied.

What is the text, and what is its mood and meaning?

Verses from the Bible (The Song of Solomon) about love.

What gives it shape or form?

The choir responds to solo tenor phrases. Three phrases of words are set in the pattern ABCBA plus a short coda.

Describe the overall style of the harmony, and study any interesting passages in detail.

Although the first chord is D major, most of the chords in the anthem have added notes – 9ths, 7ths, 6ths or 4ths. Chord changes are often achieved by one or two notes moving by step and the rest remaining the same. Some of the phrase endings are on gently dissonant chords but there are consonant chords on 'arm' (A major), 'death' (F & C without a third) and 'drown it' (C major).

> **Hint**
>
> Once you have heard a short choral work, the best way to investigate it is to ask yourself questions about it. This page contains a list of suggested questions. As an example, they have been answered for one anthem of this period.

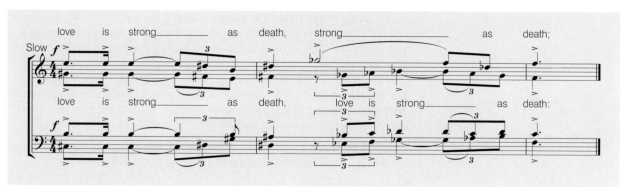

This passage (on previous page) begins on a C♯⁷ chord and moves through an **enharmonic change** to a stark F chord. There is added power from the parallel chord movements in the second bar and from the exposed treble note.

What is its tonality, and how does it change?

The anthem is centred on D major but moves freely to imply frequent changes of tonal centre. The bass line is often conjunct and this makes the moves to unrelated chords logical. The harmony often has a flattened seventh and suggests modality. The final cadence is plagal, but moves from G minor to D major, with the resolving effect of a **Picardy third**.

Describe the rhythmic style. Does it vary, and if so, why?

The crotchet beat is constant but the metre is flexible to accommodate the words. The natural rhythm of the words is followed very closely, giving rise to triplet divisions. Accents and tenuto marks encourage natural speech rhythms.

What are the characteristics of the main melodies?

The opening tenor melody sounds like an ancient chant. Melodies are mostly conjunct, making the soloist's rise to the word 'seal' more effective.

Describe the texture or textures used and say why they are suitable.

Most of the phrases are homophonic. There is a suggestion of imitation in two phrases. The main contrast is between the choir and the soloist.

What is your overall impression of the work?

This would provide a quiet and thoughtful moment in a wedding service. It is a miniature anthem, but is surprisingly powerful at its climax. The composer takes care to return to stillness at the end.

The late 20th century

Again, there is plenty of choice and you may be able to study a personal favourite. It is best to choose pieces that were originally written for choral singing. Some popular instrumental pieces have been arranged for choirs but the writing may be influenced by instruments rather than voices. The two composers selected here represent different styles but both have written a large amount of choral music as well as important works in other fields.

John Tavener, *Two Hymns to the Mother of God* (1985)

John Tavener was born in 1944 and quickly made his mark as an original and experimental composer. Much of his music is based on text, and his religious works reflect his adoption of the Russian Orthodox faith in 1977. These anthems use interesting textures, slow-moving harmonies and silence to encourage contemplation of the meaning of the texts.

A Hymn to the Mother of God

The sound of this anthem, written for two six-part choirs, is majestic and overwhelming in a large space, but it may not be obvious how this effect is achieved until you see the score:

■ Play the music for choir one. Note the chords used and the method of moving from one chord to another.

■ How does Tavener arrange the cadences, and what tonality do they suggest?

- Compare the music for choir one and choir two, and explain how they are related.
- How important is consonance? How does dissonance arise?
- How does the music express the words?
- Are there any particularly striking moments, and how are they achieved?

Hymn for the Dormition of the Mother of God

- Describe the textures used in the three sections of this anthem and consider their effects.
- What are the characteristics of the tenor melody in the first section?
- What is the harmonic effect of the SAB section?
- How does the final section differ from this?
- What can be said about the tonality or modality of this anthem?

James MacMillan, *Magnificat* (1999)

James MacMillan was born in Scotland in 1959. He achieved national recognition as a composer with *The Confession of Isobel Gowdie* in 1990 and the percussion concerto *Veni, veni Emmanuel* in 1992. He is now well known internationally and travels widely as a composer and conductor. Both his choral music and his orchestral music are often based on religious texts. The *Magnificat* was written in 1999 to a commission by Winchester Cathedral. The first performance was in an orchestral version commissioned by the BBC for the broadcast of *Choral Evensong* from Wells Cathedral on 5 January 2000.

James MacMillan described the *Magnificat* in an interview:

> There is a serenity of course but an undercurrent of destabilisation. And that clash of opposites – the serene and the unsettled going in tandem – builds up a larger architecture in the music which leads to development and a resolution of some sort.

Listen to the music and build up your notes by answering these questions. Remember that musical effects are dependent on the musical elements in the specification. It is useful to use these as a checklist when analysing the music:

- Which parts of the canticle are serene? Which parts are unsettled?
- How are these two moods achieved musically?
- Explain how the music develops. Where is the climax of the piece?
- How is a resolution achieved at the end?

Longer choral works

In the 18th century Handel created a new form of oratorio. These oratorios were dramatic settings of Bible stories for soloists, chorus and orchestra, performed in concert without costume or acting. Handel wrote for soloists and orchestra in his operas, but the oratorios also had important, exciting choruses. After his death, festivals of his works were performed by massed choirs, and they made a great impression on visitors to England. As a result, Haydn wrote his oratorios *The Creation* and *The Seasons*, and Mendelssohn wrote *Elijah* and *St Paul*.

There was an interval of 50 years before English composers began to match the quality of these works, but Elgar's *The Dream of Gerontius* (1900) set a new standard. Choral societies in schools, towns and cities have kept the tradition alive and continue to commission new works. Here are some suggestions for other 20th-century works to investigate:

- Vaughan Williams, *A Sea Symphony* (1910), *Dona nobis pacem* (1936), *Serenade to Music* (1938)
- Walton, *Belshazzar's Feast* (1931)
- Britten, *Rejoice in the Lamb* (1943), *St Nicholas* (1948), *War Requiem* (1961)
- Tippett, *A Child of our Time* (1944)
- Tavener, *Ikon of Light* (1984), *We shall see Him as He is* (1992)
- Rutter, *Gloria* (1974), *Requiem* (1985)
- MacMillan, *Seven Last Words from the Cross* (1994)
- Jenkins, Mass *The Armed Man* (1999)

This chapter gives an introduction to some of these works. Choose works from different parts of the century from this list, or from the performances, scores and recordings available to you. The methods of approach shown below can be used with any work you choose.

Elgar, *The Dream of Gerontius* (1900)

Elgar set to music a mystical poem by Cardinal Henry Newman that describes the death and judgement of Gerontius, an old man. There are three soloists: the tenor sings the part of Gerontius, the mezzo-soprano is an angel who guides him after death, and the bass plays the part of a Priest in Part One and the Angel of the Agony in Part Two. The chorus also represent characters: sometimes they are the friends praying around his bed, and in Part Two they also represent demons in hell and 'angelicals' in heaven. The oratorio is accompanied by a large symphony orchestra and uses significant returning themes or 'leitmotifs' in the same way as in Wagner's operas. The themes represent concepts, or ideas, and allow the music to represent the meaning of the words and the character's state of mind. This was a bold and innovative move by Elgar, and the result is an oratorio that rarely depicts physical action but which has great emotional and theological depth. It was first performed in Birmingham in October 1900.

Form

The oratorio is in two parts, representing the events before and after the death of Gerontius. The form is almost symphonic in its development of motifs, and the return of keys also provides structure (see Tonality, opposite). A detailed look at Part One shows that it contains forms traditionally found in oratorios. There is an orchestral Prelude introducing most of the themes, several choruses and an aria for Gerontius: *Sanctus fortis* at fig. 40. Much of the music for Gerontius is in the style of *recitative*, which allows the constant changes of mood and key needed by the text. Study an example of each style and note Elgar's handling of it.

Harmony

Elgar was a master of powerful, dignified harmony, and there is no better example than the great moment in Part Two when Gerontius at last hears the full sound of the heavenly choir (see the extract opposite).

Where the emotion is more troubled, the harmony is complex and chromatic, with restless key changes. You could analyse an extract such as fig. 12 to fig. 17 in the Prelude to demonstrate this.

Hint

Remember that you do not need to know the whole work in detail, although you should listen to it all the way through several times during the course. Select passages that will demonstrate the composer's use of the elements in the specification headings, as suggested here.

Key terms

Recitative: a musical setting of words that follows the rhythms and intonation of speech.

Instrumentation and timbre

In this section you should consider the many ways in which Elgar arranges the chorus: for example, high and low voices for 'angelicals' and 'demons'; use of semi-chorus, chant and response at Part One fig. 64; and the combination of solo voice and chorus at the end of each Part.

Melody

Contrast styles of melody used for choral prayers and for Gerontius in *Sanctus fortis*. Learn to quote two or three contrasting motifs.

Rhythm

The rhythm often provides the 'heartbeat' of the emotion – at times steady and confident, at times urgent and anxious. Identify examples of each. Contrast the rhythms used for the 'demons' and the 'angelicals'.

Texture

Collect examples of various choral textures. Part One fig. 30 to 32, and Part Two fig. 35 to 38 provide good examples of fugal writing.

Tonality

The oratorio moves from D minor to D major overall. Note the places where these keys occur during the work, and any other keys that are used for significant passages. Any interesting key changes could be noted, such as the enharmonic move from A♭ minor to E major at Part One fig. 65, used again at Part Two fig. 115.

Performers, audience, occasion

Elgar had known Cardinal Newman's poem for some years, but he only began to set it to music in January 1900 to fulfil a commission for a new work for the Birmingham Festival. It was written at great speed for performance on 10 October of that year. The first performance in Birmingham Town Hall was very unsatisfactory and badly received. Rehearsal time was short, and the death of the original choirmaster in June placed the work in less sure hands. The famous conductor Hans Richter was in charge of the first performance, and the future of the work was saved by a German choirmaster in the audience who recognised its quality and mounted further, more accomplished performances in Germany.

Hint

This analysis concentrates on the first section of the oratorio (from the beginning to fig. 15) treated chronologically and in note form. This style is useful for a revision summary, taken from more detailed notes.

Key terms

Baritone: a male voice lying between tenor and bass in range and tonal quality.

Hint

The remaining works are treated more briefly. In each case the questions indicate useful features to investigate. You can record your findings in essay form, or as notes, or under the specification headings.

Your personal view

Remember to add your impression of the piece to your notes. It is particularly valuable if you have experience of hearing it or performing it live.

Walton, *Belshazzar's Feast*

Old Testament story. Belshazzar, the king of Babylon, enslaved the Jews and used their sacred temple vessels at a pagan feast. His death was foretold by a disembodied hand writing on the wall, and he was destroyed with his court in a single night. Texts from the books of Psalms, Isaiah and Revelation describe the sorrow of the captive Jews, the pagan feast, and the Jews' rejoicing at Belshazzar's death. Mostly choral. One soloist (**baritone**) – a narrator, not a character in the story. For Leeds Festival 1931.

Beginning–7 bars before fig. 1 No overture. Prophecy of captivity in divided male voices and choral recitative. Trombone opening represents temple horn. Words illustrated by melodic shape ('Babylon') and harmony ('howl ye').

Seven bars before fig. 1–fig. 4 Lament of Jews in D minor. Divides to SSAATTB for echoes on 'wept'. Smooth, melismatic lines, gentle rhythms.

Fig. 4–7 More agitated, clashing seconds, cross rhythms ($3/4$ and $6/8$). Represents mocking by Babylonians. Two styles in conflict at six bars before fig. 6 – choir lament versus orchestra mockery. Ends *a cappella*. N.B. illustration of word 'strange'.

Fig. 7–10 Baritone solo speaks for the Jews; antiphonal response. Theme from six bars before fig. 1 begins as if in $6/8$ and changes to $3/4$ with determined crotchets in bass. Semichorus addition produces eight-part choral texture.

Fig. 10–2 bars after fig. 11 Reprise of fig. 1 shortened.

Two bars after fig. 11–fig. 13 Reprise of Fig. 4 shortened and revised.

Fig. 13–12 after fig. 14 Reprise of climax at fig. 6 to fig. 7.

Fourteen bars after fig. 14 Baritone recitative, unaccompanied and in free rhythm. Range of voice indicates mood of words – large and confident at the beginning, dark and threatening at the end.

NB ABA form with intro, centred on baritone solo, beginning and ending in D minor.

Distinct harmonic and rhythmic styles for Jews and their persecutors.

Orchestra becomes more important later in illustrating gold, silver, brass, wood etc. and in march sections after fig. 26 and at fig. 38.

Imitation between sections of choir but homophonic texture used most.

Little narration. Music creates mood and reflects emotions.

Benjamin Britten, *Rejoice in the Lamb*

Benjamin Britten's *War Requiem* is one of the outstanding works of the 20th century and you should try to hear it if you can. It has not been included here because analyses are already available, and because the score needed for detailed study is expensive to buy. Instead, here is an introduction to a shorter work that demonstrates Benjamin Britten's style of writing. It is not too difficult for a school or college choir to perform, and two of the solo sections are often set for graded examinations.

Rejoice in the Lamb was commissioned by Rev. Walter Hussey for his church in Northampton. He later moved to Chichester Cathedral and continued to commission contemporary art works of all kinds for the cathedral. The resulting sculptures and paintings can still be found in the cathedral, and he also persuaded Leonard Bernstein to compose the *Chichester Psalms*.

Make a plan of the ten sections of *Rejoice in the Lamb*, noting the position of the solos:

▦ How would you describe the choral style of the opening?

▦ Describe the rhythmic style of the second section, *Let Nimrod*. What does the organ part contribute?

▦ How does the choral texture in the *Hallelujah* help to create the mood?

▦ Choose the treble solo or the alto solo and explain how the cat or the mouse is described in the music.

▦ Analyse the harmony of fig. 18–22 and show how it helps to express the words.

▦ How does Britten create stillness in the section from fig. 30–31?

Tippett, *A Child of our Time* (1941)

Like Benjamin Britten, Sir Michael Tippett was a pacifist and Tippett even suffered a period of imprisonment for his beliefs. *A Child of our Time* is an oratorio written to his own libretto and based on a contemporary event. It describes how a young Jewish boy reacted against the persecution of his people and the suffering of his mother by shooting a government official. A greater persecution followed, but Tippett moves through the description of horror and distress to find hope at the end.

The tenor and soprano soloists represent the boy and his mother. Alto and bass soloists tell the story, and briefly take other parts. Tippett also draws on the style of Bach's cantatas, which included chorales (hymns) known to the congregation. He uses five negro spirituals to punctuate the story and to express longing, anger and eventually hope. These spirituals are sometimes performed separately from the oratorio by unaccompanied choir:

▦ Choose one of the spirituals and note how the choir and soloist(s) are used. What is the effect of introducing these familiar songs into the work?

▦ No. 6 'I have no money for my love' and no. 7 'How can I cherish my man in such days?' are good examples of solo songs to study.

▦ No. 5 'Chorus of the Oppressed' and no.19 'The Terror' show Tippett's use of contrapuntal textures to increase the drama. Follow the main themes through and note how they are used. Contrast the style of no. 19 with no. 13, 'Chorus of the Self-Righteous'.

▦ The orchestra plays an important part in creating atmosphere at the beginning of the work. Discover how this is done by choice of harmony and instruments. Instrumental interludes such as in no. 22 'The Boy Sings in his Prison' could provide useful material on texture.

▦ Linking passages are often in a recitative style. Note how Tippett uses the voice and instruments here.

Rutter, *Gloria* (1974)

John Rutter was born in 1945 and studied and taught at Cambridge. He first became known as a composer by his carols and carol arrangements, and choral music lies at the heart of his work. He writes with great understanding of the voice for both amateur and professional choirs. His *Requiem, Magnificat* and *Gloria* (1974) use texts that have traditionally been set over the centuries and are very widely performed.

The *Gloria* is set for SATB choir and can be accompanied by brass and organ or by full orchestra. The text is divided into three movements; energetic and celebratory in the first and third, and more reflective in the central *Domine Deus*. Here are some interesting features to investigate:

- Rhythms are important in creating excitement and forward momentum. How is this done in the first movement?
- Look for the interval of a fourth in harmony and in melody, and explain its effect.
- Investigate the contrapuntal textures of the *Laudamus te* and the *Cum sancto Spiritu* sections.
- *Qui tollis* is set in the style of a chorale. Analyse the harmony here, looking for chord movements, cadences and types of dissonance.
- The second movement reaches a very impressive climax on *Rex caelestis*. What contributes to its power?

■ Chamber music from Mendelssohn to Debussy

Mendelssohn wrote his first string quartet in 1823 and Debussy wrote his final sonata in 1917, so the period of study can be assumed to lie between these dates. Chamber music is written for a small ensemble playing with one person to a part. The name implies that chamber music is played at home for the enjoyment of the players, but it became more common to perform chamber works in concert during this period. The term can include:

- sonatas for piano and one other instrument, such as violin sonata or clarinet sonata

The Beethoven Trio: Russian-born US violinist Isaac Stern (1920 - 2001) in rehearsal with pianist Eugene Istomin and Leonard Rose, November 1961

- piano trios, quartets and quintets (for piano, violin and cello, plus viola, plus second violin)
- combinations of string and wind instruments, such as clarinet quintet or horn trio
- string quartets, quintets and sextets
- other combinations of a similar nature: for example, Schoenberg's String Quartet No. 2 (1907) includes a soprano voice in two of its movements.

During the latter part of the 18th century the most common forms of chamber music were the violin sonata, the piano trio and the string quartet. It is an interesting feature of this area of study that composers experimented with so many different chamber combinations. This reflects the growing versatility and importance of the piano and changing circumstances of performance, but it is still true that most chamber works were written to be played by the composer and friends. Mendelssohn was a virtuoso pianist; Schumann's piano parts were written for his wife, Clara; and Brahms wrote chamber music for his violinist friend, Joseph Joachim.

The most important composers of chamber music in this period were Mendelssohn, Schumann, Brahms, Dvořák, Ravel and Debussy. The works discussed in this chapter are chosen to introduce some of these composers, and to illustrate different combinations of instruments and various approaches to composition. It is advisable to listen to a wide range of works and then choose a representative selection for detailed study.

Mendelssohn, *Piano Trio in D minor* Op. 49 (1839)

Form

Four movements. Haydn and Mozart's piano trios have three movements: Beethoven's have four.

I Quick; sonata form

II Slow; ternary form plus coda

III Scherzo, but in a miniature sonata form (develpt. b. 46^2, recap b. 117^2). Little contrast.

IV Quick; rondo/sonata (ABACABA and coda).

First movt dominated by the two main subjects; clear divisions between sections.

First subject b. 1 D minor; Second subject b. 118^3 No exposition repeat; Develpt at b. 222^3, recap at b. 367^3; second subject D major b. 434^3; Coda b. 539^3.

Harmony

Plenty of colourful chords – all of the chords in the A2 specification can be found in the exposition of I: dim. 7ths used for colour b. 38, 41, 43; third inversion chords e.g. V^7d in b. 26; higher dominant discords V^{13} at b. 38^3; augmented sixth in b. 98, 106, 110; Neapolitan sixth at b. 213^1; dim. 7th used to intensify cadence at II/80.

Instrumentation and timbre

A well-established ensemble. Imitation between all instruments. No special techniques apart from brief pizz. in III. Piano particularly virtuosic – fast, needs fluidity and dexterity. Cello introduces both main themes in I. II starts with piano alone like a 'Song without words'.

Hints

- This work is analysed under the headings of the musical elements found in the specification and written in note form. You will also need to hear and understand each movement as a whole. To write an essay effectively you will need to locate each point in the score and learn its sound.

- Abbreviations help to make the notes more concise: for example, $I/221^3$ means first movement, bar 221, third beat.

- Long words can be shortened, such as recap, develpt, movt, appogg.

Melody

Mendelssohn was a noted melodist.

I Long, song-like melodies in I are difficult to develop except by repetition. Therefore a very long movement. Both main subjects based on triadic patterns.

II Again vocal, mostly conjunct.

III 'Fairy music' like Scherzo of *Octet* and from *Midsummer Night's Dream* – a swift and 'fluttering' melody.

IV Strong melody, almost a folk dance.

Rhythm and metre

I $3/4$ time. Melodies seem serene but there is driving momentum from **syncopation** in piano part. Briefly relaxed for second subject but even here there are alternating quavers in piano RH. Closing section of exposition and coda move into triplets, increasing urgency.

II $4/4$ time. Flows easily in semiquavers in A sections; B section b. 32^2 has two-against-three and strong accents.

III $6/8$ time. Very characteristic type of scherzo for Mendelssohn, dominated by one rhythm pattern.

Key terms

Syncopation: shifting the emphasis onto a note or beat that would normally be weak.

IV $4/4$ Also strongly rhythmic. Phrases begin on the half-bar and cadences to the strong beat are very firm.

Texture

All possible combinations of the instruments explored but piano rarely absent and often dominant. Orchestral at times – strings in octaves at I/186, heavy triplets at I/203. Some imitation between strings. III very light (the only movt with any pizz.). Lovely 'disappearing' ending.

Tonality

D minor overall – fits mood of agitation at the beginning.

I First subject in D minor, second subject in A major (dominant key) but changes to A minor in the closing section, including a partial statement of second subject in the minor. Development starts in A minor; second subject appears in B♭ (b. 263^3), C major (b. 311^3) and A major (b. 327^3). Recap. has main subjects in D minor and D major but coda turns frequently from major to minor and finally ends in D minor.

II B♭ major (turns to the subdominant side – normal). A warm, reassuring key. Middle section in B♭ minor and D♭ major.

III D major; second subject A major; devlpt moves through E min, F♯ min, C maj, B min quickly. Recap all D major.

IV D major, via F minor to F major for second theme. Third theme (b. 141) in B♭ major. This theme used in coda to help establish D major at the last.

Composer, performer, audience, occasion

Felix Mendelssohn 1809–47; German composer. Trio written in 1838. Piano part for Mendelssohn, violin probably Ferdinand David (Violin Concerto for him as well). Mendelssohn living in Leipzig as conductor of famous Gewandhaus Orchestra. Very well known as composer, conductor, pianist. Played chamber music at home with family as a boy and later with friends. One later piano trio; seven string quartets (three in 1838/39); string octet also remarkable – unusual and ambitious form, written 1825 (composer was 16).

Your personal view

All these details have still not said everything about the Trio. Your personal view of the piece is important and the examiners will be looking for evidence that you have heard and remembered the sound of the music. Make a note of your own impressions. These may change as your study progresses, so add to them when you hear the piece again later in the course.

Schumann, *Piano Quintet in E♭* Op. 44 (1842)

Robert Schumann 1810–1856; German composer. Schumann also lived in Leipzig and was a friend of Mendelssohn but was known more as a music critic and writer than a composer at the time. Wrote three string quartets and this quintet in 1842. The first ever use of this combination of instruments – piano plus a string quartet. Later examples by Brahms, Dvořák, Franck. First performance at home. Pianist was Clara Schumann, the composer's wife; violinist Ferdinand David (see above). Mendelssohn once sight-read the piano part in a performance when Clara was ill.

First movement

Allegro brillante in E♭ major and $2/2$ time. In sonata form with repeated exposition. Strong opening statement. Theme lends itself to fragmentation and development in motifs. Ambiguity of key from the beginning because of D♭ in second chord, and first cadence to E♭ is instantly contradicted (b. 9). Constantly suggesting a key and moving away – G♭ major b. 27 is very effective. Second subject b. 27 is short and immediately echoed in inversion, then used in sequence. Close of exposition based on first subject. Link passage at beginning of development returns in II/85.

Development based on opening of first subject, constantly modulating. Harmonic development here, where Mendelssohn's was melodic. Recapitulation b. 207. Texture changed but not the harmony until b. 236. Small adjustment allows second subject to return in the tonic, as expected. Rhythm – accents appear to shift the bar line in codetta from b. 320. Gives emphasis to the cadence in b. 331². Rhythm features of this type become common in Brahms.

Second movement

In the style of a funeral march in C minor and in $2/2$ time. The opening E♭ octave links with the previous movement and helps the transition of key – no cadence to C min until b. 10. Melody passed between instruments but dark colours emphasised (low violin and viola). Regular four-bar phrases but phrases overlap at b. 17. ABACABA pattern.

1–29 A Effectively **binary form**. Note change of harmony in repeat of *A* (b. 4⁴). Moves to B♭ min and F min in second half.

29–61 B Gentle contrast with three-against-four rhythms. Violin and cello mirror each other, then play in octaves. Rounded binary form shape – slight change at end of *A* in repeat (b. 37²–45¹) *A* returns at the end of *B* – marked by octaves in violin and cello. C major; passes through E minor.

61–92 A Exact repeat of *A* in C minor, plus link passage borrowed from I/116.

92–109 C Agitato in F minor – replaced an A♭ episode at Mendelssohn's suggestion. Triplets; strong accents on second beat; imitation between piano and strings at one bar distance adds to energy. Written-out binary form: first section repeats at b. 96 an octave higher.

109–132 A returns but surrounded by *agitato* material.

132–164 B repeated, but in F major.

164–193 A begins in F minor and moves back to C minor. Final cadence extended. Picardy third at end.

Third movement

A scherzo with two trios in E♭ major, ⁶/₈ time. Very swift and energetic. Features rising and falling scales.

1–44 Scherzo in **rounded binary form**. First half modulates to dominant (B♭ major); second half passes through A♭, B♭ and C majors. Strong emphasis on chords I–IV–V–I in first half, all over tonic pedal. Piano often in octaves.

44–75 Trio I. Rounded binary form. G♭ major. Features falling fifths and imitation between strings.

75–121 Scherzo. As opening, but with a two-bar link at the beginning, and without repeats.

121–195 Trio II. A♭/G♯ minor. Sudden move to ²/₄ time and folk-dance style. Pairs of strings in octaves play rushing semiquavers, based on same chord sequence (I–IV–V–I) as opening of scherzo. Middle section (b. 145–181) uses motif of rising and falling fifths, inverted from Trio I. Notation complicated because of enharmonic notation: e.g. b. 177²–181¹ is in C♯/D♭ minor.

195–264 Scherzo. Exact repeat in E♭ major to b. 239; Coda over a tonic pedal. N.B. Timbre of final chord – high piano and low strings.

Fourth movement

A long movement in **rondo** form, plus an unexpected contrapuntal conclusion. Main theme modulates to the dominant in each statement so key changes frequently.

Main returns of theme:

- *b. 1* C minor
- *b. 29* G minor
- *b. 77* E minor
- *b. 136* C♯ minor
- *b. 164* E♭ minor

■ *b. 212* C minor

■ *b. 248* C minor – as theme of a fugato

Episodes:

■ *b. 21* new idea, perhaps derived from I/29–30

■ *b. 51* Subsidiary theme in G major. Developed in b. 114–136; returns in b. 186–204 and 274–286.

■ *b. 115–130* new melodic idea combines with subsidiary theme. Returns in b. 272–288.

Two contrapuntal episodes at the end:

■ *b. 248–266* Fugato, combining opening theme with a running countermelody. Five entries, alternately in C minor and G minor.

■ *b. 321–371* Fugal exposition and stretto, combining first subjects of first and fourth movements (fourth movt theme adapted).

Entries in piano, violin I, viola, cello; false entries in violin I, violin II and violin I again. B. 355 begins stretto at two bars, moving around the cycle of fifths Bb–Eb–Ab–Db–G–C–F . Long coda to re-establish Eb major.

Your personal view

Remember to add your impression of the piece to your notes. It is particularly valuable if you have experience of hearing it performed live.

Points for further investigation

■ Thematic links between movements could be explored.

■ Use of tonality. The key changes frequently and the range of keys used is wide.

■ The importance of counterpoint, and contrapuntal techniques, such as inversion, imitation, and combination of themes.

Brahms, *Clarinet Quintet in B minor* Op. 115 (1891)

Write a brief programme note for a chamber work you have studied, including information on its form and context.

Towards the end of Schumann's life he was introduced to a 20-year-old pianist called Johannes Brahms, who played to him songs, piano pieces and string quartets that he had composed. Schumann immediately wrote a magazine article naming him as 'one man who would bring us mastery'. The two composers became friends, and Clara Schumann helped to introduce many of Brahms' works to the public. Brahms was born in Hamburg in 1833 and is regarded as a direct successor of Beethoven. He wrote symphonies, concertos, songs, piano music and *A German Requiem*. Brahms published 24 chamber works; many early works were deliberately destroyed by the composer. The chamber music

> **Hint**
>
> Here the analysis is presented in essay form. Compare the description to the music as you listen and make notes movement by movement as shown above. Later on, you will also need a revision sheet using the specification headings.

that survives was written over a long period, from 1854 to 1894, and includes piano trios, quartets and a piano quintet. There are works for four, five and six string instruments, and sonatas for violin and cello. Like Mozart, Brahms was inspired to write a clarinet quintet because he heard a particularly fine player. This was Richard Mühlfeld, who also received a clarinet trio and two sonatas from the composer.

The *Clarinet Quintet* is dated 1891 and is a warm, relaxed work in spite of its minor key. The clarinet is part of the ensemble rather than a prominent soloist, and Brahms explores the colours of its different registers expertly. There are four movements: the second in B major is slow, the third is a gentle type of scherzo and the fourth a set of variations.

Brahms was a master of traditional forms, and the first movement is a clearly defined sonata form. The key of B minor is not confirmed by a perfect cadence until bar 18, and the opening suggests D major, both melodically and harmonically. The transition (b. 25) is more marked rhythmically but the flowing style returns for the D major second subject (b. 36). The exposition demonstrates Brahms's skill as a melodist, and his liking for cross-rhythms that appear to shift the bar line temporarily (b. 58–66). The development uses two subsidiary themes from the exposition but is mainly based on the semiquaver pattern from bar 1, complete or broken into shorter motifs. The recapitulation follows the expected course except for the return of the second subject in G major. There is a short coda where the first subject is harmonised with sudden intensity (b. 195) but the movement ends peacefully.

The opening of the B major slow movement is another example of rhythmic complexity, although the effect of the overlapping rhythms is to produce a quiet background in which the effect of strong beats is softened. The middle section, back in B minor, is the only part of the work that makes virtuoso demands on the clarinettist. It is easy to miss the fact that the florid clarinet line is based on the falling phrase in the first bar of the movement. The return of the A section is disguised (b. 87) so that the calm melody is only noticed when it has begun.

There are further subtle connections in the remaining movements: the opening of the third movement is transformed into the Presto theme, and the fifth variation of the finale (in $3/8$ time) leads into a return of the mood and melody of the work's opening.

Dvořák, *Piano Trio Op. 90 in E Minor (Dumky)* (1891)

Background

Antonín Dvořák was born close to Prague in 1841 in the area then called Bohemia. He learned the violin as a boy and then studied for two years at the Prague Organ School, supporting himself by taking pupils. He played the viola professionally in an orchestra and began to compose with increasing success, helped by the friendship and support of Brahms. By the end of his life he had written nine symphonies, operas, church music, piano works, and concertos for cello and violin. There is also a large body of chamber music including two piano quintets, eleven string quartets and four piano trios. He conducted in England on 11 occasions, and paid two extended visits to America, where he was Director of the National Conservatory for Music for more than two years.

In spite of his travels, Dvořák was fiercely proud of his home country of Bohemia and the *Dumky Trio* expresses this. The word *dumka* (plural *dumky*) means reminiscence or meditation and Dvořák used it as the title of movements in several works, usually following a slow and nostalgic

Hint

This section assumes that you have studied one or two earlier chamber works by different composers and helps you to find out about this trio for yourself. Be prepared to compare this work with the Mendelssohn *Piano Trio* or a similar work to show how styles have developed over time.

section with a more lively contrast. This trio is unusual because it consists of a succession of six movements, all in the *dumka* style. Dvořák played it on a farewell concert tour before leaving for America in 1891. The violinist was Ferdinand Lachner and the cellist Hanuš Wihan, for whom Dvořák wrote his *Cello Concerto*. The composer played the piano.

What to look for

This trio was written more than 50 years later than the Mendelssohn Piano Trio. Dvořák's background, and the date of the work, suggest three main questions about it:

- Are there signs of Bohemian nationalism in the music?
- How is the work organised?
- Is there any development in the use of instruments?

Nationalism

National features could occur in imitations of folk melody or the rhythms of folk dance. You will find examples of modal melodies, irregular phrase lengths and dance sections that come to an exciting climax. Look out for pedals representing the drone of a folk instrument, and for other sounds that suggest percussion or imitate other instruments. Folk musicians often improvise: are there any passages that suggest this? What is the emotional quality of the slow sections?

Organisation

The composer has avoided the usual four-movement structure. What has he put in its place? What are the key relationships within the movements, and what changes are made from movement to movement? Is it true to say that the trio is 'in E minor'? Are there are any musical links between the slow and fast sections of each movement?

Use of instruments

Are the instruments evenly balanced or is one of them more prominent? What are the technical demands made on each player? Note any passages where the instruments use special techniques and describe their effect. Look for interesting timbres, such as extremes of range, and consider what effect the composer was trying to achieve.

Debussy, *Sonata for Cello and Piano* (1915)

Background

The composers described earlier in this area of study belonged to a continuing tradition in which each was personally known to his successor. Claude Debussy does not belong to this group, although he probably knew many of their works. Debussy was a French composer, born near Paris in 1862 and, like Dvořák, he was proud of his nationality. He resisted suggestions that he had adopted ideas from Wagner and disliked classifications of his music such as 'Impressionistic'. He was renowned for the subtlety and sensitivity of his piano playing, and famous for piano pieces, songs, orchestral music and the opera *Pelléas et Mélisande*. He died in March 1918 during the bombardment of Paris. The sonata could be approached as shown below:

Form

There are three movements entitled *Prologue*, *Serenade* and *Finale*, the second and third being linked. Identify the main melodic ideas in each movement, look for any re-appearances and devise an outline plan of each movement. Do not expect them to conform to a fixed plan.

Note down the key or tonal centre each time an idea returns. What features give unity and shape to each movement?

Harmony

Select some short passages and analyse the chords used and the types of chord progression: for example, I/bars 1–4, II/fig. 5 for six bars, III/bars 1–3, or any other passage where the sound interests you. What chords does Debussy use at cadences?

Instrumentation and timbre

Find examples of interesting use of the cello: the second movement will provide many examples. What is the effect of the cello's first entry in the *Prologue*? Identify passages where the piano has a distinctive sound, and look for different relationships between the cello and the piano. How does the use of the cello compare with its use in works by Dvořák and Brahms 25 years earlier? Describe the differences in the use of the piano between Debussy and Schumann or Mendelssohn.

Melody

How does the melody quoted below grow out of its first idea?

Look for this idea elsewhere in the movement. Write out at least one main theme from each movement and investigate its phrase structure and other characteristics.

Rhythm and metre

What replaces the normal quick–slow–quick pattern in this sonata? Consider the effect of the rhythmic changes in the first and second movements. Where does the music imply a regular pulse, and where and how is this lost?

Texture

Which predominates, harmony or counterpoint? Is it always true that the piano is a harmonic instrument and the cello melodic?

Tonality

Study the examples of melody and harmony you have copied out and discover what scales or modes they imply.

Composer, performer, audience, occasion

The cello sonata was the first of a planned set of six, and was completed in 1915 during a summer vacation near the coast. Debussy's letters of the period are a valuable source to discover his state of mind about the war and his deteriorating health. You could also investigate what became of the planned set of six sonatas to which this work belongs.

Your personal view

Remember to record your own impressions when you first hear it and when you know it well.

■ Four decades of jazz and blues 1910–50

Defining jazz

Most books on jazz begin with an attempt to define it, and there are as many definitions as there are books. At its beginning, jazz was an improvised style played in dance halls by groups or 'combos' of predominantly black musicians in New Orleans. During the period of study all of these features changed. Improvisations were written down for swing orchestras, and jazz moved out of the dance hall and into the concert hall, with more emphasis on solo performers. Jazz was adopted by musicians of any race or nationality and it spread throughout America and across to Europe. The single feature on which everyone is agreed is the development of 'swung' rhythms, which are explained below. For this area of study the definition of jazz can be broad, especially as it includes the influence of jazz on classical composers. One view of jazz is that it is more a style of playing than a defined repertory of music. The best approach for the examination is to study the performances of the great jazz musicians of the period, whatever they chose to play.

Studying jazz

This topic needs a different approach from the other alternatives because our knowledge of jazz and blues in the period 1910–50 relies more on recordings than on scores. Piano rags were written down and published, but after that we are largely dependent on recordings until the era of the swing band. The first jazz recording was made, not in New Orleans, but in Chicago in 1917. There is also a gap in recording from 1942 to 1944 during a dispute over royalties. Because of this there are no recordings of the early stages of bebop.

The best approach is to learn the main features of jazz styles and then to analyse tracks aurally. Some jazz standards have been interpreted by many different jazz musicians, and you can highlight their individual features by comparing versions. Keep a summary sheet of each track that you analyse and build up an anthology of examples. It will be helpful to listen to these tracks regularly so that you can easily recall their style and sound.

Features to listen for

The specification lists musical elements that can be applied to jazz as well as to classical music. Examination questions may focus on one or more of these elements, so it is useful to organise your notes under these headings.

Form

Ragtime was based on dances such as the mazurka and quadrille, and it follows their form. A main tune in regular four-bar phrases is played several times with episodes between. These are in the same style but have contrasting melodies and keys, typically making an ABACA pattern. There may be a short introduction and coda.

Jazz and blues numbers are built up by playing variations on a piece known to all the players. This piece can be a short sequence of chords, a complete song, or a specially composed jazz number. Variations were originally improvised, with every performance created afresh. Larger ensembles, such as swing orchestras, played from written arrangements, although these, too, may have scope for improvised breaks. The most common patterns are the blues and song form.

Blues has a 12-bar pattern, with three lines of four bars each. The simplest form of 12-bar blues uses primary triads only. In C major the pattern would be:

C		C		C		C⁷	
F		F		C		C	
G⁷		G⁷		C		C	||

By the end of the period of study this pattern could be greatly elaborated by adding notes to the chords, adding more chords in each bar or by replacing the basic chords with chromatic alternatives.

Song form was used for many of the show songs on which jazz pieces were based. It has 32 bars, made up of four eight-bar phrases. The most common pattern for the four phrases is AABA but some songs use ABAC or ABCD patterns.

Harmony

Jazz harmony is complex but it needs a notation that can be read and remembered quickly. Chords are named by their bass note with indications to show the notes above it. The example shows some of the chords that could be based on the note C with their notation.

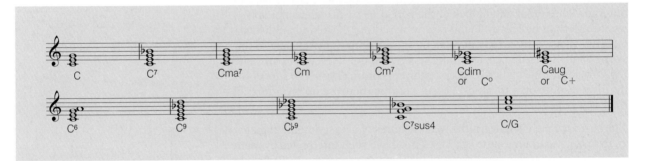

Note:

- Sevenths are assumed to be minor unless shown to be major.
- All other added notes are diatonic (belong to the key) unless stated in the chord name.
- C/G means 'a C chord over bass note G'. This would be a second inversion in classical notation.
- A small superscript circle⁰ means a diminshed chord; a plus sign+ is the convention for an augmented chord.

The sound of a jazz number comes from its chord choices and from characteristic chord moves or 'changes', which are often chromatic in the second half of the period. Songs by Jerome Kern and George Gershwin became popular jazz standards because of their interesting chord changes. A soloist can intensify the harmony in a solo improvisation by adding a 9th, 11th or 13th to a simple chord.

Some of the changes in harmony over the period can be seen in a comparison of *Tiger rag*, recorded by The Original Dixieland Jazz Band in 1917 and one of Duke Ellington's compositions, *Mood indigo*, from 1931.

Tiger rag *uses primary triads and infrequent chord changes until the 'turnaround' at the end. There are only four chromatic chords; two of these include the 'blue' third (Bb) in the final phrase of the melody.*

This extract from Ellington's Mood indigo *shows the richly coloured chords of the 1930s. There are chromatic moves in the melody and between chords.*

Instrumentation and timbre

Early jazz groups used cornet, trumpet, trombone and clarinet as solo instruments, with increasing use of saxophone. The tuba in early groups was later replaced by a plucked string bass. Piano, and guitar or banjo, provided a rhythm section, with drums. The piano emerged from the background later, and some bands had guitarists who could take solos. From the first, players were experimenting with the sounds of their instruments, and brass instruments developed a variety of mutes to colour their tone. Later, Dizzy Gillespie's unusual 'bent' trumpet was created to make the tone more penetrating.

Ensembles gradually grew in size. The sound changed from a small group of individual players to larger ensembles, with brass, reed and rhythm sections. Jelly Roll Morton and his Red Hot Peppers were seven in number. Fletcher Henderson's Orchestra had 10 or 12 members, and Count Basie expanded to 15 in the mid-1930s. Duke Ellington's band in 1940 also had 15 members: six brass (three trumpets and three trombones), five reeds (two alto saxophones and one each of clarinet, tenor sax and baritone sax) and four rhythm (piano, guitar, string bass and drums).

The development of bebop in the 1940s was marked by a reduction to small groups again, such as a five-man combo of saxophone, trumpet, piano, bass and drums. Many swing orchestras reduced in size, or disbanded, because it was difficult to continue in wartime.

Most jazz players developed an individual style and sound and you will begin to recognise, not just the instrument playing, but the name of the player, when you have heard a good selection of their work. Duke Ellington composed his works to highlight the qualities of the members of his band, some of whom stayed with him for many years.

Melody

The melody of jazz numbers is often vocal in origin, but it can be elaborated in any way by a soloist. Each new chorus (repeat of the chord sequence) challenges the improvising soloist to depart further from the basic melody. At first, the melody will be recognisable but the player is free to paraphrase it or replace sections with new melody. The only requirement is to remain faithful to the chord changes. Some jazz musicians develop characteristic melodic shapes that they use frequently.

The melody may be varied in rhythm or pitch. Ornamentation and chromatic notes may be added. In some cases, a completely new melody can replace the theme. Sometimes the melody is used for virtuoso display at extremes of the range.

Rhythm and metre

Jazz numbers of this period usually have two or four beats in a bar. The underlying pulse is firm and steady, allowing variation and complex rhythms above. Quaver patterns are 'swung', which means they are played with a relaxed, uneven feel, almost like triplets. This is sometimes known as a 'ten-to-ten' rhythm because the words give an idea of the effect. Swung quavers are difficult to notate exactly so they are usually written 'straight' and the instruction to play with swing feel given at the beginning of the piece.

There are other rhythmic characteristics in jazz, such as syncopation, which places a strong accent on a weak beat of the bar. Anticipation causes a note to be played just before its expected beat. Latin American rhythms are also found in jazz numbers.

Texture

Ragtime has a distinctive texture of a syncopated melody over a leaping, quaver-rhythm bass. Early jazz has a firm bass line and rhythm section supporting short improvised solos. If several soloists improvise simultaneously the result is a complex counterpoint above the bass. Piano textures are often distinctive to the player and can help to identify a particular pianist.

In the 1920s, soloists such as Louis Armstrong were featured more strongly within their combos. The swing bands of the 1930s often used brass, reeds and rhythm sections in answering blocks of sound, but some arrangers introduced more variety and interplay of individual instruments. The smaller groups of bebop brought back the textures of the early 1920s, but with very different musical styles.

Tonality

The majority of jazz standards of this period are in major keys, and the range of keys is smaller than in classical music, rarely venturing beyond three sharps or flats. Flat keys are preferred because clarinet, trumpet and saxophones are transposing instruments in B♭ or E♭. The sound of the major key can be affected by the use of 'blue notes', a slight flattening of the third and seventh notes of the major scale. This often hints at a darker or less certain mood. Melody may also use modes and forms of the pentatonic scale.

Composer, performer, audience and occasion

If a jazz musician writes and performs his own material, the identification of the composer is simple. More often, there are several contributors to a jazz performance. The composer of the original standard and the player who improvises on it are both contributing to the final result, and there are three people involved if the standard was arranged before performance. In the act of improvisation one member of a group may pick up an idea begun by another and the reaction of the audience may spur them on to create new variations. It is sometimes difficult to separate composer, performer, audience and occasion.

The popularity of jazz was helped enormously by the simultaneous development of sound recording. This introduced jazz to a world-wide audience, and recording royalties helped to sustain some bands through difficult times, such as the Second World War. It is important to remember that we have comparatively few recordings of early groups, so we can only speculate about parts of the history of jazz. The Original Dixieland Jazz Band, who were persuaded into a recording studio in Chicago in 1917, can hardly have thought that their performances would be studied a century later on the other side of the world.

The four decades

1910–20

In this decade, *ragtime* declined, *blues* continued and the term *jazz* was first used.

Ragtime is a style of composition and piano playing that is instantly recognisable, with a striding left hand part and a syncopated right-hand melody. Rags grew out of ballroom dances, marches and songs by composers such as Stephen Foster (1826–54) and they follow the same structure as a march or dance. The most famous ragtime composer was Scott Joplin (1869–1917). His publication *Original Rags* (1899) was immediately popular, and the *Maple leaf rag*, named after the club where Joplin played, sold a million copies. By 1910, Joplin was working as a teacher and composer in New York and he devoted himself to writing a ragtime opera *Treemonisha*. The poor reception of this work probably hastened his death in 1917.

One example which falls into this area of study is Scott Joplin's *New rag*, written in 1912.

This has the regular phrasing, leaping left hand, and right-hand syncopations that are characteristic of the style. The main theme follows a four-bar introduction and the sections follow the pattern ABACDA, with a short link before D and a four-bar coda.

The existence of printed copies does not mean that rag pianists were always faithful to the notation. Some pianists introduced more complex 'jazzy' rhythms into the left-hand parts. Among these was Jelly Roll Morton, who was playing professionally from 1904. Ten years later he led the most successful band in Chicago, but his recordings date from the 1920s (see page 193).

Ragtime developed into *stride piano*, whose greatest players were James P. Johnson and Thomas 'Fats' Waller. You can get a good idea of his style from Waller's composition *Honeysuckle rose*, although this was recorded later.

Fats Waller, *Honeysuckle rose*

This shows Waller's outgoing, fun style, which made his versions of many types of music popular. *Honeysuckle rose* is in 32-bar song form: each *chorus* or repeat of the theme has four lines of eight bars in the pattern AABA. Count the bars, thinking in $2/4$ time. The piano's left-hand part is similar to the style in the Joplin example above. You will soon find it easy to sense the change of line and the beginning of a new chorus. The structure is very clear in the second chorus because the vibes play the 'A' lines and guitar takes the 'B' line. There are six more choruses after this, featuring saxophone (with a repeated piano riff), piano, trumpet, drums, piano and the whole band. Often the featured soloist enters just before the end of the previous chorus.

Blues has a long history and probably preserves some features of African music as well as spirituals and work songs. The tempo is slow and the mood nostalgic, longing for a lost past or a distant happy future. Melody is usually in the blues scale – a major scale with a tendency to flatten the third and seventh notes. This cannot be notated exactly, and it is best to learn its sound by listening to blues performances. The effect is to 'soften' the semitone steps in the scale (making the third and fourth notes, and the seventh and eighth, more than a semitone apart). It also approaches the sound of the **Dorian mode**.

Written blues may alternate the natural and flattened versions of the third and seventh notes to indicate that they are 'blue notes', but in practice the performer will alter them subtly and not by a whole semitone.

Early jazz was an exciting way of playing new or established tunes with a small combo improvising together. The Original Dixieland Jazz Band was a quintet of white players formed in New Orleans and led by Nick LaRocca (cornet). The other instruments were clarinet, trombone, piano and drums. Their fame spread, leading to a move to Chicago, and they played in New York in 1917 on the recommendation of Al Jolson. Their first recording sold a million copies. The band stayed together, with some personnel changes, until 1925, and some of the members returned when Nick LaRocca formed a swing band in 1936. The playing of LaRocca influenced later players, such as Bix Beiderbecke. Once groups were recorded, it became possible for young enthusiasts to model themselves on a player they had never heard live.

The Original Dixieland Jazz Band, *Livery stable blues*

The first jazz recording ever issued featured this number, coupled with *Dixie jazz one-step*. It was recorded in 1917 and is a 12-bar blues with a four-bar introduction and ten choruses. These are arranged in pairs. The third and fourth, and seventh and eighth choruses have more forceful drums. Beginning at number five and number nine, the band plays in **stop-time**, while the clarinet, cornet and trombone imitate the neighing of horses, making it something of a novelty item. Clarinet, cornet and trombone are prominent and the piano very much in the background.

■ Key terms

Dorian mode: the scale made by the white notes on the piano starting on D.

Stop-time: a characteristic feature of jazz in which the band plays on occasional beats, leaving space for a soloist to improvise unaccompanied.

The blues chords begin simply in each chorus, but the second and third lines move round a cycle of fifths to reach the final cadence. The performance sounds improvised but was actually well prepared and rehearsed in detail before recording.

1920–30

In this decade, great soloists emerged as leaders or members (sidemen) of the best bands. Joseph (King) Oliver played cornet in Kid Ory's band in 1918, but then founded Oliver's Creole Jazz Band. Louis Armstrong (1901–71) replaced Oliver in Kid Ory's band and then went to join him in Chicago in 1922. Armstrong, who played cornet and later trumpet, was commonly known as 'Satchmo' and remains unmatched as a soloist for his fine tone and high range. His improvisations were dramatic and often broke away from the original melody to introduce new phrases. He was also an excellent vocalist and scat singer. He was still capable of producing a number one hit in 1964, when he sang *Hello Dolly* and displaced the Beatles from the top of the charts, but his greatest importance was as a jazz improviser. His best recordings were made between 1925 and 1928 with the small groups known as the 'Hot Five' and 'Hot Seven'. The opening solo in *West End blues* is one of the most famous moments in jazz history, but it was probably based on the virtuoso cornet playing he had heard in brass bands.

Other important soloists at this time were the clarinettist Sidney Bechet (1897–1959), and Bix Beiderbecke (1903–31). Beiderbecke, like Armstrong, played the cornet but he specialised in middle range rather than the high notes loved by Armstrong. He had a delicate, dreamy style which was influential later in the 1950s in the music of Miles Davis and Bill Evans. He absorbed the moods and harmonies of Debussy in his compositions, using the whole-tone scale in *In the mist*.

Jelly Roll Morton's Red Hot Peppers, *Grandpa's spells*

This was recorded as a piano solo in 1923, but Jelly Roll Morton arranged it for his seven-piece band in 1928. It is easy to recognise its background in ragtime, but the arrangement is unusual in its variety. Changes of texture are made every few bars, and not just at the end of a chorus.

Louis Armstrong, *West End blues*

Form

Twelve-bar blues with an improvised solo introduction. There are five choruses.

Harmony

Follows the standard blues sequence with some variation, e.g. second line turns to subdominant minor and end of each chorus varies the chords. Piano chorus has more adventurous harmonies with chromatic slips.

Instrumentation and texture

Six players: the 'Hot Five' plus Earl Hines on piano. Clarinet, trombone, banjo, drums, plus Louis Armstrong as lead trumpet and vocals. Armstrong now playing trumpet more than cornet. The five choruses feature trumpet, trombone, clarinet, plus scat vocals, piano solo and trumpet, with piano leading in the final line. NB: second line of fourth chorus is in Earl Hines's 'trumpet style' of piano playing – forceful and in octaves, less pianistic. Surprising to find piano unaccompanied in fourth chorus – tribute to Earl Hines. Note light percussion in second chorus.

> **Hint**
>
> This is a very famous recording, analysed in a number of books on jazz. Here the information is organised under the specification headings to help you to revise and prepare for the examination.

Melody

Many variations on the chord sequence, mostly with short phrases. Armstrong explores high register.

Rhythm and metre

Slow four time, no variation in pulse. Staccato chords establish pulse at first – later it is 'understood' but not always sounded. Double-time by piano and trumpet in some lines. Swung rhythms used by Armstrong – these were a new feature and became accepted universally.

Texture

Clear variation between choruses. Call-and-response between voice and clarinet in third chorus; piano has some stride style in fourth chorus. Trumpet has sustained high pedal note in fifth.

Tonality

Major, without change, but enlivened by chromatic harmonies, especially in piano chorus.

Composer, performers, audience and occasion

Written by Joe Oliver, recorded June 1928 in Chicago. Featured performers are Louis Armstrong (trumpet and vocals), Jimmy Strong (clarinet), Fred Robinson (trombone), Earl Hines (piano). Influential recording – early example of scat singing, and Armstrong's solo introduction admired and copied by many players.

1930–40

Jazz became more widely popular in the 1930s, helped by the availability of recordings and radio broadcasts. The centre of jazz moved again to New York and small combos grew into swing bands, which have fewer opportunities for individual soloists. Some feel that swing is not true jazz because the arrangements were written down, but composers, such as Duke Ellington, sometimes developed their numbers in an improvisation session with the band and then wrote them down. The most prominent bands of this period were those of Duke Ellington (1899–1974), Count Basie (1904–84) and Benny Goodman (1909–86). The 1930s also saw the rise of great song-writers such as George Gershwin, Cole Porter, Harold Arlen and Jerome Kern. Their songs cannot be classed as jazz in their original forms, but they became standards for all the bands. The arrangers enjoyed their inventive, varied chord changes, and their melodies were instantly recognisable. Great songs encouraged great singers such as Bing Crosby, Ella Fitzgerald, Billie Holiday and Jimmie Rushing.

Duke Ellington

Duke Ellington stands alone as the greatest jazz composer of the 20th century. He produced over a thousand compositions, about a quarter of which were written in collaboration with members of his band or other musicians. They cover a huge range of styles, from ragtime and blues to longer, more ambitious works and arrangements of classical pieces. He wrote very specifically for the players in his band, as in *Concerto for Cootie* for his trumpeter Cootie Williams. Williams, along with Bubber Miley, experimented with playing in a 'growl' style and colouring his sound with a variety of mutes. These can be heard on the Latin-American-influenced *Caravan* and in *East St Louis toodle-oo*, which was the band's signature tune until 1941. Johnny Hodges (alto sax) and Joe 'Tricky Sam' Nanton (trombone) were also important members of the band.

Any collection of Duke Ellington recordings will show the diversity of his work. It is interesting to contrast two or more different works from a similar time, such as *Mood indigo* (1930) and *It don't mean a thing (if it ain't got that swing)* (1932). In each case note:

- the complexity of the chord changes
- the overall structure
- the role played by each section of the band and the use of individual instruments from sections
- the style of melody used by each improvising soloist.

As an example of his longer works, you may want to refer to *Reminiscing in tempo*, a four-movement work in slow tempo composed in memory of his mother. The breaks between movements were enforced by the length of a record side. In practice, the piece makes a 12-minute whole, retaining the same tempo and musical ideas throughout.

Count Basie, *Lester leaps in* (1939)

Count Basie's band was famous for its precise rhythm section and its easy swung rhythms. This track was recorded by a small group of soloists with Basie on piano and the rhythm section playing a crucial role in providing the energy behind the performance. It demonstrates a number of standard jazz techniques:

- *Walking bass:* a constantly moving bass line roving around the chord changes.
- *'Comping':* the pianist supplies short chords at the changes, leaving space for the soloists to improvise without competition from the piano.
- *Trading fours:* two soloists alternate at four-bar intervals.

1940–50

Many swing bands struggled to survive in the 1940s. The Second World War brought petrol rationing, midnight curfews and high taxation. The large bands, with mixed-race membership, suffered from racial discrimination in America, at venues, hotels and restaurants, making touring difficult. Sometimes, world-renowned black players were banned from dance halls or had to enter hotels by a rear entrance. When the recording ban was lifted in 1944 it became apparent that small groups playing a new kind of jazz had formed in the meantime. The new style was called *bop* or *bebop* and was a fast and furious style, once again featuring improvisation. It also had complex harmonies and a high level of virtuosity. The greatest players were Charlie Parker (1922–55) on alto sax, Dizzy Gillespie (1917–93) on trumpet, and the pianist Thelonious Monk (1917–82). Parker and Gillespie recorded together in the 1940s and, when they separated, Gillespie was replaced by the young Miles Davis (1926–91). All had careers lasting several decades, but only their recordings up to 1950 need be considered for this examination. Improvisation became freer and more daring, and Gillespie began to feature Latin-American rhythms in his compositions.

Here are some famous examples from the late 1940s, with hints on how to investigate them. If you do not have recordings of these examples you could use similar questions with other tracks from the period.

Duke Ellington and his band performing jazz sacred music at Grace Cathedral, San Francisco, 1965

Dizzy Gillespie, *Cubana Be and Cubana Bop* (1947)

■ The title suggests the influence of Cuban music. How does this appear in the music?

■ Comment on the use of instruments and voices, including the instrumental textures used.

■ Describe the style of the harmony throughout the track. Why is the ending a surprise?

Thelonious Monk, *Misterioso* (1948)

■ How does the idea stated in the introduction (rising sixths) appear later in the number?

■ Make a plan of the form, basing it on 12-bar blues with a four-bar introduction.

■ The piano style is very individual in this piece. Explain its role, referring to melody, harmony and rhythm.

■ What can be said about the textures in this piece?

■ Describe the vibraphone solo.

Looking ahead: Miles Davis, *Israel* (1949)

This is one of the first examples of 'cool jazz', which developed further in the 1950s. Miles Davis used a nine-man group with four brass (including French horn and tuba), two reeds (alto and baritone sax), piano, bass and drums. There was no tenor sax, and no guitar. The saxophonists were Lee Konitz and Gerry Mulligan. Konitz played with a softer sound than Charlie Parker, exploring high register and using a slower vibrato. *Israel* is again based on 12-bar blues and has a complex contrapuntal texture.

The meeting of jazz and classical styles

Jazz and classical styles met in two ways. The longer works of Duke Ellington moved towards a concert style, such as the suite *Black, Brown and Beige*, first performed in 1943 in Carnegie Hall. This was his first extended work and it has a serious subject: the history of black people in North America. Several classical composers moved towards jazz by introducing elements of jazz rhythm, harmony or instrumentation into their works. Examples include:

- piano pieces by Debussy, such as *Minstrels* and *The Golliwog's Cakewalk*
- Stravinsky's *Ragtime for Eleven Instruments*, *Piano-Rag-Music* and *Ebony Concerto*
- the ballet *La Création du Monde* by Darius Milhaud
- *Piano Concerto in G* by Ravel.

Between these two directions stands George Gershwin, who began his career as a pianist demonstrating songs for sale, and in later years took composition lessons from Arnold Schoenberg. He wrote three pieces of 'symphonic jazz': *Rhapsody in Blue*, *An American in Paris* and *Piano Concerto in F*.

Gershwin, *Piano Concerto in F* (1925)

The concerto was commissioned immediately after the success of *Rhapsody in Blue* and written in 1925. By this time, Gershwin was sufficiently confident to orchestrate the work himself, and he adopted a classical pattern of three movements, quick, slow and quick. Jazz rhythms are evident from the fifth bar and the orchestration often favours the woodwind or brass sections as contrasting blocks of sound. The first movement follows the outline of sonata form, saving the main theme for the piano in a dramatic entry beginning with a two-octave glissando.

The second subject follows at fig. 9, development at fig. 14 and the recapitulation, marked *Grandioso*, is at fig. 29.

The slow movement rests the piano at first and gives a long, bluesy solo to the trumpet, which is later muted with a felt hat. The accompaniment to this theme, for two clarinets and bass clarinet in parallel harmonies, is exactly like the reed section of a swing orchestra. The tempo picks up when the piano enters, and a further theme builds to a grand ending.

The finale is fast and exciting with its own themes, but gradually ideas from earlier movements are woven into the new tempo. The third theme from the slow movement appears at fig. 13, the piano's second movement theme at fig. 19. Continuing to work backwards, the *Grandioso* idea from the first movement is heard at fig. 22 and the opening timpani strokes return in the final bars.

■ Types of questions

Before you begin

You will be asked to write your answer as an essay and there will be a choice of questions. Tell the examiner which question you are answering by writing down its number. There is no need to write out the question, but you should read it carefully and consider exactly what is being asked before beginning. Allow time to plan your answer, as a well-constructed argument will save time and score more marks than a collection of observations, even if they are correct. Much of the advice given in Chapter 12 also applies here, but there are some extra points to consider.

Understanding the question

As for the set work, there are several types of question that may be asked:

- Writing a detailed account of one work from the area of study, including its context: 'Choose one chamber work which marked a new departure in style or form during the period. Give an account of your chosen work.' Describe the whole work in your answer, but leave plenty of time to highlight and explain the new features.

- Writing about the use of one or two musical elements, such as rhythm or instrumentation in a number of different works: 'Show how the size and composition of jazz ensembles changed between 1920 and 1950. What effect did these changes have on the arrangement of the music?' Refer to specific examples at each stage.

- Discussing the work of one important figure of the period: 'Assess the contribution of one composer to the development of choral music during the period.' Choose carefully. It would be possible to discuss a composer who wrote a number of works over a period, or a single work which was very influential.

- Responding to an opinion in a quotation: 'Mendelssohn played the piano because it was his nature. He possessed great skill, certainty, power and rapidity of execution [and] a lovely full tone (F. Hiller).' 'Explain how the style or form of the chamber works you have studied were affected by the players for whom they were written.' The quotation is rather distracting here. You may write about Mendelssohn's works and refer directly to the quotation, or you could choose any other composer and describe the context and technical demands of the music.

Writing the essay

Here are some practical points to help you:

- Because you are free to make your own choice of works from the period you must identify clearly the works you are discussing. References to 'the Dvořák quartet', 'the Howells *Magnificat*' or 'the Ellington number' do not give enough information for the examiner to check that what you say is accurate. In Options A and B name the key, title or opus number of the work and in Option C name the performers, the title and the approximate date, if possible.

- Use your essay plan to measure out the time you spend on each section. It is better to cover the whole question than to spend too much time on one part. Allow time to write out musical examples and to check through at the end.

■ Your mark could be reduced by poor use of language. The examiner will be looking for accurate spelling and grammar and well-constructed sentences. Use paragraphs to structure your writing, and use technical language and musical terms correctly and precisely. Aim for a flowing style of writing that reads easily.

■ It is important that your handwriting is legible. If you are concerned about this, experiment with different pens beforehand to find a type that is reliable, comfortable and has a suitable thickness of nib. Writing can also deteriorate if your hand and arm become cramped when writing for some time at speed. Stop briefly and relax your hand, arm and shoulder if this happens. A slight change in sitting position may help.

14   Developing your composing skills for A2

Learning objectives:

■ to understand and use more complex chords

■ to learn the distinctive features of one or more musical styles and apply them in practice, or develop a consistent style of your own

■ to learn to structure longer pieces.

Key terms

Tonal system: the system of major and minor keys used in much recent Western music.

Modal system: music based on other types of scales such as the Renaissance modes and folk scales.

The additional chords needed for this unit – listed in the specification – are covered in this chapter. Features of style and advice on structure can be found under the relevant brief in Chapter 15.

Harmony

When we analyse harmony for the examination it is useful to remember that we are trying to describe a process that was probably instinctive for the composer. Composers were not working from textbooks when they created new and adventurous sounds, and the labels given to chords are only for the convenience of later students and commentators. Sometimes a modern-day analysis would mean nothing to an earlier composer who may have been thinking in a **modal** rather than a **tonal system**, or building chords on a harmonic bass rather than planning chords below a melody.

Some chords and progressions are so widely accepted that they can be categorised and named, but there will always be passages of music that defy analysis because they were not created in a calculated way. However, analysis can be useful for stimulating ideas and discussion for your own compositions. It can also help you understand which passages followed the conventions of the time and which would have startled a contemporary audience.

The specification adds the following more complex chords and progressions at A2 Level.

Third-inversion chords

When a seventh is added to a triad it creates the possibility of a third inversion: that is, an arrangement of the chord with the seventh in the bass. The tendency of the seventh to fall a step to resolve is emphasised in this position, so a third-inversion chord can only be used if the bass can step down into the following chord.

The most common example of this progression is V^7d (the third inversion of the dominant seventh), which resolves to chord Ib.

V⁷d can be used to introduce a modulation from the tonic to the subdominant: for example, the addition of a B♭ below a C major chord leads naturally to Ib in F major and to a cadence in that key.

Major and minor sevenths

The addition of a seventh to the dominant chord is already familiar. It is possible to add a seventh to any other triad in a key, producing minor sevenths on chords II, III, VI and VII and major sevenths on chords I and IV.

In Baroque and Classical harmony, the seventh is regarded as a dissonance and must be prepared by sounding as a harmony note at the same pitch in the previous chord, and resolved by falling a step into the next chord. Resolution rising by a step is also found occasionally.

After chord V⁷, chord II⁷ is the most common example in the Baroque period, often forming a cadence pattern with chord II in first inversion: II⁷b–V–I.

Bach - *Chorale No. 297*

A chain of sevenths can also be produced, where each chord resolves the previous seventh and prepares the next one.

The use of seventh chords became freer during the Romantic period until composers such as Debussy used them as a colour in their own right, without the need for resolution. In jazz, seventh chords are an essential part of the language. In a standard such as Gershwin's *The man I love* there is a seventh in almost every chord. Notes, which would earlier have been regarded as dissonant, feature prominently in the melody.

Key terms

Diatonic: music in which all notes belong to the prevailing key.

Chromatic: music with notes added from outside the key, to give extra colour.

Diminished seventh chords

In a minor key, the seventh on chord VII produces a chord known as the diminished seventh, which has a number of special features:

■ It is the only **diatonic** seventh chord to have the interval of a diminished seventh between its top and bottom notes.

■ The interval between each note and the one above is a minor third.

■ Because of its symmetrical structure it does not change its character when inverted.

■ There are only three possible diminished seventh chords, but they often look different because inverted or notated in different ways.

Bach and his contemporaries used the diminished seventh in its diatonic position as VII^7 in a minor key. The VII^7 resolves to chord I because the bass is the leading note, which needs to rise, and the seventh resolves by falling a step. This is shown in the example from chorale no. 297 on the previous page. It could also arise in passing, as shown below. All diminished intervals tend to resolve by 'collapsing' inwards.

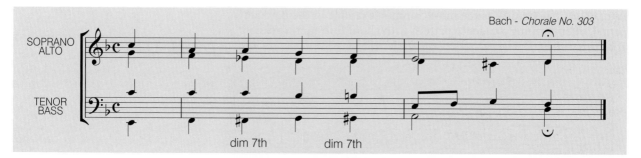

In Classical and Romantic harmony the diminished seventh chord is often used as a **chromatic** chord: that is, as a chord outside the prevailing key. It adds a moment of tension or colour without changing the key, as in this extract from the first movement of Brahms' *Clarinet Quintet*.

The diminished seventh can also be used as an aid to modulation. It can be transformed into any one of four dominant seventh chords by moving one of the notes down a semitone, and this enables passage to a new, often remote, key. In the example below, from Dvořák's 'American' *String Quartet*, a diminished seventh (F#–A–C–Eb) approached from A minor changes into V^7d in C# minor (F#–G#–B#–D#) and resolves into the new key. The only note changed is A moving to G#: other notes are written differently but do not change their sound.

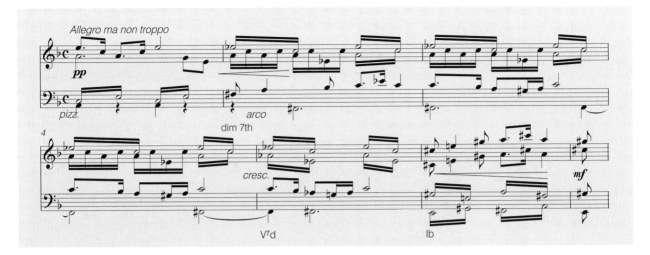

Chromatic harmony

The diminished seventh chord can be used as a diatonic chord (a chord belonging to the key) or as a chromatic chord. The word chromatic means 'colourful', and chromatic chords use notes not belonging to the key to create extra colour.

Major and minor substitutions

The simplest chromatic change is to change a chord from major to minor, or minor to major:

- Chord II is changed from minor to major by sharpening the third in a major key, or by sharpening the third and the fifth in the minor. This commonly happens at a perfect cadence in Bach's chorale harmonisations. Usually, chord II is in first inversion and the chromatic note is contradicted by adding a seventh to the dominant chord.
- At the end of a minor key movement the final chord is sometimes made major. This is known as a Picardy third or *tierce de Picardie*.

Both of these techniques are illustrated in the example below.

It is also possible to change chord IV from major to minor. In a 12-bar blues pattern, the subdominant chord, in bars five and six, is sometimes changed in this way.

The Neapolitan sixth

When chord IIb is used to approach a perfect cadence it can be transformed into a major chord by leaving the third unchanged and flattening the root and fifth. This produces an E♭ major chord in D minor, instead of an E minor chord in the Mendelssohn example shown below.

The chord is said to have originated in operas written in Naples at the end of the 17th century and is therefore called a Neapolitan sixth. It is defined as the major chord on the flattened supertonic. This chord is best used sparingly, but it is very effective in producing a sudden darkening of the sound.

The augmented sixth

A further interesting approach to a perfect cadence is the chord of the augmented sixth. This is based on the sixth note of a minor key or the flattened sixth of a major key (A♭ in C major or C minor). It has three forms, known as Italian, French and German. All add a major third and an augmented sixth above the bass. The Italian form doubles the third, the French sixth adds a fourth, and the German sixth adds a perfect fifth. They resolve to chord V. In the case of the German sixth chord, Ic often precedes V to avoid consecutive fifths.

Heard alone, the German sixth sounds the same as a dominant seventh chord. They can be distinguished by their context, by their notation (F# and not G♭ in the Mozart example) and by their resolution. In a dominant seventh, the seventh note will fall to resolve. In an augmented sixth chord, the augmented interval resolves by moving outwards. In this example, the F# in the treble moves up a step to G and the A♭ in the bass moves down to G. Composers have taken advantage of this ambiguity in modulation. A chord that begins as a dominant seventh can be re-interpreted as an augmented sixth and resolved into a fresh key.

Unessential notes

You could also be asked to recognise unessential notes, such as accented passing notes, suspensions and notes of anticipation in the listening questions.

Like any **passing note,** an accented passing note is a short note moving by step but it falls on a strong beat, making a dissonance with the chord. In the Bach example below the quaver G in the alto at bar 1^2, the quaver C in the treble at bar 2^2 and the quaver B in the treble at bar 2^4 are all accented passing notes.

In the final cadence, the note G in the alto is a **suspension**, prepared at bar 2^4, suspended at the beginning of bar 3 and resolving into chord V on the second beat of the final bar. There are three types of suspension – a fourth above the bass resolving to a third (4–3 suspension), a seventh resolving to a sixth (7–6) and a ninth resolving to an octave (9–8). The 4–3 suspension is the most common, and is shown below.

Further examples of suspensions and of notes of anticipation can be found in Chapter 5 (see page 88 and page 140 (Chapter 11)).

Further examples of suspensions and of notes of anticipation can be found in Chapter 5 (see page 88 and page 140 (Chapter 11)).

Key terms

Unessential note: a note that sounds against a chord to which it does not belong. Examples include **passing notes, suspensions** and appoggiaturas.

Bach - *Chorale No. 5*

The set works and topics for Unit 4 focus on music from the 19th and 20th centuries, and you will find many examples of the chords and techniques described above in them. In the listening questions you may be asked to recognise them. The best way to understand them fully is to practise writing them and listen to the results. They will also give new variety and interest to your composition. They open up possibilities of expressive colour, modulation to distant keys and more adventurous structures that should be explored at this level.

Things to do

Play this extract from Chopin's *Nocturne in F minor* Op. 55 No. 1. You should be able to find in it:

■ a dominant pedal

■ an appoggiatura

■ a chromatic appoggiatura

■ a Neapolitan sixth chord

■ two augmented sixth chords in different keys.

Learning objectives:

Learning objectives:

- to understand the choices available in this unit

- to look at examples that may suggest useful ideas and techniques

- to develop checklists that will help you to monitor and improve your work.

Key terms

Pastiche: writing in the style of an existing composer. The style used could be from an earlier period, for example using the harmonic language of Bach or Mozart, or you could adopt the style of a contemporary band, jazz player or music theatre composer.

Overview of the options

The three options available in this unit will help you develop further the skills you learned in Unit 2. Although Briefs A, B and C in Unit 5 follow on from Briefs A, B and C in Unit 2, you do not have to choose the same type of brief in the second year of the course. The choice will depend on your interests, your performing experience and the development of your compositional skills so far. You should also take into account the advice of your teacher and the future direction of your musical studies after A Level.

The options are:

- Brief A (Compositional techniques): Completion of a chorale harmonisation in the style of Bach, and of a string quartet extract in a classical style.

- Brief B (Free composition or **pastiche**): Composing a single movement, or a group of two or three related pieces, with a total duration of five to eight minutes. There is no restriction on the choice of voices and/or instruments to be used, live or electronic, from a solo instrument to a large ensemble.

- Brief C (Arranging): Arranging a given piece of 'classical' music, from the Baroque period onwards, in a recognised pop, rock or jazz style. The ensemble of voices and/or instruments must include drum kit or percussion, double bass or bass guitar, and guitar or keyboard. It may be for live instruments, electronic sound sources or a mixture of the two. It should last between five and eight minutes.

The three briefs allow considerable flexibility, and the final choice need not be made at the beginning of the year. Studying the Classical string quartet for Brief A might lead to composition of an original quartet movement in pastiche style for Brief B. Experiments in writing in a free rock or jazz style for Brief B might be strengthened by using the given material and submitting an arrangement for Brief C.

In Briefs B and C there is the option of writing an annotation of the composition if it is not possible to produce a score. This has been described in Chapter 7 (see page 109).

In addition, you will need to write a review of the composition, whether or not you have produced a score. This will explain the background to the composition and evaluate its success. There is further advice on writing the review in Chapter 16.

■ Brief A: Compositional techniques

Composers have always learned their craft by studying the work of earlier masters. The study is particularly valuable when great composers have worked at a particular genre over a long period, exploring its possibilities to the full and refining their technique constantly. Bach and Haydn are examples of this, as each remained with the same employer for several decades and both were required to compose repeatedly for the same circumstances and ensembles. The chorale harmonisations of Bach and the string quartets of Haydn, Mozart and their contemporaries, provide an encyclopaedia of compositional practice in the 18th century and teach skills that can be used in any style of composition.

Question 1: Harmonisation of a Bach chorale melody

Johann Sebastian Bach was a devoted member of the Lutheran church from his earliest years as a choirboy. At his death he was still working as an organist, choirmaster and school teacher in Leipzig. He composed for the Lutheran liturgy throughout his life, apart from a short period, from 1718 to 1723, when he worked as a chamber musician.

The singing of hymns, known as chorales, lay at the centre of Lutheran services, and hymns for all occasions in the church year were familiar to the congregation. Bach wove these hymn tunes into many of the cantatas he was required to write, often in elaborate settings for chorus and orchestra and with a different arrangement for each verse. The cantatas also included recitatives and arias for solo voices, setting religious poetry that commented on the Biblical text set for the day. Almost 200 of Bach's cantatas survive, and many more have been lost. Frequently, the final movement of a cantata, summarising its meaning, is a choral setting of the chorale melody. The melody is stated simply and without elaboration, but the harmonising parts are full of interest and very inventive. Similar settings can be found at intervals in Bach's settings of the *Passion according to St John* and *St Matthew*.

Bach's chorale harmonisations were collected and published for study from 1764 onwards. The best way to learn about them is to play or sing them from a printed edition such as the *371 Harmonised Chorales* edited by Albert Riemenschneider, and to listen to them in their original context in Bach's cantatas and passions. They are also available from a website (www.jsbchorales.net) and can be downloaded in score or as a sound file.

General features

■ The melodies are simple and are not by Bach. They are the traditional tunes intended for congregational singing, although Bach's settings are for choir and their range is sometimes more suitable for trained voices.

■ The ends of lines are marked by pauses, indicating cadences.

■ It is clear that Bach chose his harmonies to express the text, but, in many cases, the original text is unknown. No text will be supplied in the examination, and any suitable harmonisation within the style will be accepted.

■ Bach's harmonisations are adventurous and inventive. They must have seemed complex and even shocking to contemporary listeners. Bach's repertory of chords consists of all the root-position and first-inversion chords in the key, and second inversions used at the cadence as Ic V, and in passing during a phrase. Sevenths appear on chords V and II but they are always introduced as suspensions or passing notes, then resolved. Diminished sevenths occur diatonically as VII^7 in a minor key or in passing, as illustrated in Chapter 14 (see page 202). Augmented sixths and Neapolitan sixths are extremely rare in chorales and can be disregarded in this style.

Principles of the style

It is not possible to give hard and fast rules to meet every situation, but a number of principles can be stated to guide you. Bach was not composing from a set of rules and he sometimes made daring or surprising choices, but he would know his choir and their capabilities well. If you choose a selection of examples to study, you will soon discover the essential features of his style:

- Bass lines are important, with a strong sense of direction and a wide range.
- All voices are arranged so that they can sing the words in the style of a hymn.
- The chord usually changes every crotchet, although it may change on a quaver, especially at a cadence. Minims in the melody often have a change of harmony on the crotchet beat.
- Perfect and imperfect cadences are most common, but plagal and interrupted cadences are also found. Cadences are points of strength and often have a leaping bass line. The most common perfect cadence patterns are IIb–V–I and Ib–V–I or Ic–V–I. There are a number of approaches to chord V at an imperfect cadence, including IVb–V, known as the Phrygian cadence.
- In the course of a chorale Bach usually moves through several related keys, although these may not be obvious in the melody.
- Cadences are decorated by passing notes and suspensions.
- A repeated phrase will be re-harmonised on its second appearance.
- Parts may cross if it makes sense to do so melodically. Sometimes the bass line rises above the tenor, but this is because the bass line was doubled by instruments at the octave below. The bass line remains the harmonic bass even when it moves above the tenor.
- A flowing texture is achieved by adding passing notes, auxiliary notes, suspensions and other quaver movement to alto, tenor and bass parts in turn.
- At a perfect cadence Bach often allows the leading note to fall to create a richer sound in the final chord.
- Chorales in a minor key usually end with a Picardy third.
- Certain features are characteristic of the style and can be learned and practised. Examples of common harmonic patterns are given in Chapter 11 (see page 138) and you should become very familiar with these.

An example

Here is a complete chorale as an example of Bach's work. Try these exercises:

- Play the melody alone. You will find that the only essential modulation is to C major in phrase 4. Note how Bach has introduced more interest by suggesting Bb major and G minor.
- Play the melody and bass line together and note how often they move in contrary motion.
- Copy out the cadences and learn their patterns. They are all commonly used by Bach.

■ Compare phrases one and two with phrases five and six.

■ Look for passing notes, accented passing notes, suspensions and a diminished seventh chord.

Bach - *Chorale no. 311*

F major - but Bach hints at B♭major briefly, even in the first phrase.

V⁷b   I

V   V⁷   I
with
suspended 4th

Ib   V   modulating to C major   iib   V   I

passing modulation to B♭ major . . . . .and to G minor

Ib   V   returning to F major.

Strong perfect cadence decorated by a suspension and the dominant seventh

Hint

You will find more examples and exercises on chorales and string quartets in the related online materials.

Question 2: The Classical string quartet

The string quartet (two violins, viola and cello) became the most popular form of ensemble chamber music in the 18th century. It replaced the trio sonata in importance, eliminating the continuo part for a keyboard instrument that was so fundamental to ensembles in the Baroque period. The earliest players would have been groups of friends performing for their own enjoyment, and this tradition continues among string players today. From the 19th century onwards string quartets began to be played in concert. Some of Beethoven's quartets could be attempted only by the finest players of the day, and 20th century quartets by Bartók, Shostakovich, Britten and Tippett are very demanding technically.

String quartet in performance

The style set for the examination belongs to the 18th and early 19th centuries and to domestic performance, although the setting could be grand. Haydn's quartets were written for the magnificent palaces of his employer, Prince Esterházy, but were probably played informally, with the prince sometimes playing the cello part. Mozart's quartets were often tried out at home as soon as they were completed. On one remarkable occasion, the quartet included Haydn as second violinist and the composer playing the viola. Good quartet writing has the atmosphere of a lively and interesting conversation between friends.

General features

- The set question will be an extract from a string quartet movement. The style could be a quick movement, a slow movement or a dance-like minuet or scherzo.

- The parts should be instrumental in range and style. They should not be confined to a narrow compass or to largely conjunct movement as in vocal writing.

- There are many possible textures to explore as the instruments blend so well together. There is a tendency for the first violin to lead and for the viola to play accompanying parts, but important lines can be found in any instrument. Texture changes from phrase to phrase, from four parts, to two or three. A two-part texture could be created by two solo instruments or by two pairs of instruments playing in octaves.

- Playing techniques, such as pizzicato and **double-stopping,** may be included but should not be overused. Discover which double-stops are most effective, and which are difficult or impossible to play.

- The given melody may include decorative appoggiaturas with some chromatic notes. It is important to distinguish between these and accidentals that indicate a change of key.

Key terms

Double-stopping: a string technique in which the player sounds two notes at once on different strings.

The harmonic rhythm depends upon the tempo of the movement. Slow movements will change chord more frequently than quick movements, and the harmony can help to make the triple metre clear in minuets and scherzos. In the example above, the rate of chord change is slow but the energy of the dance is provided by the cello part, outlining chords and adding passing notes. Notice how the articulation of the cello part emphasises the first beat of the bar.

Principles of the style

The phrase structure is clear in classical style. Locate the phrase endings and identify cadences and changes of key at an early stage.

Cadence patterns are often characteristic and you can practise some common patterns. The cadential six–four (Ic–V and Ic–V–I) is very common in Classical style.

The music will modulate to closely related keys, most probably moving to the dominant first. A movement in a minor key may move first to the relative major. Haydn sometimes moves abruptly between the tonic major and tonic minor.

The full range of harmonies described in Chapter 14 can be found in classical string quartets. Chromatic chords are often used to highlight moments of surprise or intensity, which may be indicated by a dynamic such as *sfz*.

Homophonic textures are common, but the instruments are also often independent and may have countermelodies or imitation.

Ideas from the melody may be included in the other parts as accompanying motifs. They can be developed in **sequence** and by inversion, as when a rising scale is answered by a falling scale. More rarely, ideas may be used in augmentation (note values doubled) or diminution (note values halved).

An example

Here is an extract from a Haydn string quartet to study. There are some points to note:

The melody looks complex, but the underlying harmonies are comparatively simple. It is important to distinguish between harmony notes and unessential notes when choosing harmonies: for example, bar 4 needs to end on chord V to lead back to the repeat of the melody in bar 5, so Ab and F are treated as accented passing notes.

There are a number of accidentals in the melody but the key does not change. E naturals belong to the key of F minor, and the F# is a chromatic passing note.

The rhythm of the accompaniment complements the rhythm of the melody, adding the missing strong beats and maintaining the movement when the melody has a sustained note.

Changes in dynamic are not haphazard but are supported by other features of the music. The two *forte* bars occur when the melody reaches its highest point (bar 8) and at the most intense harmony – the German sixth in bar 9. The *piano* marking at bar 10 occurs when the articulation becomes detached and the texture is simplified by viola and cello playing in octaves.

The texture is lightened by rests. An idea which enters after a rest has more effect than the same idea contained in a continuous phrase. There are many instances in Haydn's music where he used silence as a dramatic feature.

Schloss Esterházy in Eisenstadt where Haydn was employed

■ Brief B: Free composition or pastiche

Brief B allows composition for any ensemble, in a structure of your own choice and in any musical language that meets the guidelines of the specification. This is an opportunity to write for your own instrument or for an ensemble with which you are familiar. Whatever the choice, you should make good use of the early part of the course to practise techniques, structures and instrumental textures. Practice exercises can be tried out in performance, and there is much to learn from live sounds and from the comments of your teacher and the performers. By the time the controlled time begins you should have a clear idea of the type of piece you intend to write and of your chosen ensemble.

Genre

Although all genres are permitted, a very small ensemble, such as one or two melody instruments, is restricting. Great skill is needed in this genre to demonstrate the range of harmonies and techniques required at an advanced level. A very large ensemble, such as full orchestra or concert band, will need more time for scoring. Timed practice in advance will make orchestration swifter and will indicate whether you will be able to complete and score a substantial composition in the 20 hours allowed. Electronic compositions also need complete familiarity with the technology in advance, and careful timing. It can be very time-consuming to achieve the correct mix and balance of sounds and this must not take precedence over the need to develop the piece further.

Duration

Constructing a single piece of five to eight minutes' duration is demanding and needs study and experiment. A movement with only one or two themes will require interesting development to reach this length. If more material is used it needs intelligent organisation so that relationships between sections are evident. Examiners are likely to penalise compositions that:

▨ contain unvaried and unnecessary repetitions

▨ appear to be a collection of themes with little sense of direction, or

▨ adopt an unnaturally slow tempo to meet the required duration.

It is useful to study movements of the correct length that feel satisfying and to investigate their construction. Many attractive forms, such as Romantic piano pieces and 1960s pop songs, achieve their aim within three minutes: in the latter case because of the length of a seven-inch single record. Building longer structures needs more advanced skills. The following ideas could help you to construct a longer piece:

▨ Devise melodic material which has a strong character and which has potential for development. It may use a distinctive rhythm or melodic shape which can be used in different ways. Common methods of development are to extend a phrase in sequence, to fragment it, to expand or contract intervals and to use it in inversion.

▨ Use contrasting styles in themes. Sonata form movements often have an energetic, motivic theme as the first subject and a more lyrical melody as the second subject. These can be developed into contrasting sections of the movement.

▨ Control the rhythm to vary tension and release, and to build moments of climax or relaxation.

▨ Modulate to different key areas, making sure that the return to the tonic at the end is secure.

- Vary instrumentation, timbre and texture to reflect structural changes.
- Follow the narrative of a text. This will give a sense of progress, but the musical development must be explicable without reference to the text.
- Vary the intensity of the harmonic language: for example, provide a more complex harmonisation when a theme is repeated.

As an alternative, it is possible to compose a group of two or three related pieces. This would be effective where the genre chosen is naturally short, such as songs, or Baroque dance forms. The group of pieces should be written for the same ensemble but they should demonstrate the same variety and skills as a longer piece, such as in mood, tempo and different structures.

Content

Musical content should go beyond the harmonic vocabulary listed for Unit 2 and explore the chromatic harmony explained in Chapter 14 (see page 200). The choice of harmony will depend on the genre and style chosen, especially if writing in a pastiche style. In this case, you can prepare by analysing the characteristics of the style of your chosen composer. Piano pieces in the style of Bach or Debussy will use different selections of chords, but understanding of chromatic harmony can be shown in both cases. A composition which is confined to primary triads will be penalised. If study of your chosen style reveals a very restricted chord vocabulary it would be wise to choose a more adventurous model.

Brief C: Arranging

This brief is a natural development from Brief C in Unit 2. It may also provide an interesting project if you want to write in a pop, rock or jazz style but are looking for material on which to base your composition. The composition must be in a recognised pop, rock or jazz style. To prepare, you can analyse examples of the style and find its characteristic features. In the review you can explain how you have used ideas and techniques from your chosen style.

Genre

The best approach is to model the piece on the work of a named group, band or combo. The ensemble must include drum kit or percussion, double bass or bass guitar and guitar or keyboard. Any other instruments or voices that belong to the style may be added. The choice of model will guide the structure and style as well as the instrumentation. Jacques Loussier's jazz arrangements usually state their Bach original exactly before breaking into improvisation on it. Apocalyptica's rock arrangement of *The Hall of the Mountain King* by Grieg takes an instantly recognisable fragment and builds a substantially new piece on it. Either of these approaches is possible for the examination.

Duration

Many pop and jazz arrangements are shorter than the minimum of five minutes needed for this composition. The supplied brief is likely to be short and part of the task is to identify ideas within it which can be developed. Suggestions for development can be found under Brief B, in examples of the style you are following, and in the example at the end of this chapter.

Things to do

- Use the music you study in Unit 4 and your own performing and listening to gather ideas for composition.
- Write short practice compositions for the voices, instruments or software you will be using.
- If you are writing for live performers, arrange a workshop performance of your practice pieces and discuss where they are most effective.

Content

The brief and your choice of style will guide much of the content of your composition. In an effective arrangement the listener will usually recognise the original immediately, or after an introduction. Traditional jazz arrangements often begin with a simple statement of the theme or chorus and build successive variations on its chord structure. There is more freedom in pop and rock styles and in later jazz to extract motifs and to transform the structure and pace. Another possibility is to begin with fragments from the original and to work towards a full statement of the theme. An interesting example of this, though not strictly within the requirements of this unit, is *St Thomas' Wake* by Peter Maxwell Davies. It is based on a Pavane by John Bull, which eventually emerges at the end of the piece.

An example

The Schumann piano piece printed below offers a number of possibilities, which can be combined to make a piece of the required duration.

▣ Arrange the music literally for the chosen ensemble.

▣ Re-harmonise or elaborate the melody.

▣ Develop new melodies over Schumann's chord sequence.

▣ Use motifs from the melody such as the rising sixth or the dotted rhythm.

▣ Develop the sequence that begins in bar 9.

▣ Use the triplet rhythm of the inner part as a riff.

▣ Use the first four bass notes (G–C#–D–F#) or the bass notes of bars 9 and 10 as an ostinato.

▣ Extract the first two chords (G major and C#dim 7th) and use them dramatically.

▣ Consider the idea of 'foreignness' in the title and allow it to influence the mood and progress of the piece.

Things to do

■ Choose a classical piece and list all the features that could be used in an arrangement.

■ List the main features of the pop, rock or folk style you are intending to follow in your composition.

■ Write some short practice compositions to experiment with the features you have listed.

■ If you are writing for live performers, arrange a workshop performance of your practice pieces and discuss where they are most effective.

Robert Schumann - *Von fremden Ländern und Menshen (Of Foreign Lands and People)*

Here is the opening of an arrangement of this piece in the style of a Scott Joplin rag. The introduction does not relate specifically to the brief, apart from its use of triplets, but it establishes the ragtime style. Bars 8–15 are built directly on the chord sequence of bars 1–8 in the brief.

16 Writing the review

Learning objectives:

- to learn to review the development of a completed composition and assess its success

- to be able to write informatively about the process of composition and the resulting work.

You must complete the composition process by writing a review of the work to be submitted. The maximum length of the review is 500 words. If time permits, this can be written in the controlled time, when the review process may lead you to reconsider some details of the composition, which can then be altered. Otherwise, you may write the review after the controlled time has ended. No changes can be made to the composition at this stage: the final version will have been submitted and you will have no further access to it.

The purpose of the review is to help the examiner understand your aims and the process of composition. It need not describe features which are obvious in the score, but should illuminate the way in which you reached your final version.

Brief A: Compositional techniques

For Brief A, the review may be comparatively short as the form and style of the compositions are prescribed. It would be useful to discuss any phrases of the chorale where various alternative harmonisations were tried or cadences used which could be treated in different keys. Explain the options that were available and why you made your choice. Point out any features which are typical of Bach's style. In the string quartet, the review should show understanding of the character of the movement, the harmonic structure, and the use of instruments. In both cases, the review should use appropriate technical language and evaluate the success of the harmonisation.

Example comments might be:

Chorale

- I chose an interrupted cadence at this point because I did not want to anticipate the final perfect cadence two bars later.
- I experimented with adding a seventh to this chord but removed it because it could not be prepared.

String Quartet

- The *sfz* mark suggested some emphasis. A chromatic chord was not possible so I used double-stopping.
- My first attempt at this cadence seemed too static so I introduced movement in the cello part.

Brief B: Free composition or pastiche

For Brief B, the review will need to give more information about your aims and choices. The following should be included, if relevant:

- Explain the reasons for your choice of ensemble, genre and harmonic style.
- Give an account of your preparatory work, especially if it had an influence on the finished submission.
- Explain the aim of the piece, the way in which it developed, and any lessons learned in the process.
- If it is intended for particular performers, describe any constraints this imposed.
- Point out any musical features that are not immediately apparent to the listener, such as hidden relationships between themes.
- If the piece is descriptive, give the ideas or text on which it is based.
- In a pastiche composition, name the composer, band, or style on which it is based. List any pieces or tracks that have been studied in preparation. If they are not widely known, include a sample of the style, recorded or in score, with your submission.
- Identify the particular features that have been adopted from your model in a pastiche composition.
- Where a live performance is recorded, account for any differences between the recording and the score, indicating which represents your intentions most closely.

Where an annotation has been written because there is no score for a composition, some of the material for the review may be covered in the annotation. In general, the annotation should describe the content of the composition and how it was composed. The review should explain its background and preparation and evaluate its success. It is not necessary to repeat material from the annotation in the review.

Brief C: Arranging

Much of the guidance for Brief B also applies to Brief C. The following points must be covered in the review:

- Name the pop, rock or jazz style on which it is modelled.
- Provide a sample of the style, recorded or in score.
- Point out particular features of this style that have been included in your arrangement.
- Identify the ideas from the brief that have been used constructively in the composition.
- Explain the plan of the arrangement, if this is not already included in an annotation.
- Discuss any problems that arose and were overcome in the process of composition.
- Evaluate the aims and success of the arrangement.

17 Introduction to performing

Learning objectives:

■ to understand the nature of each of the three options available

■ to understand the administrative requirements in terms of the paperwork needed to accompany the submission

■ to appreciate the method of assessment within this section.

There is a wide choice within this unit and you must, therefore, work to your strengths and spend time considering the possible options. You are required to choose *one* performance option from the three available and it must last between 10 and 15 minutes. You have to choose a programme that shows variety in style, technique, period and/or approach. The options are:

■ (a) solo acoustic performances

■ (b) technology-based performances

■ (c) one solo performance and one technology-based performance – each performance to be at least five minutes.

For the last option, the instruction that you can play one long piece or compile a programme of two or more shorter pieces still holds good: the most important aspect is that of *variety*.

For all options, you can perform one or more of your own compositions if the standard of technical expertise and expressive control is considered suitable: always consult your teacher about this before deciding.

■ What you need to submit

In each case, your performances are to be submitted on CD or minidisk and there will be a candidate record form to complete.

You must also be able to submit either:

■ a score of the music you have played, or

■ a detailed annotation/lead sheet, or

■ a recording of the original work (this is a useful option if you have learnt the piece by listening to the recording rather than using notated music/TAB).

However, you must still make it clear what your role is in the performance so that your part can be identified by using your annotation/lead sheet and listening to the recording of your performance.

If relevant, you must also submit any additional information required by the technology-based options.

■ How the performing options are assessed

Performing is one of the three assessment objectives for all Music specifications. At A2, it is worth 15 per cent of the final A Level grade (30 per cent of the marks available during your A2 year). Many of you will be very good performers and, as at AS, it is hoped and anticipated that you will do well. It is again paramount that you prepare thoroughly and take full account of the requirements of your chosen options.

Assessment objective 1 (performing/realising) requires you to:

> interpret musical ideas with technical and expressive control and a
> sense of style and awareness of occasion and/or ensemble.

These requirements are reflected in the assessment criteria, and you
should read these carefully as you choose your programme and prepare
your performance(s).

Option A: Solo acoustic performances

As for AS Level, these are assessed under four headings:

- level of demand
- accuracy
- communication
- interpretation.

Option B: Technology-based performances

These options have different sets of assessment criteria, though they
remain the same as at AS.

Technology-based performance 1: sequencing and multi-tracking

This is assessed on five requirements:

- accuracy of pitch and rhythm
- use of timbre, balance and panning techniques
- evidence of close attention to performing and expressive detail
- awareness of style required
- ability to use the facilities available within the software and hardware
  to produce a valid result.

(See also Chapter 21, page 236.)

Technology-based performance 2: multi-track/close microphone recording

This is assessed on:

- balance
- dynamic range, including use of compression
- manipulation of mixing desk
- use of effects, such as reverb or delay
- quality of the recording across a wide range of frequencies.

(See also Chapter 21, page 236.)

Option C: One solo performance and one technology-based performance

Here, you have the opportunity to divide your performance assessment
between acoustic and technology-based, though each must last at least
five minutes.

18 Developing your performing skills

Learning objectives:

- ■ to appreciate the ways in which the standard required at AS has increased for A2

- ■ to learn ways of gaining additional skills for the acoustic performances

- ■ to understand the criteria for assessment of acoustic performances

- ■ to learn how to gain the required skills for technology-based performances

- ■ to understand the criteria for assessment of technology-based performances.

AQA Examiner's tip

Try to make early decisions as to where the 'variety' will come within your performance. Remember, you can choose for that variety to be of style, technique, period or approach; or any combination of these.

■ Acoustic performances

Standard of performance expected

The standard of your performances is, naturally, expected to be at a higher level for A2 than it was for AS. This is reflected in the way that marks are awarded for level of demand. Six marks are available – again, a fairly low proportion of the total of 60 – but to achieve even the lowest marks you need to play at about Grade 5 standard. If all the music you perform in Option (a) is at Grade 5 standard, or its equivalent, you will gain two marks. If your programme includes pieces just below this standard, you will probably gain only one mark and, if your music is consistently easier than Grade 5 – say at Grade 4 or below, it is unlikely that you will receive any marks out of six.

As the difficulty of the music you perform increases, so your mark will climb, with the full six marks being awarded where your programme is of pieces consistently *above* Grade 7 standard (or its equivalent). However, the same advice given at AS holds good here: do not attempt pieces that are beyond your technical and interpretative abilities – your 'comfort zone', if you prefer – as you are more likely to be nervous and prone to error.

Part of the work you will do during your A2 year is, therefore, to improve your level of technical competence and widen the range of music you perform and listen to. This work will enable you to tackle harder pieces well and also to understand the characteristics of particular pieces and genres of music. Your instrumental/vocal teacher should be made aware of the requirements of the course and this option, and help you plan a programme of work that will enable you to acquire the extra skills needed and to plan the final programme.

As at AS, your performance will be assessed on its technical accuracy, fluency and security. You will be expected to observe the composer's performing and expressive directions and be able to communicate the music to the audience in a committed, convincing and assured manner. You will also have to demonstrate that you understand the requirements of the music in terms of its period and style.

Improvisation is allowed within the scope of this examination but it must be clear what the basis for the improvisation is: a chord sequence, a riff, a melodic fragment or longer phrase, a specific scale or mode, and so on. Pieces that rely almost exclusively on improvisation are not recommended.

Improving technique

In consultation with your instrumental/vocal teacher, you should identify, at an early stage, which areas of your technique need to be addressed and how you can best achieve improvements and advances. Obviously, you should never ignore the basic, 'everyday' practice schedule, which should include scales, arpeggios, long notes, techniques specific to your instrument or voice, and so on. Scales can be made more interesting by introducing a variety of rhythms into their performance, rather than sticking with the regularity of quavers. Here are some suggestions (which can be applied to arpeggios, too):

Playing techniques can also be used to vary scale and arpeggio practice, including playing legato, staccato, accented and marcato, among others. For example:

You should identify the particular techniques needed in your chosen programme, and plan a series of exercises to address these. They may cover such matters as long phrases, wide leaps, changes of register, a wide range of dynamics, particular problems of articulation, and so on. This element of forward planning is another reason why identification of your final programme, as early as possible, is essential. If you cannot determine the whole programme, then at least you will soon be able to start practising one of the pieces you will perform.

The solo performance

The acoustic performance option is for solo performances, defined in the specification as:

■ a single unaccompanied part

■ a part which is accompanied by piano, guitar (or similar), a backing track, or a small unit of other players.

Solo performance : alone or as part of a group

The first item on the above list should be taken as applying only to works written specifically for a solo instrument, rather than merely omitting the accompanying part of other pieces, which would not be musically acceptable at this level. Some instruments will have a rich repertoire of music written for them to play alone; most others will be much less fortunate and it is always important to remember that 'variety' is a key word within this unit.

A very important skill in solo performance at this level is that of working with an accompanist (or a small unit of other players). This is another area that will need careful attention as you prepare for this unit and decide which pieces will become a part of your final programme. It is important, even vital, that you will be able to practise regularly with your designated accompanist or with the small group of players who will join you for the performances. Try to keep organisational matters as simple as possible: in other words, aim to do all of your pieces with the same accompanist, backing track facility, or small group of players.

On the subject of 'backing tracks', bear in mind that the backing track dictates all aspects of the performance – tempo, dynamics, articulation, and so on – and, as such, is rarely the best medium to use at this level. This is not to state that it should never be used – it is, after all, there as an option – but you need to be fully aware of the extent to which you will be able to demonstrate the techniques and understanding needed to access the highest marks.

Assessment

Assessment focuses on three main areas, each worth a potential 18 marks. These are accuracy, communication and interpretation. If you have already taken this new AQA Music course at AS, you will see that the descriptors are exactly the same as for the acoustic performances at that level, though you will now be tackling music of increased difficulty.

Traditionally, candidates score highly for performing at A Level Music, so you need to ensure that your marks will be as good as they possibly can be. Your success will depend on the way in which you go about improving and consolidating your skills during the first part of your A2 year. Remember that for this examination, you will be submitting a recording of your performances and so you also need to practise recording yourself playing/ singing. This is not just to ensure that your pieces record well but to get a 'feel' for how you sound and, if necessary, explore any ways that might lead to the recorded version being a truer reflection of your live performance.

■ Technology-based performances

For both options, the minimum requirements have increased from AS, as is to be expected. In each option, you must now include at least six independent parts, and each option has additional requirements.

Technology-based performance 1: sequencing

As at AS, you are to use a combination of sequencing and multi-tracking/close microphone recording to create one or more recordings. At least one of your recordings should be of a pop/rock/jazz ensemble and should include a drum kit: so, there should be at least six vocal/instrumental parts, one of which is to be a drum kit.

Again, as at AS, your recording will combine sequenced and audio tracks. There is no instruction or requirement as to how many of each – the final decision is yours – but there must be *at least one* of each type. As it is most likely that you will submit more than one piece to form a programme, the specification goes on to add further information:

■ each piece must be 48 or more bars in length

■ pieces in 'classical' style will feature a solo part

■ pieces in a pop or jazz style will feature a vocalist

■ there must be evidence of the use of sound sources other than general MIDI (such as plug-ins or sound modules)

■ there must be at least one VSTi (virtual studio instrument) track.

You are to provide a recording on CD or minidisk, giving full details of the equipment used, including the use made of the various facilities available within the hardware and the software.

Thus, for A2, you are to extend the skills acquired at AS and show your competence at this higher level. Assessment will again be based on your ability in five areas. You must be able to:

■ ensure accuracy of pitch and rhythm

■ choose appropriate timbres, effectively balance the parts and use appropriate panning techniques to separate members of the ensemble and similar sounds

■ show close attention to performing and expressive detail

■ achieve the stylistic requirements of the music

■ use the various facilities available within the software and hardware.

You will acquire these skills over time, by working through short examples of sequencing and multi-tracking. Your submission will combine both recorded audio and MIDI sequenced tracks with a minimum of six tracks required. You must decide just *how many* of each type of track to include, but both must be present and at least one track must be a VSTi.

You will need to decide how to divide your tracks between sequenced and audio, but you might initially prefer to work on short examples using greater numbers of each to hone your skills in both sequencing and recording/mixing. Although the audio parts can be provided by yourself and/or others, you must input the sequenced tracks.

Reference should be made, at this stage, to the comments and observations made under Unit 3, the AS equivalent of this component, with regard to equipment and procedures (see Chapter 10, page 122).

The style of music must include at least one piece in a pop/rock/jazz style, involving at least six vocal/instrumental lines, one of which must be a drum kit. If you have not recorded a drum kit before, it will pose new problems for you in terms of balance and ensuring clarity. Part of your preparation should, therefore, include the recording and subsequent manipulation of drum kit tracks.

A further requirement is the inclusion of at least one VSTi. Normally, a VSTi is a plug-in program needing a 'host' sequencer program for it to operate, though there are a few which can operate as standalones. Free ones are available via the internet: try a search on 'VSTi' or 'virtual instrument' to located sites with useful downloads.

The more advanced ones available nowadays produce very high-quality sounds, derived from a collection of audio samples of the actual instrument itself. The incorporated managing program is capable of organising and/or processing the sounds. They are based on audio (although these are triggered by MIDI messages) and this helps in the creation of master audio mixdowns. They can also be used with the far superior audio processors found in top-flight sequencers.

An additional possibility is to record a performance of music of a more 'classical' nature. The basic requirements of having both sequenced and audio tracks remains with the additional condition that there must be a solo part. This may be a new type of recording situation for you and, if so, should be one in which you tackle a range of short tasks to improve your skills relating to combining tracks and manipulating the mixing-desk.

Technology-based performance 2: multi-track/close microphone recording

For this option, you are to produce one or more recordings based on initial recordings of at least six parts, which must include independent instrumental and vocal lines. Your submission will include the original recording and the final mix.

Thus, at A2, the minimum requirements are for:

■ six independent lines, at least one of which must be vocal
■ each piece to be at least 48 bars in length
■ a demonstration of the appropriate use of both time-based and dynamic effects, plus the use of stereo field/panning at mixdown.

This, in turn, leads to the five areas for assessment, which are the same as at AS. There must be evidence of:

■ care taken to ensure good balance
■ use of an appropriate dynamic range
■ use of panning to obtain a clear recording and, where necessary, to separate sounds that utilise similar frequency ranges
■ use of effects where appropriate, such as reverb, delay or echo
■ quality of recording across a wide range of frequencies.

As at AS, the following advice holds good at A2: your main starting point will be your intentions in terms of the performers to be involved in the 'initial recordings'. Accuracy is a vital element and you will also be deciding on your own role within performances:

- will you be a single element (in other words, playing one of the parts)
- will you take a much fuller role (anything up to performing all the tracks yourself), or
- will you confine yourself purely to the recording and processing side of the performance?

The choice is yours as the assessment is based on your manipulation of the mixing desk to improve the initial recording to its final mix. The actual style of music will depend on your own interests and the performers available to you. As the extension from AS is the increase in the number of audio tracks, your preparatory work will probably centre around short recordings of at least six tracks and then experimentation with the mixing desk and its functions, to try out different effects. For example, adjusting dynamics, using panning, compression and EQ and then appraising the results. Careful record-keeping will be vital to help build up a list of the best possible conditions for recording your final chosen ensemble and then mixing down that initial recording so that you know what the effect of adjustments will be.

As you have to provide details of the equipment used and the recording process, it is good practice to get into the habit of using the same equipment each time you record anything; keeping a log of what you do and backing up any recordings that you make so that you listen to them and check the result of adjustments against the process you went through.

19 Choosing a performing option

Learning objectives:

- to be in a position to make an informed choice as to which option to take

- to fully understand each option

- to understand how the recital can be programmed.

The options at A2 Level are as follows:

- solo acoustic performances
- technology-based performances
- one solo performance and one technology-based performance, each of which is to last at least five minutes.

Solo acoustic performances

If you are a good performer and can play confidently at Grade 6 or higher, then there is little doubt that this would be a good option. If your abilities are slightly lower it would still be possible, but you should weigh your skills in this area against any technology skills you have. Although playing pieces at Grade 5 will still earn you a third of the marks available for level of demand, conversely it means that your highest achievable mark is now 56 rather than 60. Again, there can be no 'blanket' advice here: it will depend very much on your individual circumstances.

You will need to be able to play pieces that demonstrate variety: this can be in terms of approach, period, style or technique, or any combination of these. Your programme of pieces must last between 10 and 15 minutes. You must play at least two pieces to enable you to show variety, though these may be two movements from the same work if there is sufficient contrast. For example, one might be a quick movement, requiring a lively, detached manner of playing the music, another a movement that might enable you to display a much more legato and cantabile style.

You might contrast a Baroque piece with one from the Romantic period, a Classical piece with a modern one. You might include arias from opera, or oratorio with lieder, or songs from a musical. You might choose to 'showcase' two types of Prelude such as one by Bach and one by Gershwin. The possibilities are virtually endless and you should look at repertoire with your instrumental/vocal teacher. Lists provided by The Associated Board of the Royal Schools of Music, Trinity/Guildhall and Rock School could provide valuable sources for ideas, though you do not need to limit your choice to these publications.

If you play within a 'small unit of other players', you need to ensure that the parts you perform will be substantial elements in the pieces: a subsidiary role will not qualify as a 'solo part'. There is plenty of music available for small ensembles in which you can play an important part – instrumental chamber music, small vocal ensembles, and so on. It is preferable, should you be contemplating this particular route, that you are already part of an established small ensemble and/or that the chosen ensemble will have many opportunities to practise and decide on repertoire suitable for all members.

Technology-based performances

As with AS, there are two technology-based routes and, although it is not immediately obvious from the specification, it is possible for you to do, in effect, one of three 'sub' options:

- all performances within technology-based performance 1: sequencing
- all performances within technology-based performance 2: multi-track/ close microphone recording
- a combination of performances from both options provided that each lasts at least five minutes.

Thus:

- You can continue to improve your skills in sequencing, where the use of a sequencer and a multi-track recorder is assessed.
- You can concentrate on the recording of audio tracks and the subsequent refinement of the initial recording into a really impressive final mix.
- You can decide to do at least five minutes within the parameters of each technology-based option.

If you decide to do your entire recording within either technology-based performance 1 or technology-based performance 2, there must be some variety present, either of approach, period, style or technique, or any combination of these.

If, however, you do at least five minutes of recording for each option, variety will automatically be there in the manner of achieving the recordings and count as variety of approach and, to a certain extent, technique, although multi-tracking is present in both options. You can produce two or more shorter pieces to fulfil the 'at least five minutes' condition for each of these options, rather than one long piece, and it might well be easier to do so in terms of initial recording and subsequent editing.

Your choice here will depend on your own interests and the availability (either at your centre or by other means) of the necessary software and hardware. Remember that, at the end of the sequencing, recording, multi-tracking and refining process, you and your teacher have to verify this as your own work and, therefore, it is vital that your teacher sees the work in progress and can discuss the process you are undertaking with you on regular occasions.

■ One solo performance and one technology-based performance

Although this option refers to 'one solo performance' and 'one technology-based performance', it is quite in order to submit two or more shorter pieces to form a short programme, each elemenet of which is to last at least five minutes. The element of variety will come from the juxtaposition of the two types of submission, although you might also want to include further variety within or across the programmes. Alongside the solo performance element, you can choose either of the two technology-based options (but not a sample of each type).

Thus, within this option, there are again 'sub' options:

- ■ solo performance plus technology-based performance 1: sequencing
- ■ solo performance plus technology-based performance 2: multi-track/close microphone recording.

The same 'rules' apply to each of these elements as applied if one or other were being submitted alone, except for the 'variety' condition, as already outlined. Thus:

- ■ Your acoustic performances will be assessed with a level of demand mark out of 6 and then under the same three headings of *accuracy*, *communication* and *interpretation*, each marked out of a maximum of 18. The standard of performance expected remains the same.
- ■ Your technology-based performance will be assessed against the relevant criteria for either performance 1 or performance 2, with a maximum of 12 marks available for each assessment area, and a total out of 60 given.
- ■ These two totals will then be added together and divided by two to give a final mark out of 60, as with options (a) and (b).

Unless you are convinced that you will be able to give a really good account of yourself within each option, this is a choice to be taken only after long and careful reflection, including discussion with instrumental teachers and your class teacher(s). The real advantage, if you can meet the standard, is that there is less to prepare in each option: in other words, a minimum of five minutes' music for each rather than a total of 10–15 minutes. The disadvantage is that you need to be of a very high standard in two very different areas of performing.

Again, it is worth bearing in mind that your programme for each option can be made up of two or more shorter pieces rather than one that meets the full time duration required. However, it is not possible to submit a longer programme (well over five minutes) in one option and a much shorter programme (less than five minutes) in the other, even though this would give a total of ten or more minutes.

20 Preparing acoustic performances

Learning objectives:

■ to become aware of procedures for preparing acoustic performances

■ to become familiar with the elements within the assessment

■ to learn about recording and annotating performances

■ to understand the requirements of the Candidate Record Form.

Most of the advice given for Unit 3 Interpreting Musical Ideas (see Chapter 9) holds good here, and the salient points are virtually reproduced.

Preparing for the performance

Take time to warm up

For all acoustic performances, take sufficient time to warm up and to tune the instrument carefully; whether it be to your accompanist, or to other members of the ensemble. If one instrument is of 'fixed' tuning (such as the piano), you must tune to that, otherwise you either use the pitch given by the best player or one of the many electronic tuning aids available. Stringed instruments will take longer to tune simply because of the number of strings to be checked. Time taken here will be rewarded within the context of the performance.

Focus on the characteristics of the music

It is during the final stages of preparation that you deal with the main characteristics of the music, focusing on its style and the composer's instructions for dynamics and/or articulation. If you are playing Baroque music, most such indications will be editorial and it is up to you, your teacher, your accompanist and/or the rest of the ensemble, to determine to what extent these are followed or adapted. Whatever you decide, make sure that the score you submit matches your intended interpretation.

During performance, dynamics should be exaggerated a little so that they can be heard easily (without, of course, going to absurd extremes!). Articulation should equally be made obvious: short, clean *staccato* notes; strong, clear accents and so on. Tempo markings, where given, should be strictly observed and changes carefully practised. Where no tempo mark has been given, you should determine this by listening to music in a similar style, or recordings of the actual piece, and ensure that your decision is written on the score.

Having chosen your pieces and practised them, both individually and with your accompanist, it is time to apply the 'finishing touches'. (It has already been emphasised how important it is that you and your accompanist have ample opportunities to work together in order to appreciate how the different parts fit together and complement each other and to know *each other's part* in the music.)

Practise performing under exam conditions

As at AS, it is important that you become used to performing your programme under examination conditions. (It is worth noting that, as in public music examinations, it is quite acceptable to omit repeats unless they are an important part of the structure or add something to your performance/interpretation, such as when the convention of the piece allows for embellishment or other forms of improvisation during repeated sections.) Such performances should be to people who have not yet heard you play or practise so far: perhaps you have a relative who is musical; perhaps you can organise a performance to a group of pupils in your school, in their classroom or in an assembly; perhaps there are other teachers in your school who are interested in music and would be prepared to give up some of their time to listen to your performance; perhaps there is opportunity at your church or club: be imaginative!

Whatever you manage to arrange, try to perform your pieces as a unit on more than one occasion. You are quite likely to be nervous in this new situation but, if you find that you are having problems with passages, then it is vital that you return to personal practice. Having gone through this process at AS, nerves should be less of a problem, hopefully (though it is true that some players are always nervous and some feel that the nervousness actually helps them give a better performance!). However, if you really do suffer from performing nerves, there is all the more reason for you to play 'in public' as often as possible as preparation for the recording.

You will need to decide whether any problems you encountered were minor and can, therefore, be remedied quite easily, or whether they are of a more serious nature, to the extent that a possible revision of your intended programme is necessary. This is another reason why early preparation of your pieces for acoustic performance is so important.

Pay attention to the style of the music

When you are playing, remember that you now have an audience and let your manner of performing the music really communicate its meaning to them. You need to be confident, not only with the notes, but also with the style of the music.

Close attention to stylistic features is paramount. Whatever music you choose to play falls into a particular genre and so brings with it various expectations and conventions. The scheme of assessment gives credit for your ability to convey these characteristics through your performance, so you must be clear what they are. It is vital that you play as much music as possible from different periods and listen to recordings: it is all part of your wider musical education.

If you are playing Baroque music, dynamics will be contrasted (tiered); in particular, a repetition of a short phrase will almost inevitably be at a different dynamic from the first playing (usually quieter) as in the example below; trills will start on the *upper* note; repeats will give you the opportunity to decorate the melody appropriately; dotted rhythms might be interpreted as 'double-dotted' or as *notes inégales*.

(The brackets indicate the usually editorial nature of all such dynamic markings in Baroque music.) Contrapuntal passages must be played in such a manner that each line is clearly delineated.

Music from the Classical period needs a balanced approach, with poise and a sense of elegance. There will be opportunities to include dynamic shading within phrases, as well as changes of tone quality and articulation. Melodies should sing out; examples of the Alberti bass should flow. You should listen to some of the great recordings of music from this period – preferably of the pieces you are to play – but listen to more than one: each performer will do things slightly differently – a slightly different tempo; a change of emphasis; a variation in phrasing. Notice the differences and then decide on how your understanding of the style of this period will influence *your* interpretation.

Music from the Romantic period (most of the 19th century) will invariably require a greater depth and range of emotions to be portrayed. Certainly, a wide range of dynamics will be covered and the music could need a *cantabile* and *legato* approach, a dramatic, *pesante* mode of playing, or styles that are shades or combinations of these. Playing techniques will be different from earlier music and your teacher will be able to advise you on the correct approach. However, there must always be evidence that you have tried to bring some of your own character and interpretation to the music.

Modern music will often call upon additional skills, such as the interpretation of 'swung' rhythms, the articulation of the 'stride' bass, or the use of pitch bend. Some more '*avant-garde*' or experimental music will be even more demanding – but equally rewarding.

Communicating with the audience

As with the acoustic performances at AS, there is a section of marks awarded for communication: the ability to give a committed, assured, convincing and well-projected performance of the music – a maximum of 18 marks at A2. In this unit, your recorded performances are sent off to an examiner appointed by AQA. In any live performance, your confidence will come partly through your sense of conviction that the way you are performing the music is not only valid but also correct, and partly through your body language during that performance. An introverted player cannot communicate the meaning of the music. This is not to say that you have to be excessively physical during your playing/singing! Even though it is just an audio recording, on CD or minidisk, that is sent to the examiner, it is important that you *look* confident and make eye contact with members of the audience, your accompanist and/or other members of the small ensemble: this will help you feel confident! Do not 'hide' behind your music. If you are singing, it is invariably better to have memorised the songs, as your facial expressions are important in your interpretation and communication of the music to the audience.

Eye contact is a vital element of communicating with your audience

AQA Examiner's tip

Make sure that you have fully complied with the specification in terms of length of programme. If you submit substantially less music than required it is unlikely that you will be able to access the higher bands of marks. However, there is no need to exceed the maximum recommended time: if you haven't managed to show your abilities within 10–15 minutes, there is little chance that you will do it in a longer programme.

■ Finishing – recording and annotating

You need to submit:

■ a recording on CD or minidisk

■ either a score, a lead sheet/detailed guide to the music or, if the learning process was based on this, a recording of the original work

■ a Candidate Record Form (CRF).

The recording

The recording should be as clear and balanced as possible. Time should be taken to ensure that microphones are positioned to optimise balance and clarity. Short passages should be recorded to test balance and dynamic levels: performances must be clear, neither too faint nor too distorted. You should take all practical steps to ensure that your recorded performances match the live ones as closely as possible.

It is not part of this examination to rely on just one 'take' of your performance. However, beware of attempting to play the pieces too often: it is much better to be fully prepared and in just the right frame of mind, having warmed up and played through any passages you particularly wish to look at 'for the last time', and then approach your performance as if it was 'the big occasion' and the climax of all your careful practice and endeavour (which of course it is!).

Do not spend too long warming up or playing through the pieces over again, especially if you are a brass player. Make sure that the music stand, if you are using one, is at the correct height and is carefully put together; a stand that collapses part way through your performance is the last thing you want!

Your teacher will make sure that the room set aside for the recording will not receive interruptions during the performing and recording process so, as far as you can, when it comes to the actual examination performances, relax and enjoy yourself. You *know* the pieces, you are well prepared, you have played them on many previous occasions to a range of audiences and this is what it has all been leading towards. And you can always rest secure in the knowledge that, if the worst does happen and something unexpectedly does go wrong, all is not lost: you can have another go!

The score or detailed guide to the music

If you have played from standard music notation, then this score should be submitted. Wherever possible, enclose the full score, whether it is of your part plus piano or a complete ensemble score (if working in a small group of players). This makes it much easier for the examiner (who will be listening to your *recorded* performance) to hear and appreciate how your part fits in with the rest of the musical texture.

If you do not use standard notation there are various other options open to you, but, whichever one you choose, you must give the examiner enough information to be certain of what instrument you are playing during the performances.

Remember that, while a tab score is fine for indicating the pitches of notes by showing their positions on the strings, it does not give a clear indication of rhythm and will rarely show any dynamics or phrasing. Wherever possible, you should add extra information and make sure that, on the recording, your part is clearly audible (do short test recordings first). Where there is possible confusion because of a similarity of timbres between your part and that of another player, give clear details to enable the examiner to follow your part.

The candidate record form

On the CRF, you must fill in:

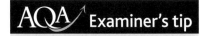

Examiner's tip

Double-check that you are submitting *everything* that is required for this examination component.

- the name and number of your centre
- your full name and candidate number
- if appropriate, the track number from which your submitted recordings begin
- the options you have chosen, by listing the titles of the pieces you have played in the appropriate boxes
- the instrument/voice you have performed upon and what either accompanied you or made up the rest of the small group of players
- your signature and the date (and your teacher must also sign and date the CRF).

Make sure, whichever options you choose, that your teacher receives the materials in good time – it is in nobody's interests to leave things till the last minute!

As part of your submission, you need to provide, for the examiner, a guide that explains how each aspect of your coursework has been created.

21 Preparing technology-based performances

Learning objectives:

- to become aware of procedures for preparing technology-based performances
- to become familiar with the areas of assessment
- to learn about recording and annotating performances
- to understand the requirements of the Candidate Record Form.

What you need to prepare will depend on which of the technology-based performances you are submitting.

Technology-based performance 1: sequencing

If you decide to opt for performance 1: sequencing, you will have to think in terms of exactly what hardware and software you will be using. This will extend to consideration of a whole range of items, including the sound module, interface, keyboard, microphones, multi-track recorder, mixing desk, external effects, two-track stereo mastering recording and any other equipment.

You will probably need to spend time familiarising yourself with the chosen equipment and trying out a range of shorter sequencing and audio recording tasks, so that you can experiment with various effects and improve your skills. Just how much time you need to spend on this will vary according to your initial skills level. Obviously, the increase in the number of tracks required at A2 and the longer minimum time for any single recorded piece may mean that you need to spend a reasonable amount of time sequencing more parts or getting audio recordings of more parts.

At first, you might decide to concentrate on adding to your sequencing skills and then turning your attention to improving audio recording techniques. Eventually, you will have to combine these, using a minimum of six tracks overall: it is entirely your decision just how many tracks will be MIDI sequenced and how many will be audio recordings *but both must be present.*

You should take note of the range of facilities available within the software and/or hardware you are using and ensure that you make optimum use of these. Above all, the assessment criteria will reward well-judged use of timbres, balance and panning techniques, so it will be well worth your while to experiment with these and produce several versions of the same initial recording for either self-assessment or assessment by your peers/teacher.

As for AS, you should ensure that at least basic equipment is available:

- a sequencing software package such as Cubase SX or Logic Pro 7
- a notation/scoring package such as Sibelius or Coda Finale 2005
- a mixing desk
- condenser and dynamic microphones
- all the necessary cabling and connections
- good-quality headphones and speakers
- a good system to 'back up' work in progress
- keyboard: this could be a 'controller keyboard', a 'synthesiser' with GM/XG capacity and/or a 'soft synth' – a VST instrument that operates from within the computer (VST or VSTi = virtual instrument, such as Hypersonic)
- a processor/external effects, such as that provided within the Behringer series.

For A2, the use of a VSTi for at least one track is mandatory.

You should refer to the information given within the section in Unit 3: Performing, for further details on this equipment (see Chapter 10, page 129).

Sequencing skills needed and other considerations

- data input methods
- note accuracy
- articulation
- expression (dynamic) and phrasing
- tempo handling
- convincing drums
- individual note editing
- listen and imitate
- panning
- balancing: with either a solo part in classical submissions or a vocal part in pop/rock/jazz submission.

A sequencer

For this option, you will have used a combination of sequencing and multi-tracking/close microphone recording to create one or more pieces of music. Although your music can be in any style, at least one recording must be of a pop/rock/jazz ensemble:

- there must be at least six independent vocal/instrumental parts
- there must be a combination of recorded audio and MIDI sequenced tracks (though it is for you to decide the ratio of one type to the other)
- a piece must be at least 48 bars long
- pieces in a 'classical' style must feature a solo part
- pop or jazz music should feature some use of a drum kit
- there must be at least a moderate level of dynamic variation.

Remember also that your submission within this option must include 10–15 minutes of music. Your submission must include variety, as with the acoustic performances. This can be of approach, period, style, technique or any combination of these. Thus, you must submit at least *two* pieces, and the likelihood is that you will submit more than this – probably three or four. This will be easier for you to handle as you plan, build up and then combine and edit the tracks to produce your final version of each piece.

As you plan each piece, decide on the balance of resources you will use:

- will the accompanying parts be MIDI-generated with a single solo audio track (a voice or solo instrument)?
- will there be just one line, such as the percussion, generated via MIDI, with the other five parts being audio tracks?
- will your ratio be three and three?

Other questions you will have to answer include:

- What will be the best order in which to lay down the tracks?
- If your piece is in a 'classical' style, how will you ensure that it meets the requirement to have a solo part? What problems will this pose?
- If your piece is in a pop or jazz style, how will you incorporate the drum kit? What problems will this pose?

■ How will you decide on the ratio of MIDI tracks to audio?

■ Are there any additional problems with using a VSTi?

You need to look carefully at the facilities available within the software and hardware that you will be using and decide to what extent you will be able to use them in the production of your recordings. The main areas for assessment have been outlined earlier (see Chapter 18, page 222) and you need to be fully aware of these as your work progresses. It is best always to aim to meet the criteria of the top band of marks: to aim lower is to risk not even achieving at that level.

Remember that, although you can play on one or more of the audio tracks, you might decide to direct other players. However, you *must* input all sequenced tracks, including the VSTi.

Key areas to be assessed

You need to demonstrate the ability to:

■ ensure accuracy of pitch and rhythm

■ choose appropriate timbres, effectively balance the parts, and use appropriate panning techniques to separate members of the ensemble and similar sounds

■ show close attention to performing and expressive detail

■ achieve the stylistic requirements of the music

■ use the various facilities available within the software and hardware.

Following the same approach as at AS, you should aim to meet the descriptors for the top band in each area of assessment.

Accuracy of pitch and rhythm

Excellent accuracy of pitch and control of all rhythmic elements to produce a musically satisfying performance.

You are responsible for obtaining the various tracks that make up the performance. Most recording machines of the standard needed to tackle this option will have a facility that enables you to adjust the recorded pitch so that it will come in line with that of other instruments and MIDI channels used. Additionally, there is a 'transpose' function within most sequencing packages. Rhythmic accuracy from MIDI tracks may well involve some use of the quantising facility, while rhythmic accuracy from players/singers on audio tracks needs to be assured through careful practice and rehearsal. The inclusion of a VSTi should not greatly increase problems here. The degree to which you will be able to adjust such elements will depend on the software/hardware being used and this is why it is vital to give such information on the Candidate Record Form (CRF).

Use of timbre, balance and panning techniques

Judiciously chosen timbres set within a well-balanced and effective recording.

Obviously, the choice of timbres is your own, but it must be appropriate to the genre of music being performed – this is where the extent to which your choice is *judicious* can be assessed.

Your recording must be *well balanced*, with no track being either overpowering or unacceptably faint. This will be done through your work at the multi-track recorder and/or at the sequencer. You will, where necessary, use panning techniques to separate the tracks and produce an effective recording. Careful use of panning will enable you to produce a 'spacious' sound with the tracks being 'placed' either centrally or at different degrees to the left or right. Given the sounds and effects being used, it may even be effective to convey the sense of a sound 'moving' from one side of the aural spectrum to the other – that is, panning across, from left to right for example. However, this is an effect that needs careful thought.

Your final result will be an *effective recording*: it will, within the parameters of your chosen genre, combine appropriate timbres to produce a performance where each line is clear and at an appropriate level, and clearly audible because of your attention to this and to panning techniques.

Evidence of close attention to performing and expressive detail

Comprehensive evidence of close attention to all aspects of performing and expressive detail to create a musical performance.

This will credit your close attention to matters of dynamic contrast, articulation, phrasing, shading and tempo control. There will need to be aural evidence of all of these elements in your recorded performance if you are to access this top band of marks. You will also have outlined the steps you took to effect these areas in your accompanying guide for the examiner.

Awareness of style required

Complete awareness of the stylistic requirements of the music and the ability to achieve this through the careful editing of data.

Stylistic awareness is an awareness of the characteristics of the music allied to an understanding of how to interpret them. You should refer to some of the points made on this matter under the comments on the acoustic performances above. It is likely that you will have listened to various existing recordings in order to work out the characteristics which you need to incorporate into your recording.

Ability to use the facilities available within the software and hardware to produce a valid result

Complete understanding of the measures needed to use the facilities within the software and/or hardware to produce an authentic recording.

This assesses your ability to make full use of the chosen software and/or hardware to produce what is referred to as *an authentic recording*. On the CRF, you have to identify just what the software and hardware can do. This is where you show your skill in utilising those properties in order to effect a final recording which reproduces and, where appropriate, enhances the original sounds and performance situation. In other words, whatever you set out to achieve through your recording, this measures the level of your success in achieving that goal.

Technology-based performance 2: multi-track/ close microphone recording

For this option, an important feature is that you will submit the *original* recording of your chosen ensemble and also your *finished* version. It is the difference between these two that forms the basis of the assessment: that is, what you have done via the available technology to improve on the initial recording.

There must be six or more independent vocal and/or instrumental parts. Your initial planning will involve making decisions about track allocation.

You will have to take care in your preparation of the music and allow sufficient setting-up and recording time. Finally, and very importantly, you must allow yourself enough time to do the actual mixdown and transfer the final version to a two-track stereo recorder.

The examiner will listen to the original recording and then to the final mix before starting the assessment. Again, there are five different areas and these are the descriptors you must meet in order to attain at the highest level:

Key areas to be assessed

You need to provide evidence of:

- care taken to ensure good balance
- use of an appropriate dynamic range
- use of panning to obtain a clear recording and, where necessary, to separate sounds that utilise similar frequency ranges
- use of effects where appropriate, such as reverb, delay or echo
- quality of recording across a wide range of frequencies.

Following the same approach as at AS, you should aim to meet the descriptors for the top band in each area of assessment:

Balance

- Excellent sense of balance throughout the recording.

This is where you ensure that each of the parts is clear and that none overpowers or is obscured by another. Always bear in mind the fundamental truism that the only way to 'undo' poor recording is to redo it.

Dynamic range, including use of compression

- Excellent management of dynamics in ways completely appropriate to the music.

It will be expected that a range of dynamics will be evident in your final mix. As you record the individual tracks, the use of a compressor may be needed, especially if pop music instruments and/or the voice are used. (If you are recording a more 'classical' piece, there should be a wide range of dynamics anyway.) A compressor is, basically, an automatic volume control which turns down the signal level when it gets too loud and turns it up when the parts get too quiet: judicious use of this is important and level of use should be shown within the information included with your submission. Notice the phrase 'in ways completely appropriate to the music': this will have a direct and important bearing on what you do in this area.

Manipulation of mixing desk

- Excellent use of mixing desk which enables all aspects of the recording to be appreciated.

This is where you demonstrate your ability to bring together your recorded tracks into one finished, coherent musical work. You need to work on each channel separately, then in conjunction with others. Think how the instruments/voices would be grouped on a stage and apply appropriate panning. Keep logical sections of your mix (such as the drum kit) together so that you can adjust their overall level together. What use have you made of EQ, of further compression?

Use of effects, such as reverb or delay

▦   Judicious and appropriate use of effects throughout the piece.

Notice the important words 'judicious' and 'appropriate': don't overdo your use of effects, especially reverb, as this can take away the contrast you need to enhance your mix. However, you will lose marks if there are sections of your mix where the use of effects has been unsuccessful, or their use would have enhanced the mix, but they are missing.

Quality of the recording across a wide range of dynamics

▦   An excellent recording with clear use of a wide range of frequencies.

This is where your use of equalisation or EQ is assessed: this is the function that allows you to adjust the relative balance of the frequencies present in your audio recording. EQ channels are present on even the most basic mixing desks with three sections – low, mid and high. Low and high (or bass and treble) enable you to cut or boost frequencies above or below a specific point (usually below 100Hz for the bass and above 10Hz for the treble). Bands of mid EQ control the range between these extremes. In the information you present as part of your submission, the range of frequencies used should be shown.

If you did the AS submission, you will have seen the list of suggested books and other resources. If not, you should refer to the relevant section now (see Chapter 10, page 134).

▦ Finishing: recording and annotating

You need to submit:

▦   your recordings on CD or minidisk; there should be no material included on the CD/minidisk apart from your performances for assessment

▦   a copy of the music performed, either in standard notation, or as a lead sheet/detailed guide or, if neither reflects accurately the way in which the music was learnt prior to performance, a separate recording of the original work

▦   a Candidate Record Form (CRF).

The CRF must contain:

▦   the name and number of your centre

▦   your full name and candidate number

▦   if appropriate, the track number from which your submitted recordings begin

▦   the options you have chosen (do this by listing the titles of the pieces you have recorded in the appropriate boxes)

▦   details of the equipment used

▦   information as to the facilities available within the chosen software and hardware (performance 1)

▦   details of the recording process (performance 2)

▦   your signature and the date (and your teacher must also sign and date the CRF).

Make sure, whichever options you choose, that your teacher receives the materials in good time – it is in nobody's interests to leave things until the last minute! You will need to liaise with the other performers but, in many cases, it might well be true that the performers themselves would

AQA Examiner's tip

Make sure that you have fully complied with the specification in terms of length of programme. If you submit substantially less music than is required, it is unlikely that you will be able to access the higher bands of marks. However, there is no need to exceed the maximum recommended time: if you haven't managed to show your abilities within 10–15 minutes, there is little chance that you will do it in a longer programme.

welcome an earlier opportunity to do their recording rather than leaving everything to that period when demands on time grow ever greater.

As part of your submission, you need to provide, for the examiner, a guide that explains how each aspect of your coursework has been created.

Technology-based performance 1: sequencing

It is important that the examiner can fully appreciate and follow the steps you have taken during your work in this option. A series of headings is suggested as a framework around which to build your outline. Areas to be addressed should include:

■ identifying the hardware and software
■ explaining how the musical data was entered into the sequencer
■ explaining how the sequencing software was used to shape a musical performance and create the style of the chosen piece
■ explaining how the audio was added and blended with the sequence.

Identifying the hardware and software

Under this heading, you will need to cover areas such as:

■ make, name, model/version and their capabilities/facilities
■ details of any Interface used
■ details of the sound module, keyboard and microphones
■ details of the VSTi used
■ details of the multi-track recorder, the mixing desk, the two-track stereo mastering recorder
■ any external effects
■ use of a DI box or other equipment.

Musical data entry into the sequencer

This will cover matters such as:

■ how the data was entered initially – using real time or step time? Metronome or grid/piano-roll editor?
■ any subsequent overdubbing, correcting, use of quantise.

Use of the software to shape a musical performance and create the style of the chosen piece

This is where you will need to cover your use of controller data to manipulate elements such as:

■ dynamics, expression, articulation, panning, phrasing, sustain, velocity
■ your efforts to imitate 'live' performers through measures such as breathing (wind players), bowing (string players), strumming (guitars) or pedalling (pianists)
■ use of reverb
■ tempo, balance, choice of timbre.

How the audio was added and blended with the sequence

Finally, you need to refer to:

■ the process of integrating MIDI with audio
■ the recording method used – room, equipment, number of takes

- the order of recording
- the use of foldback and effects
- the final mixdown process.

Technology-based performance 2: multi-track/close microphone recording

As no sequencing is involved in this option, the guide you need to produce will cover slightly fewer areas. The main 'headings' under which to structure your response might well be:

- details about the equipment used
- the recording process used to achieve the initial recording
- the process of producing the final mix.

Details about the equipment used

Here you will need to give full information on:

- microphones, headphones and monitor speakers
- multi-track recorder and mixing desk
- effects unit and dynamic processing unit
- two-track stereo mastering recorder
- any other equipment used.

The recording process used to achieve the initial recording

Some of the main issues that need to be addressed include:

- the order in which tracks were recorded: a detailed track listing, indication of the number of 'takes', decisions as to the final choices for use
- venue
- microphones, DI, use of foldback
- recording levels, microphone choice and positioning (consider supplying photographs and/or diagrams)
- any initial use of compression
- the performers – how did you get the best from them (and/or yourself)
- problems encountered and overcome.

The process of producing the final mix

This is where you explain how you transformed the initial recording into the final mix. Remember that this is the focus of the assessment in this unit and, therefore, it is essential that you give full details of the process you went through. You will need to cover the following, as they apply to your work:

- effects used – preferably for each track – and including, where applicable, compression, EQ, reverb, and so on. Give your reasons for such use.
- the style of the piece – what did you need to address? Did you listen to any specific recordings? Did you receive any specific advice?
- use of panning and the stereo field
- balancing
- refining the mix and setting the master recording levels
- transferring your mix onto a two-track stereo master.

AQA Examiner's tip

Double-check that you are submitting *everything* that is required for this examination component.

Glossary

A

Acciaccatura: Also known as 'crush notes': a type of grace note where the note is literally 'crushed in' and played in as short a time space as possible. It is notated as a small note with a diagonal line through the stem.

Aria all'unisone: In this, the voice is doubled by the instrumental line: an example is *The people that walked in darkness* from Handel's *Messiah*.

Aria cantabile: A quiet, slow song, tender in mood and with a relatively simple accompaniment. Convention was that the solo singer would decorate the vocal line.

Aria di bravura or ***aria d'agilità***: Generally an *Allegro* aria, with passages designed to showcase the vocal talents and powers of the particular singer. These are found more in operas than in the works covered by this area of study.

Aria di mezzo carattere: Often in da capo form, this tended to be quite passionate and have a rich and varied accompaniment; the main section was often, though not always, *Andante*, with the middle section slightly faster. Oboes and other wind instruments would often join the strings.

Aria d'imitazione: This covers a wide range of styles and includes war-like airs with trumpet obbligato, echo songs, airs with *obbligato* woodwind passages of a descriptive nature (imitating birdsong, for example).

Aria di portamento: A sedate and dignified rather than passionate aria with symmetrical phrases and a restrained accompaniment.

Aria parlante: This had a more declamatory style and often expressed deep passion or other strong emotion.

Arioso: A type of vocal piece that combines the declamatory style of the recitative with the more formal style of the aria.

B

Baritone: A male voice lying between tenor and bass in range and tonal quality.

Binary form: A movement in two sections, each repeated, producing an AABB pattern. The form was common in dances of the Baroque period and continued into the Minuet and Scherzo.

Book: The name given to the adaptation of the original novel, poems or historical events that provide the plot for the musical and the basis for the lyrics.

Bridge passage: In sonata form this provides the link from the first subject to the second and effects the modulation needed.

C

Cadence: The end of a phrase where the music comes to rest. The final chords in the phrase can be chosen to make the moment of rest seem partial or complete, natural or unexpected. See page 3 for more information about cadences.

Cantabile: Literally 'song-like'; to be played in a flowing manner as one would sing.

Canto fermo or ***cantus firmus***: The literal meaning is 'fixed song' and refers to the melody that a composer has taken from another source and then added other melodies in counterpoint against.

Cavatina: Really an *aria cantabile* without its contrasting central section.

Chaconne: The term derives from an obsolete dance, probably of Spanish origin. It was usually in triple time, with an accent on the second beat, at a slow tempo, and constructed as a series of variations on a ground bass, usually eight bars in length.

Chorus: Music sung by the choir, traditionally in four parts: SATB – soprano, alto, tenor and bass.

Chromatic: Music with notes added from outside the key, to give extra colour.

Coda: An optional 'tail-piece' at the end of a movement. It may contain further development of the themes, and resolves any remaining conflicts of key.

Codetta: A short 'rounding-off' section.

Col legno: With the wood of the bow.

Coloratura (or *fioratura*): Florid ornamentation of the melody in vocal music.

Consecutive fifths and octaves: When one chord moves to another and the same two voices/instruments are a fifth apart in both chords, the consecutive intervals can sound too prominent. The same applies to consecutive octaves.

Countermelody: the addition of a second melody to the original.

Crescendo: Getting gradually louder.

D

Development section: The central section of a sonata-form movement, in which the themes are fragmented, extended or otherwise developed. The music usually passes through a number of keys.

Diatonic: Music in which all notes belong to the prevailing key.

Diminished seventh: A chord formed using intervals of a minor third. For example E–G–B♭–D♭.

Diminuendo: Getting gradually quieter.

Diminution: A rhythmic feature in which note values are halved so that an idea is played at double speed.

Dominant: The fifth note of a scale – for example, the note C in F major.

Dominant pedal: A sustained or repeated bass note on the fifth note of the scale above which the harmony changes.

Dominant seventh: Chord built on the dominant or fifth chord of the key. For example, in the key of C, the chord of G with a minor 7th added to give the chord G–B–D–F.

Dorian mode: The scale made by the white notes on the piano starting on D.

Double-stopping: A string technique in which the player sounds two notes at once on different strings.

Enharmonic change: A change in notation that does not alter the sound of the note. For example, a chord is written first as D♯ major and then as E♭ major.

Exposition: The first section of a sonata-form movement, in which the main themes are announced. In the Classical period there were two themes or groups of themes in contrasting keys, known as the first and second subjects. They were linked by a bridge passage or transition. Normally, the second subject was in the dominant key and the exposition was marked to be repeated in full.

f: forte: Italian for 'loudly'.

False relation: Two conflicting notes, such as F♯ and F♮, which are heard close together in different parts.

Figured bass: A notation used for the keyboard continuo part in music of the Baroque period. The bass line was written on a stave, with numbers to indicate the harmonies. The player improvised a part from this skeleton.

First inversion: A chord with the third in the bass part.

First subject: The first main theme or group of themes.

Fugue: A strict contrapuntal composition in three or more parts. Each part or *voice* enters in succession with the main theme or *subject*. Alternate entries are in the tonic and dominant keys. Entries in the dominant are known as an *answer* and may be exact (a *real answer*) or adjusted (a *tonal answer*). Entries are usually accompanied by a secondary theme, the *countersubject*. When all voices have entered (the *exposition* section) the material is developed in various keys alternating *episodes* and *middle entries* of the subject. The *final entry* in the tonic key is often highlighted by *augmentation* (long note values), *stretto* (overlapping entries) or a pedal.

German augmented sixth: This chord is formed by taking the sixth note of the scale, flattening it, adding a third, a fifth and an augmented sixth. It resolves here to the dominant:

Aug. 6th.   V in C   Aug. 6th.   Ic

Ground bass: A repeating pattern in the bass over which the composer weaves melodic and harmonic variations. The ground bass – often 2, 4 or 8 bars long – is usually heard either alone or just with simple harmonies at the beginning of the work.

Half-diminished seventh: This is built up: minor third – minor third – major third (whereas a diminished seventh is built entirely of minor thirds).

Harmonic series: The series of notes that can be played on a brass instrument just by altering the pressure of the lips on the mouthpiece. As the pitch gets higher, so the available notes are closer together.

Harmony note: A note that belongs to the prevailing chord.

Hemiola: A device where the rhythmic emphasis is shifted so that two bars of triple time sound more like three bars of duple time – for example, three minim beats across two bars of three crotchets.

Homophonic: (literally 'one sound' or 'same sounding' from the Greek): A chordal texture building upon a bass line or adding chords below a melody.

Imperfect cadence: One that ends on the chord of the dominant. Often the two chords are simply I (tonic) to V (dominant).

In this cadence, or half-close, chord I is used in 2nd inversion (Ic) to resolve by step to the dominant, giving Ic–V.

Italian augmented sixth: Formed by flattening the sixth note of the scale and adding above it a major third and an augmented sixth – for example A♭–C–F♯.

Legato: Smoothly.

Lyrics: The words of the song.

Major 7th: Where the interval of a major seventh is added above a major chord, for example CEGB.

Male alto: The male alto or countertenor voice is a falsetto voice, normally used for the alto line in cathedral choirs.

Melisma: A passage of melody that sets several notes to one syllable.

Minuet and trio: The minuet was a stately dance in $^3/_4$ time that originated in the 17th century. Composers would pair the minuet with a second dance that contrasted in style and texture, called the trio, before returning to a repeat of the minuet. Note that 'trio' does not refer to the number of players in this instance – although the orchestration would usually be lighter, there would usually be more than three people playing. The term 'trio' is also used to refer to a lighter, contrasting section in the middle of a scherzo movement.

Modal system: Music based on other types of scales such as the Renaissance modes and folk scales.

Mode: A particular scale pattern. The most familiar are the major and minor modes. Other scale patterns are found in music of the Renaissance period and earlier and in folk music. Each mode creates its own mood or sound in the music.

Modulation: A move from one key to another. See page 8 for more information about modulations.

N

Notes inégales: French for 'unequal notes'. They are characteristic of music of the French Baroque style and would often be performed as if the music were in $^9/_8$ rather than $^3/_4$. Thus, the opening

would be played:

O

Ostinato: A short phrase, persistently repeated.

P

p: *piano*: Italian for 'quietly'.

Passacaglia: An early Italian or Spanish dance, similar to the chaconne, constructed over a ground of 2, 4 or 8 bars. If anything, the passacaglia seems to be of a more solemn character than the chaconne.

Passing note: A note that moves by step between two notes of a chord.

Pastiche: Writing in the style of an existing composer. The style used could be from an earlier period, for example, using the harmonic language of Bach or Mozart, or you could adopt the style of a contemporary band, jazz player or music theatre composer.

Pentatonic: A five-note mode common in Scottish folk music, negro spirituals and music from Eastern Europe and the Far East. It can be found easily by playing the black notes on a keyboard.

Perfect cadence: A 'final' cadence that uses the progression V–I (dominant to tonic), though V^7–I is shown in this example:

Pesante: Heavily.

Picardy third or *tièrce de Picardie*: A major chord used as the final chord of a minor key passage.

Pitch bend: A device, usually a wheel, on a keyboard that enables the user to 'bend' the pitch of the note up and down.

Pizzicato: Plucking the strings rather than playing with the bow (*con arco*).

Polyphonic: From the Greek 'many sounds', where many different melodic lines combine and interweave. Also known as counterpoint.

R

'Real' time: The music is played in via a keyboard or other instrument connected to the sequencer; the sequencer records what is played in terms of pitch, rhythm and dynamic (velocity).

Recapitulation: The third section of a sonata-form movement. It follows the exposition closely, but resolves the conflict of keys. Usually, both subject groups are in the tonic key.

Recitative: A musical setting of words that follows the rhythms and intonation of speech.

Recitativo accompagnato/recitativo stromentato ('accompanied recitative'): The accompaniment is orchestral and a more dramatic situation is the result: the text covers rapidly changing emotions and the orchestra both reinforces this through its accompaniment and adds brief instrumental passages, punctuating the text.

Recitativo secco (literally, 'dry recitative'): Here, the text is set as simply as possible, with the melodic line tending to follow the vocal inflections and rhythms of the text and the accompaniment being slow-moving chords with a sustaining bass instrument, written in the form of a figured bass. This type of recitative was used to deliver long passages of text in a short time, with no repetition.

Reprise: The repetition of a song at a different stage in the musical where its new position means that its dramatic significance has changed, casting new light on a character and/or a situation.

Resolution: Moving from a dissonant harmony to a consonant harmony, i.e. from tension to rest.

Ritornello: An important theme that returns several times during a movement. Many concerto movements in the Baroque period have a *ritornello* for full orchestra and episodes for the soloist. The pattern was also used in keyboard pieces and vocal music.

Rondo: A movement that has a main theme at the beginning which returns at intervals during the movement. There is fresh material in the intervening episodes, making a pattern such as ABACADA.

Root: The note on which a chord is built, usually by the addition of intervals of a third and a fifth.

Rounded binary form: A binary form movement in which the A section returns to conclude the B section.

Sacred: Written with a religious or devotional purpose.

Scherzo: Literally, a joke. In the symphony, a quick movement in triple time. Originally it followed the binary-form pattern of the minuet and trio.

Second inversion: A chord with the fifth in the bass part.

Second subject: In sonata form, the second tune or 'subject' in the dominant; this is traditionally a gentler, more cantabile or 'feminine' melody.

Secular: Non-religious.

Sequence: Repeated use of a short phrase moving up a step on each repetition. Descending sequences are also used.

Staccato: To play the notes crisply, detached. Dots are placed above or below notes to be performed in this style.

'Step' time: This is where each note of the music is entered from a keyboard, and you select duration as you enter.

Stop-time: A characteristic feature of jazz in which the band plays on occasional beats, leaving space for a soloist to improvise unaccompanied.

Stride bass: A bass/left-hand pattern typical of ragtime music; it consists of a single bass note followed by a chord:

Sus: Shortened form of 'suspended' or 'suspension'. It refers to the device of holding on to, or sustaining, a note from the previous chord and delaying its resolution.

Swung rhythms: In jazz and blues, where a rhythm notated as dotted quaver/semiquaver or two quavers is to be played as a triplet crotchet/quaver as in these examples:

Written

Played

Symphony – Classical pattern for four movements: In the Classical period the pattern of a four movement symphony was:
1. a quick movement in sonata form
2. a slow movement in binary, variation or short sonata form
3. a minuet and trio or scherzo and trio
4. a quick movement in sonata or rondo form.
The order of the second and third movements may be reversed. All movements are in the tonic key except for the slow movement, which is usually in the subdominant key.

Syncopation: Shifting the emphasis on to a note or beat that would normally be weak.

Texture: The relationship of the different parts in a passage of music.

Third inversion: A seventh chord played so that the seventh is the lowest pitch, the bass note.

Timbre: The particular quality of sound of a voice or instrument. Timbre often changes in different parts of the range: for example, low notes may be gentle and high notes more penetrating.

Tonal system: The system of major and minor keys used in much recent Western music.

Tonic: The 'home note' of a scale – for example, the note F in F major.

Tremolando: The rapid repetition of a note (or the rapid alternation of two different pitches) designated by several lines being drawn through the stem of the note affected.

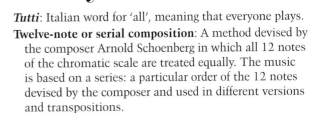

Tutti: Italian word for 'all', meaning that everyone plays.

Twelve-note or serial composition: A method devised by the composer Arnold Schoenberg in which all 12 notes of the chromatic scale are treated equally. The music is based on a series: a particular order of the 12 notes devised by the composer and used in different versions and transpositions.

Unessential note: A note that sounds against a chord without being part of it. Examples are passing notes, auxiliary notes and suspensions.

Word-painting: Illustrating the words by the sound or look of the music: for example, using a rising phrase for *he ascended* or a long note on the words *for ever*.

Reference works

Books

Boyd, Malcolm (2000) *Bach Chorale Harmonisation and Instrumental Counterpoint*, Kahn & Averill, London

Bukofzer, M.F. (1975) *Music in the Baroque Era*, J.M. Dent & Sons, London

Cooke, Deryck (1980) *Gustav Mahler – An Introduction to his Music*, Faber, London

Evans, M. (2006) *Musicals: Facts, Figures & Fun*, Hewitt, NJ

Everett, W. A. and Laird, P. R. (2002) *The Cambridge Companion to the Musical*, Cambridge University Press, Cambridge

Grout, D. (2005) *A History of Western Music*, W.W. Norton, New York

Harman, A., Milner, A. and Mellers, W. (1988) *Man and His Music*, Barrie & Rockliff, New York

Hefling, S. E. (2002) *Nineteenth Century Chamber Music*, Routledge, London

Jacobs, A. (1972) *A New Dictionary of Music*, Penguin Books, Harmondsworth

Jacobs, A. (ed.) (1978) *Choral Music*, Penguin Books, Harmondsworth

Keys, I. (1978) *Brahms Chamber Music*, BBC, London

Kennedy, M. (1977) *Mahler*, J M Dent & Sons, London

Kennedy, M. (1980) *The Works of Ralph Vaughan Williams*, Oxford University Press, Oxford

Lockspeiser, E. (1980) *Debussy* (Master Musicians Series), J.M.Dent & Sons, London

Long, R. E. (2003) *Broadway, the Golden Years*, Continuum, London

Ottaway, Hugh (1980) *Vaughan Williams Symphonies*, BBC, London

Pedler, D. (2003) *The Songwriting Secrets of The Beatles*, Omnibus Press, London

Robertson, A. (1965) *Chamber Music*, Penguin, Harmondsworth

Robbins Landon, H. C. (1968) *Haydn Symphonies*, BBC, London

Sadie, S. (1986) *Mozart Symphonies*, BBC Publications, London

Sadie, S. and Tyrrell, J. (eds) (2001) *New Grove Dictionary of Music & Musicians*, Macmillan, London

Schuller, G. (1986) *Early Jazz*, Oxford University Press, Oxford

Schuller, G. (2005) *The Swing Era: The Development of Jazz 1930-45*, Oxford University Press, Oxford

Sisman, E. (1993) *Mozart: The 'Jupiter' Symphony*, Cambridge Music Handbooks/Cambridge University Press, Cambridge

Sutro, Dirk (2006) *Jazz for Dummies*, John Wiley & Sons, US

Tovey, D. F. (1975) *Essays in Musical Analysis 1*, Oxford University Press, Oxford

Westrup, J. A. (1966) *Bach Cantatas*, BBC Music Guides, London

Zaslaw, N. (1988) *Mozart's Symphonies: Context, Performance Practice, Reception*, Clarendon Press, Oxford

Scores

Bach, J. S. *Christmas Oratorio*, Novello & Co.

Bach, J. S. *Mass in B minor (Hohe Messe in H moll)*, Edition Peters

Bach, J. S. *Sleepers, Wake! (Wachet Auf)*, Novello & Co. Ltd

Bart, L. *Oliver!* Lakeview Music Co.

Bernstein, L. and Sondheim, S. *West Side Story (vocal selections)*, Leonard Bernstein Music Publishing Company Ltd.

Bock, J. *Fiddler on the Roof (vocal selections)*, The New York Times Music Corp.

Handel, G. F. *The King shall Rejoice*, Novello & Co. Ltd

Handel, G. F. *Messiah*, ed. Watkins Shaw, Novello & Co. Ltd

Haydn, G. F. *String Quartets (four volumes)*, Dover Publications

Lloyd Webber, A. *The Andrew Lloyd Webber Anthology*, foreword by Melvyn Bragg: A Really Useful Group Production

Mahler, G. *Symphony No. 4*, miniature score Ernst Eulenburg Ltd

Mozart, W. A. *Complete String Quartets*, Dover Publications

Mozart, W. A. *Symphony No. 40*, Ernst Eulenburg Ltd

Purcell, H. *Ode on St. Cecilia's Day (1692)*, Novello & Co. Ltd

Purcell, H. *Rejoice in the Lord Always (The Bell Anthem)*, Novello & Co. Ltd

Riemenschneider (ed.) *Bach: 371 Harmonised Chorales*, Schirmer

Rodgers, R. and Hammerstein, O. *Oklahoma!* Williamson Music

Schönberg, C.M. and Boubil, A. *Les Misérables*, Wise Publications

Vaughan Williams, R. *Symphony No. 5*, Eulenberg miniature score

Websites

Encyclopaedia Britannica: www.britannica.com

Microsoft Encarta: http://www.encarta.msn.com

Music Teacher's Resource Site: www.mtrs.co.uk

www.redhotjazz.com

www.jsbchorales.net

www.rvwsociety.com

Index

A

Able MIDI Editor **126**
acciaccaturas 6, 24
accompaniment **114–15, 224**
acoustic performances
  assessment criteria **111, 120**
  choosing options **114–16, 228, 230**
  communicating with the
    audience **233**
  developing skills **113–14, 222–4**
  practice 117
  preparing **117–21, 231–3**
  recording and annotating **122–3,
    234–5**
All around my hat
  (Steeleye Span) **76**
Almond, Mark **78**
Always on my mind
  (Pet Shop Boys) **79**
America (from *West Side Story*) **58**
Another brick in the wall (Pink
  Floyd) **75**
anthems **167**
  Baroque period **50–4, 86**
  English 20 century choral music
    167, 169–70, 171–2, 172–3
appoggiaturas **6, 141**
aria all'unisone **43**
aria cantabile **43**
aria di bravura (aria d'agiltà) **43**
aria di mezzo carattere **43**
aria di portamento **43**
aria d'imitazione **43**
aria parlante **43**
arias **43–4**
arioso **43**
Armstrong, Louis **193**
  West End blues **193–4**
arrangement **105–6, 215–17, 219**
assessment, of performing options
  111–12, 221
atonality **142**
augmented intervals **141**
augmented sixth **29, 204**

B

Bach, Johann Sebastian **82, 208**
  chorale melodies **202, 208–10**
  Christmas Oratorio **41, 47, 47–9**
  Mass in B minor **42, 46, 49–50**
  Wachet auf **41**

backing tracks **224**
Ball, David **78**
baritone 176
Baroque period
  choral music **38–9, 40–54**
  pastoral music **85**
  style of music **119**
Bart, Lionel **59**
Basie, Count
  Lester leaps in **195**
Beatles **70–4**
bebop **189, 195**
Bechet, Sidney **193**
Beethoven, Ludwig von **82, 152**
Beiderbecke, Bix **193**
bell anthem (Purcell) **50–1**
Belshazzar's Feast (Walton) **176**
Bernstein, Leonard **58**
binary form 182
bitonality **142**
blues **187–8, 191, 192–4**
Blur **79**
Bock, Jerry **61**
Böhm, Georg **41**
book 58
bop **195**
Boublil, Alain **64**
Brahms, Johannes **183–4**
  Clarinet Quintet in B minor Op.
    115 **184, 202**
bridge passages 19, 21, 30
Bring him home (from *Les
  Misérables*) **68**
British popular music 1960 to the
  present day **39–40, 70–81**
Britpop **79**
Britten, Benjamin
  Rejoice in the Lamb **176–7**
Buxtehude, Dietrich **41**

C

cadences 3–4, 32, 33, 84, 85, 88–90
Candidate Record Form (CRF) **110,
  135, 235**
canons **4**
Can't buy me love (The Beatles) **71**
cantabile **119**
cantatas **41–2, 208**
canticles **167, 168–9**
canto fermo (cantus firmus) **41**
Castle on a cloud (from *Les
  Misérables*) **66–7**

cavatina **43**
cello programmes **115**
chaconne 42
chamber music, from Mendelssohn
  to Debussy **179–87**
Child of our Time, A (Tippett) **177**
choral music
  20th century English **167–78**
  Baroque period **38–9, 40–54**
chorales **208**
chords **84, 200**
  cadences **3–4, 32, 33, 85, 88–90**
  chromatic harmony **203–4**
  creating interesting sequence of
    86–7
  cycle of fifths **140**
  describing **164**
  diminished seventh **28, 29, 34,
    202–3**
  dominant seventh **20**
  German augmented sixth **29**
  half diminished seventh **22**
  identification **4**
  jazz and **188–9**
  major and minor seventh **201**
  picot **91**
  and texture **90, 91**
  third inversion **28, 29, 200–1**
  using changes to create harmonic
    rhythm **90**
chorus **45–6**
Christmas Oratorio (Bach) **41, 47,
  47–9**
chromatic music 202, 203–4
clarinet programmes **115**
Clarinet Quintet in B minor Op.
  115 **(Brahms) 184, 202**
Classical period
  orchestras **15, 17–18**
  pattern for four-movement
    symphonies **19**
  style of music **14–15, 119**
Classical string quartets **210–13**
clefs **163**
click tracks **124**
coda 20, 150
  Mahler's *Symphony No. 4 in G
    major* **150, 151**
  Vaughan Williams *Symphony No.
    5 in D major* **157**
codetta 24–5
col legno **162**

coloratura 46
communication, with the audience 233
composing options
    arrangement 105–6, 215–17
    compositional techniques 97–102, 208–13
    free composition or pastiche 102–4, 214–15
    overview 96, 207
    preparation 107
    recording and annotating 109
    review of submitted work 218–19
    using controlled time effectively 108
composition 82–3
    colour, texture and timbre 91–2
    harmony 200–4
    instruments 92–3
    musical language 84–7
    notation 94
    structure 88–91
    unessential notes 205
    voices 93
compound time 138–9
compressors 134
computer sound cards 130
consecutive fifths and octaves 98
Consider yourself (from *Oliver!*) 60
context, music in 145
contrapuntal music 9, 15, 16, 46, 99
Corelli, Arcangelo
    Trio Sonata Opus 3 No. 7 101–2
countermelodies 21
counterpoint see polyphony
crescendo 20
CRF (Candidate Record Form) 110, 135, 235
'crush notes' 6, 24
Cubana Be and Cubana Bop (Gillespie) 196
Cubasis VST 125
cycle of fifths 140

D

Dark Side of the Moon, The (Pink Floyd album) 74–5
Davies, Miles 195
    Israel 196
day in the life, A (Beatles) 73–4
Debussy, Claude 185, 197
    Sonata for Cello and Piano 185–6
Depeche Mode 77
development section 19, 90–1, 149
    Mahler's *Symphony No. 4 in G major* 149
    Mozart's *Symphony No. 41 in C* first movement 25–9
    Vaughan Williams' *Symphony No. 5 in D major* 156

diatonic music 202
    completion of diatonic melody 7–8
    harmonisation of 16-bar diatonic melody 97–8
diminished intervals 141
diminished seventh 28, 29, 34, 202–3
diminuendo 20
diminutions 159
Do you hear the people sing? (from *Les Misérables*) 64–5, 69
dominant pedal 22, 139, 140
dominant seventh 20
Don't Believe the Truth (Oasis album) 79
Don't cry for me, Argentina (from *Evita*) 63–4
Dorian mode 141, 192
double-stopping technique 211
Dream of Gerontius, The (Elgar) 174–6
Duran Duran 77
Dvořák, Antonin 184
    Piano Trio Op. 90 in E Minor (Dumky) 184–5
dynamics
    acoustic performances 117
    technology-based performances 134

E

Eleanor Rigby (The Beatles) 72
electric guitar programmes 116
Elgar, Edward
    The Dream of Gerontius 174–6
Ellington, Duke 194–5, 197
English choral music, 20th century 167–78
enharmonic changes 172
ensembles
    acoustic performances 114–15, 116, 120
    arranging for 105–6, 215–17
    composing for 102–3, 104, 210–13, 214–15
equalisation (EQ) 134–5
Eurythmics 78
Evita 63–4
exposition 19, 20, 148
    Mahler's *Symphony No. 4 in G major* 147–8
    Mozart's *Symphony No. 41 in C* first movement 20–5
    Vaughan Williams' *Symphony No. 5 in D major* 155–6

F

f: forte 20
false relation 90

falsetto 9, 169
farmer and the cowman, The (from *Oklahoma!*) 57
Fiddler on the Roof 61–2
figured bass 86
fioratura 46
first inversion 87
first subject 19, 20
flute programmes 115
folk rock 76
free composition 102–4, 214–15, 219
Freund Hein 150
From me to you (The Beatles) 71
fugue 46–9

G

Genesis 75
German augmented sixth 29, 204
Gershwin, George 197
    Piano Concerto in F 197
Gillespie, Dizzy 195
    Cubana Be and Cubana Bop 196
Gloria (Rutter) 178
Gloria (Vivaldi) 89, 90, 91
Grandpa's spells (Jelly Roll Morton's Red Hot Peppers) 193
ground bass 42

H

half-diminished seventh 22
Hammerstein, Oscar 55
Handel, George Friederic 173
    anthems 51–4, 85–6
    Messiah 43–5, 46, 47, 49, 85, 92
    Water Music 98–9
hard day's night, A (The Beatles) 71–2
harmonic series 22, 30
harmonisation
    of a 16-bar diatonic melody 97–8
    of a Bach chorale melody 208–10
harmony 200–4
    analysing 162, 200
    and counterpoint 90
    homophony 9–10, 15, 90, 91
    jazz 188
harmony notes 99
Haydn, Franz Joseph 17
    string quartets 211, 212–13
hemoila 44, 52, 90, 139, 157
historical study
    British popular music 1960 to present day 39–40, 70–81
    chamber music from Mendelssohn to Debussy 179–87
    choral music in Baroque period 38–9, 40–54
    English choral music in the 20th century 167–78

jazz and blues 1910-50 187–97
methods of study 38, 166–7
musicals from 1940-1980 39, 54–69
types of questions 198–9
homophony 9–10, 15, 45–6, 90, 91
Honeysuckle Rose (Waller) 192
Hutchings, Ashley 76
Hymn for the Dormition of the Mother of God (Tavener) 173
Hymn of Praise (Mendelssohn) 100
Hymn to the Mother of God (Tavener) 172–3
hymns 208

I

I don't know how to love him (from *Jesus Christ Superstar*) 62–3
I dreamed a dream (from *Les Misérables*) 65–6
I was glad when they said this unto me (Parry) 169–70
imitation 5
imperfect cadences 3, 4, 32, 88
improvisation 113
independent record labels 80
instrumentation 8–9
instruments
    Classical orchestra 15, 17–18
    jazz 189
    recognising 8–9
    suggested programmes for specific 115–16
    techniques affecting sound of 143
    transposing 162–3
    tuning 117
    virtual 130
    writing for 92–3
internet and popular music 80
interpretation 145
interrupted cadences 3, 4, 88
intervals 7–8, 12–13, 141
inversion chords 87
Israel (Davies) 196
Italian augmented sixth 204
It's a sin (Pet Shop Boys) 78

J

jazz
    defining 187
    features of 119, 187–91
    four decades 1910-50 191–7
Jesus Christ Superstar 62–3
Joplin, Scott 191

K

key signatures 87, 164
keys (modes) 84, 141–2
king shall rejoice, The (Handel) 51, 52–4

Krieger, Philipp 41
Kuhnau, Johann 41

L

Lamb Lies Down in Broadway, The (Genesis album) 75
Ländler 150
LaRocca, Nick 192
legato 119
Lennox, Annie 78
Les Misérables 64–8, 69
Lester leaps in (Count Basie band) 195
listening skills 2–13, 138–43
Livery stable blues (The Original Dixieland Jazz Band) 192–3
Lloyd Webber, Andrew 62–4
Lonely room (from *Oklahoma!*) 57
Love me do (The Beatles) 71
lyrics 55

M

MacGowan, Shane 77
Macmillan, James 173
    Magnificat 173
Magnificat in G major (Stanford) 168–9
Magnificat (Macmillan) 173
Mahler, Gustav 146, 154
    Symphony No. 4 in G major 145, 146–54, 163
major seventh 7
male alto 169
Maria (from *West Side Story*) 59
mass 49–50
Mass in B minor (Bach) 42, 46, 49–50
Master of the house (from *Les Misérables*) 69
melisma 44, 86
melody 84–6
    completion of 7–8
    harmonisation of 97–8, 107, 208–10
    jazz 190
    melodic dictation 143
Mendelssohn, Felix 178, 181
    Hymn of Praise 100
    Piano Trio in D Minor Op. 49 179–81, 204
Messiah (Handel) 43–5, 46, 47, 49, 92
MIDI sequencers 124
MIDI sound modules/keyboards 130
minuet and trio 15, 32
    Mozart's *Symphony No. 41 in C* third movement 32–5
Misterioso (Monk) 196
mixing desks 134
modal system 200

modes 84, 141–2
modulations 8, 14, 85, 91
Monk, Thelonious 195
    Misterioso 196
mordents 11
Morton, Jelly Roll 192, 193
Mozart, Wolfgang Amadeus 16–17
    Symphony No.41 in C, first and third movements 16, 20–35
multi-track/close microphone recording
    choosing as option 128–9
    developing skills 126–7, 226–7
    performance preparation 129–30, 133–5, 239–41
    performance recording and annotating 135, 137
    see also sequencing
music sequencers 124
musicals 1940–1980 39, 54–69

N

Neapolitan sixth 203–4
Neumeister, Erdmann 41
New rag (Joplin) 191
notation 94, 123
notes inégales 52, 119
notes, unessential 6, 99, 100, 205

O

Oasis 79
Oh, what a beautiful morning (from *Oklahoma!*) 56
Oklahoma! 55–7, 68–9
Oliver! 59–61
Oliver, Joseph (King) 193
On my own (from *Les Misérables*) 67
One hand, one heart (from *West Side Story*) 59
oratorios 43–9, 173–8
orchestras, Classical 15, 17–18
Original Dixieland Jazz Band 192
    Livery stable blues 192–3
ornamentation 10–11
ostinato 5

P

p: piano 20
Pachelbel, Johann 41
panning techniques 132
Parker, Charlie 195
Parry, Sir Hubert 167
    I was glad when they said this unto me 169–70
passacaglia 42, 155, 160
    Vaughan Williams' *Symphony No. 5 in D major* 160–1
passing notes 6, 98, 100, 205
pastiche 102–4, 214–15

pastoral music **85**
pedals **5, 22, 139–40**
pentatonic mode 106, 141
perfect cadences 3, 33, 88, 203, 204
perfect intervals **12, 13**
performances
   acoustic **113–23, 222–4, 231–5**
   assessment **111–12, 221**
   options available **220, 228–30**
   technology-based **124–37, 225–7,
   236–43**
   what to submit **110–11**
pesante **119**
Pet Shop Boys **78–9**
phrases and phrasing **14, 88–90**
piano, programmes for **116**
Piano Concerto in F (Gershwin) **197**
Piano Quintet in E flat Op. 44
   (Schumann) **181–3**
Piano Trio in D Minor Op. 49
   (Mendelssohn) **179–81, 204**
*Piano Trio Op. 90 in E Minor
   (Dumky)* (Dvořák) **184–5**
Picardy third 172
Pink Floyd **74–5**
pitch
   technology-based
   performances **132**
   transposing instruments
   and **162–3**
pitch bend 119
pivot chord **91**
pizzacato **25, 26**
plagal cadences **3, 88**
Please please me (The Beatles) **71**
Pogues **76–7**
polyphony 9–10, 15, 45–6, 90, 91
polyrhythms **139**
Pore Jud is daid (from *Oklahoma!*) **68**
popular music 1960 to the present
   day, British **39–40, 70–81**
practice, importance of **114, 117**
Prior, Maddy **76**
punk rock **76–7**
Purcell, Henry **41–2, 50**
   Rejoice in the Lord alway (bell
   anthem) **50–1**

R

ragtime **119, 187, 190, 191–2**
'real' time **125**
Reason software **130**
recapitulation **19, 20, 149**
   Mahler's *Symphony No. 4 in G
   major* **149**
   Mozart's *Symphony No. 41 in C*
   first movement **30–1**
   Vaughan Williams' *Symphony No.
   5 in D major* **157**
recitative style 44–5, 174

*recitativo accompagnato (recitativo
   stromentato)* **44**
recitativo secco **44, 45, 48**
recordings
   of acoustic performances **122–3,
   234**
   of compositions **109**
   of technology-based
   performances **135**
Red Hot Peppers, Jelly Roll Morton's
   Grandpa's spells **193**
Rejoice in the Lamb (Britten) **176–7**
Rejoice in the Lord alway (Purcell)
   50–1
reprise 56, 61
resolution 87
reverb **134**
rhythm **138–41**
   choral **169**
   jazz **190**
   rhythmic devices **5, 13**
   technology-based performances **132**
Rice, Tim **62, 63**
riff **5**
ritornello 91
rock musicals **62–8**
Rodgers, Richard **55**
Rolling Stones **74**
Romantic period **119**
rondo 182
root (of a chord) 87
rounded binary form 182
rounds **5**
Rutter, John **178**
   Gloria **178**

S

sacred music 167
scales **84, 141–2**
scherzo 155
   Symphony No. 4 in G major
   (Mahler) **150–1, 151**
   Vaughan Williams' *Symphony No.
   5 in D major* **157–8**
Schoenberg, Arnold **142**
Schönberg, Claude-Michel **64**
Schumann, Robert **181, 183**
   Piano Quintet in E flat Op. 44 **181–3**
scores of acoustic performances **123**
second inversion 87
second subject 19, 22, 30
secular music 167
sequence 5, 13, 140, 212
sequencing
   assessment criteria **112**
   choosing as a option **127–8**
   developing skills **124–6, 225–6**
   performance preparation **129–30,
   131–3, 236–9**
   performance recording **135–6**

*Sergeant Pepper's Lonely Hearts
   Club Band* (Beatles' album) **73–4**
serial composition 143
Set me as a seal (Walton) **171–2**
set works
   analysing the music **16**
   key musical features **14–15**
   Mahler's *Symphony No. 4 in G
   major* **146–54**
   methods of study **14, 144–5**
   Mozart's *Symphony No.41 in C,*
   first and third movements **16,
   20–35**
   types of questions **36–7, 162–5**
   Vaughan Williams' *Symphony No.
   5 in D major* **154–61**
Sex Pistols **76**
Soft Cell **78**
software for technology-based
   performances **125–6, 129, 130, 133**
solo performances, acoustic **114,
   115–16, 117–19, 224**
Sonata for Cello and Piano
   (Debussy) **185–6**
sonata form **19–20, 147, 155**
sonatas **19**
Sondheim, Stephen **58**
song form **188**
sound cards **130**
South Pacific **55**
Spandau Ballet **77**
staccato **21**
Stanford, Sir Charles **167**
   Magnificat in G major **168–9**
Steeleye Span **76**
'step' time **125**
Stewart, Dave **78**
stop-time 192
stride bass 119
stride piano **192**
string quartets **210–13**
style of music, and performance **119,
   133**
Supper's ready (Genesis) **75**
Surrey with the fringe on top (from
   Oklahoma!) **56, 56–7**
sus (suspension) 31, 140, 205
Sweet dreams (are made of this)
   (Eurythmics) **78**
swung rhythms 119
symphonies, Classical **19–20, 147**
Symphony No. 4 in G major
   (Mahler) **145, 146–54, 163**
Symphony No. 5 in D major
   (Vaughan Williams) **140, 145,
   154–61, 163**
Symphony No. 41 in C (Mozart) **16,
   20–35**
syncopation 180
synthesisers **77**

T

Tavener, John **172**
Two Hymns to the Mother of God
172–3
technology-based performances
assessment criteria **112**
choosing options **127–9, 229, 230**
developing skills **124–7, 225–7**
preparing **129–35, 236–41**
recording and annotating **135–7,
241–3**
useful resources **134**
texture 91
and composing **91–2, 99–102**
jazz **190**
listening to **9–10, 15, 142**
theorbo **50**
third inversion 28, 29, 200–1
tierce de Picardie **172**
timbre 91–2, 143
jazz **189**
technology-based performances **132**
time signatures **12, 138–9**
Tippett, Sir Michael
A Child of our Time **177**
tonal system 200
tonality **8, 141–2, 190**
tonic pedal 139–40
Tonight (from *West Side Story*) **59**
tremolando 24
triads **86–7**
trills **10–11**
trio
minuet and trio **15, 32, 34–5**
in a scherzo movement **15, 150,
151**
Trio Sonata Opus 3 No. 7 (Corelli)
101–2
trombone programmes **115**
trumpet programmes **115**
turns **11**
tutti **21**
twelve-note composition 142

U

unessential notes 6, 99, 100, 205

V

Vaughan Williams, Ralph **141, 154,
156**
Symphony No. 5 in D major **140,
154–61, 163**
violin programmes **115**
virtual instruments **130**
virtual sound modules **130**
Vivaldi, Antonio
Gloria **89, 90, 91**

voices
composing for **93**
recognition **9**
suggested programme for **116**
VSTi (virtual studio instruments)
130, 226

W

Wachet auf (Bach) **41**
Wall, The (Pink Floyd album) **75**
Waller, Fats
Honeysuckle Rose **192**
Walton, William **171**
Belshazzar's Feast **176**
Set me as a seal **171–2**
Water Music (Handel) **98–9**
West End blues (Louis Armstrong
recording) **193–4**
West End girls (Pet Shop Boys) **78**
West Side Story **58–9**
Who will buy? (from *Oliver!*) **59–60,
60–1**
Wonderwall (Oasis) **79**
word-painting 44, 46, 168

X

xylophone programmes **115**

Y

Yesterday (The Beatles) **72–3**

Z

Zachau, Friedrich Wilhelm **41**

Acknowledgements

The authors and publishers wish to thank the following for permission to use copyright material: pv Getty Images; p9 DK Images; p16 Corbis/Ali Meyer; p42 Alamy/Chuck Perley; p59 Getty Images; p62 Flickr/Purpleslog/The West Allis Players; p83 Corbis/Yuriko Nakao/Reuters; p93 iStockphoto; p103 Alamy/Celtic Collection-Homer Sykes; p108, 118 and 125 Fotolia; p125 Cubasis VST/Steinberg/Yamaha Ltd; p133 and 138 iStockphoto; p146 (Mahler silhouette) Alamy/Lebrecht Music and Arts Photo Library; p146 (Vienna Opera House) iStockphoto; p154 Flickr/RT Peat; p156 Getty Images; p161 Nattional Youth Orchestra/Kiran Ridley; p178 The Beethoven Trio; p196 Corbis/Bettmann; p210 Fotolia; p 213 Flickr/Pentchett & Wetzer; p224 iStockphoto; p233 Fotolia; p237 iStockphoto.

P7 'Bali Ha'i' from SOUTH PACIFIC; Lyrics by Oscar Hammerstein II, Music by Richard Rodgers. Copyright (c) 1949 by Richard Rodgers and Oscar Hammerstein II, Copyright Renewed. This arrangement Copyright (c) 2009 by WILLIAMSON MUSIC. WILLIAMSON MUSIC owner of publication and allied rights throughout the world. International Copyright Secured All Rights Reserved.

P8 'The Lonely Goatherd' from The Sound of Music; Lyrics by Oscar Hammerstein II, Music by Richard Rodgers, Copyright (c) 1959 by Richard Rodgers and Oscar Hammerstein II. Copyright Renewed. This arrangement Copyright (c) 2009 by WILLIAMSON MUSIC. WILLIAMSON MUSIC owner of publication and allied rights throughout the world. International Copyright Secured All Rights Reserved.

P56 and 57 'Oklahoma', 'I Cain't Say No', 'Oh, What A Beautiful Mornin'', 'The Surrey With The Fringe On Top', 'Lonely Room' and 'The Farmer And The Cowman' from Oklahoma! Music by Richard Rodgers; lyrics by Oscar Hammerstein II. Copyright © 1943 by WILLIAMSON MUSIC; Copyright Renewed, International Copyright Secured. All Rights Reserved;

P58 and 59 'America' and 'Maria' from West Side Story. Music by Leonard Bernstein, lyrics by Stephen Sondheim; © Copyright 1956, 1957, 1958, 1959 by the Estate of Leonard Berstein and Stephen Sondheim. Copyright renewed. Leonard Berstein Music Publishing Company LLC. Publisher Boosey & Hawkes, Inc, Sole Agent.

P60 'Who will buy?' From the Columbia Pictures – Romulus Film Oliver! Words and Music by Lionel Bart © Copyright 1960 (Renewed) 1968 (Renewed) Lakeview Music Co., Ltd., London, England TRO – Hollis Music, Inc., New York, controls all publication rights for the U.S.A. and Canada. Used by Permission.

P61 'Fiddler on the Roof' from the musical Fiddler on the Roof. Words by Sheldon Harnick, music by Jerry Bock. Copyright (c) 1964 Jerry Bock Enterprises and Mayerling Productions, Ltd. Copyright Renewed 1992. This arrangement Copyright (c) 2009 Jerry Bock Enterprises and Mayerling Productions, Ltd. All Rights for Mayerling Productions, Ltd. Administered by R&H Music, International Copyright Secured All Rights Reserved.

P64 to 67 'Do You Hear the People Sing', 'I Dreamed a Dream',' Castle On a Cloud' from Les Misérables; Music by Claude-Michel Schönberg, Lyrics by Alain Boublil, Jean-Marc Natel and Herbert Kretzmer; Music and Lyrics Copyright (c) 1980 by Editions Musicales Alain Boublil, English Lyrics Copyright (c) 1986 by Alain Boublil Music Ltd. (ASCAP). This edition Copyright (c) 2009 by Alain Boublil Music Ltd. (ASCAP). Mechanical and Publication Rights for the USA Administered by Alain Boublil Music Ltd. (ASCAP) c/o Stephen Tenenbaum & Co., Inc., 1775 Broadway, Suite 708, New York, NY 10019, Tel. (212) 246-7204, Fax (212) 246-7217. International Copyright Secured. All Rights Reserved. This music is copyright. Photocopying is illegal. All Performance Rights Restricted.

P67 'On My Own' from Les Misérables; Music by Claude-Michel Schönberg, Lyrics by Alain Boublil, Jean-Marc Natel, Herbert Kretzmer, John Caird and Trevor Nunn; Music and Lyrics Copyright © 1980 by Editions Musicales Alain Boublil. English Lyrics Copyright © 1986 by Alain Boublil Music Ltd. (ASCAP). This edition Copyright © 2009 by Alain Boublil Music Ltd. (ASCAP). Mechanical and Publication Rights for the U.S.A. Administered by Alain Boublil Music Ltd. (ASCAP) c/o Stephen Tenenbaum & Co., Inc., 1775 Broadway, Suite 708, New York, NY 10019, Tel. (212) 246-7204, Fax (212) 246-7217. International Copyright Secured. All Rights Reserved. This music is copyright. Photocopying is illegal. All Performance Rights Restricted.

P71 'Love me do' Words & Music by John Lennon & Paul McCartney © Copyright 1962 MPL Communications Limited. Used by permission of Music Sales Limited. All Rights Reserved. International Copyright Secured (does not include US rights).

P71 'Please please me' Words & Music by John Lennon & Paul McCartney © Copyright 1962 Dick James Music Limited. Universal/Dick James Music Limited. Used by permission of Music Sales Limited. All Rights Reserved. International Copyright Secured (does not include US rights).

P72 'Eleanor Rigby' Words & Music by John Lennon & Paul McCartney © Copyright 1966 Sony/ATV Music Publishing (UK) Limited. Used by permission of Music Sales Limited. All Rights Reserved. International Copyright Secured.

P73 'She's Leaving Home' Words & Music by John Lennon & Paul McCartney © Copyright 1967 Sony/ATV Music Publishing (UK) Limited. Used by permission of Music Sales Limited. All Rights Reserved. International Copyright Secured.

P75 'Another Brick in the Wall': Warner Chappell Music UK/Roger Waters (permission provisionally granted at time of going to press: credit to be confirmed at reprint).